TRUTH THAT SETS US FREE

Nirmal Mozumdar

Invincible Publishers

First published in India in 2016 by Invincible Publishers

ISBN: 978-93-86148-06-3

Invincible Publishers

F-55, Sushant Lok II, Hong Kong Bazar Lane Sector 57, Gurgaon-122003

Opposite Kasturba Ashram, Radaur Distt Yamuna Nagar, Haryana- 135133

Dedicated to- Intriguing circumstances and perfect family ensuring my perseverance through bumpy road to success. My gratitude to all those on this earth, for inspiring, guiding and verifying my personal experiences while walking this obscure path. Dolores Cannon, Barbra Ann Brennan,Dr. Brian Weiss ,Jas Jasmin, Doreen Virtue, Dr. Deepak Chopra, Walter Semkiv.and the list is long to mention all of them here .

My gratitude to my Reiki Guru Dr. NK Sharma and Dr. Savita Sharma , Gnostic Teacher Dr. Amit Jain, Shaman Teacher Gurpreet Singh ,Past Life Therapy Teacher Shasta Sirohi".

To my family and friends , I live in gratitude of each one of you. For the time we share here has not only enriched my soul but also taught me the invaluable lesson in the emotional expression of the human heart.

My husband Susnigdho tested my patience and sought confirmation at every step. In spite of not being convinced initially, he not only gave me time to pursue this obscure field but also became a channel to view the reality of our life from a different angle.

My son Ayan crushed my ego at the outset by revealing the mysterious bitter truth in his session. Accepting these not only healed our life and made me more humble, loving and none prejudiced but also enfolded the path for further evolution.

My son Rohan silently supported my work by assisting me in computer operation making it easier for me to be more connected and creative.

Greatness arises from within when making positive choices on our day-to-day events. Though the choices may not appear beautiful at first, as the right-side door at the covers; but it will be fruitful and beautiful when you actually get into the journey with those choices.

Acknowledgement

I acknowledge the guidance from those Spirit Guides, who have been arranging for the earthly beings to come to me with stories of pain and tragedy, seeking guidance and healing . I did my best to place their minds and heart to rest and body to recoup, In return, I was rewarded with the wonders of 'Higher Wisdom ' which aided in my evolution . Circumstances of my life woven into the tapestry of time, now providing evidence and comfort that in trials and tribulations, I was never alone.

Chapter one:Inner Calling

❋ ❋ ❋

As one of the spirit guide Samuel says, 'The Grace of God needs the recipient in order to be complete, you are held in the hands of God and totally loved, when that circle is completed'.

My Introduction To Past Life Regression Therapy.

Karma, destiny, coincidences, circumstances, desires and obstacles are prefect mirror to each other .The root cause of any problem is in its past. Many past life therapists are working to prove the continuity of life through past life regression therapy. Some of them are doing to validate history, and some are healing present life problems, originated in the past life.

Dr. Brian Weiss is a famous Psychiatrist who accidentally stumbled into a past life of his client . Now he is a renowned reincarnation doctor in the West as he has written many books on his experiences in past life therapy. I had read his First book, Many Lives Many Masters in 1999 with great interest. I was awestruck by his work since I have been fascinated by the mysteries of past life and its consequences on present life as I understood it through the Karma philosophy. Though I was interested in pursuing spirituality for further evolution, but I was not very keen to undergo one set of rigid doctrine and accept one Guru for the whole of life.

Then Reiki with its simple and safe healing techniques came my way. I was not interested in healing self and others. I just wanted to learn how to concentrate my mind and do proper meditation to grow spiritually. Without any deeper knowledge and any firm belief , regular practice of Reiki healing brought some very subtle transformation within me. I started viewing negative aspects of my life as a means to enfold more creativity and progress. That was the time when I made myself open to the knowledge which I needed the most. I would relate each and every quote , story or an article like a message for me.

Dr. Deepak Chopra's writings have greatly inspired me.

Same time I also read two books by Ruth Montgomery on the subject of life after death as she had described it through her personal experiences in channeling the higher spirit by automatic writing. I was fascinated and convinced of the truth in it as it went well with my belief in Bhagavad Gita's karma philosophy of "cause and effect". I had the desire to know about my past life but did not know if anyone in India was doing this therapy at that time (1999). It wasn't a mere coincidence that same year I picked up a book from a book store in Shimla "Conversation with a spirit " by Dolores Cannon. In which she had described various mystic phenomena, guides,walk in souls,different planes of existence , aliens, ghosts by her direct access to this higher knowledge through regression session.

In 2006, I got an opportunity to interact with some of the world famous past life regression therapist in Habitat center, Delhi. Dolores Cannon, Trutz Hardo, Walter Semkiv, and many others. I had also started practicing this therapy by this time in my healing. Their knowledge had greatly enhanced my understanding of the mysterious working of life. By mentioning about the opportunity to meet them, I am not only showing my gratitude to them but also acknowledging universe speaking to me through their words.

My own regression sessions

In November 2005, I got the opportunity to learn Past Life Regression therapy .The day I was going to join the course, I had requested my teacher to take my session. I was so excited that the previous night I had a dream that I am being regressed and in regression, I am feeling the physical pain of some past experience, probably of labor pain, (delivering a baby) during that session.

Next day when I had the session, I could not go into any of my past lives. There could be many reasons for this according to my teacher Mrs. Shamta Sirohi . First was that I was above forty years. Secondly, I was meditating (healing), thus people meditating tend to erase memories from their past life.(One of the main purposes of Healing). Third was that mentally strong people are not ready to give the control of their mind to another person easily, that is why it takes time and few sessions for them to go back to their past life. Last explanation by her was that you are an alien, meaning that you are from another planet that is why you don't have any past life. After doing many cases myself and going into the depth of success and failure of past life session, I fully agree to all of the explanations. I have explained the same in my book Mystic Life revealed , 'Can everybody view his past life?

In my first regression session with her, I could only see one big continuously moving golden ball emptying and emerging into itself ,.Second was the feeling of waves flowing over me when she had guided me to move back in time. I was very disappointed as I had expected my past life story enfold in that session. Afterward as I was reflecting on the outcome of my session.,I presumed that moving golden ball type thing must be Oum, the sound, which is considered the universal and natural sound of the Creation and the waves were Great Time signifying that I am an old soul. There after I had four, five sessions with her but there was nothing for me to see, to the point that even when she asked me to at least imagine any place and situation, I could not hold my thought in any imaginative situation . It is not that I am a mentally strong type of personality who needs the real flower to feel or imagine about the flower. I have had few visions during my healing meditation and I had started comprehending some of the meaning full dreams. So my that faculty was open to see what lies beyond physical eyes.

My another session was a group regression by Trutz Hardo renowned specialist in this field in the month of March 2006 during the inauguration of a book by Walter Semkiv, titled ' Reincarnation 'Born Again'? Again I could not see anything other than one very old tree with small reddish fruit on it, a Goldfish and a snow clad mountain very far away .

One of the significant session I had with my Reiki Guru Dr. N. K Sharma in April 2006 .There was no vision , though I did see the vastness of my soul in a higher dimension . I learned so much and felt relieved of the unnecessary burden of taking responsibility for others to the point that I was holding myself guilty for their sufferings as in spite of my sincere effort ,I was not able to heal them . I learned that it was my subtle ego which wanted to be fed by making me feel successful in every project.

Exactly after one month I had gone into one of my past life on my own, during my routine healing meditation. Before transcending into that experience, I was having a telepathic conversation with Guruji as if I am seeking confirmation from him about people who don't have any guides coming to them during sessions .As I had decided to invoke every body's guide at the time of regression, so that one may feel safe and secure in the presence of Higher Beings , with whom they are spiritually connected .This was a sort of intuitive breakthrough. Now I contribute it the intervention of these Higher beings so that I can learn more about the mystic world. As earlier like many others, I also believed that there is nobody in the sky with the names what we believe or hear the names of God on earth. Later my experiences in healing through regression revealed that irrespective of one's belief in this life in any of such mystic beings , there were guides for ninety percent of people .This proved the continuity of life and our approach through different paths , meeting different Higher Beings at the end of our life time. We may not remember them consciously in this life, but our subconscious is witness to our connection and arranges the spiritual encounter.

My belief in Higher Power

I had a feeling ,without any experience that there is some power operating and influencing us here on earth. People personify him as God with different names, claim that they have seen or felt his presence. But he never gave me any proofs that he has any form. Some call him formless, but I am fazed why do scriptures describe different names and forms of God? I could not fully come to any firm conclusion in this regard .I wanted to know the truth but did not feel deserving and capable of grasping such worth knowledge. As I started healing through Reiki, I started having few visions,which initially had been of light, mountains, colors etc and later I had a glimpse of some events and people, which are mentioned in detail in the special section on visions in my book Mystic Life Revealed . I started taking note of my visions and contemplating on the messages these wanted to convey to me.

As we are advised to be optimistic, because wise men know that we create our own destiny, what we think we get and become. So by thinking positively, we will definitely change the outcome of any circumstances for our higher good. I have had my experiences of frustration, negativity, and feeling of helplessness, as I was healing myself through Reiki, I was becoming optimistic slowly. Now even the past issues which were hurting me, I started acknowledging these events as they were teaching me some lessons.

I started viewing my family's resistance to my work as a lesson to me, in two ways. First was that I should not restrict myself to my family of this life only. I am not seeking such deeper wisdom and doing healing for limited people whom I know and love in this life. It is for wider application. Secondly, I had to still go deep in search of the obstacles they were imposing on me by not acknowledging my ways of doing things .Now when I look back, I find, that time I had picked up this attitude just to convince myself and not to feel hurt, but now I know how both the feelings were true.

Initially, it was my son Ayan through whom mystic mysteries were revealed to me in his healing sessions, which I was unaware of or I did not want to believe in such complicated ,fearful phenomena for two reasons. One was that it is frightening to know that something invisible can also affect us.

Secondly, my logical mind did not accept any such possibilities without any proofs and verifications. As I continued healing the mystic mysteries of Life were being revealed to me and to those who were having such sessions with me to see the real cause of their life's circumstances beyond blame and physical appearance of the substance.

Declaration–This book is based on true stories of Healing through Reiki and Past Life Regression session. Most names have been changed to protect their identity. I am thankful to few close associates, who have agreed to reveal their identity. But for them, my documentary work on the truth about mystic nature of our life wouldn't be appealing .I have tried my best to preserve the authenticity of the cases by describing words and events as they occurred. I have bracketed my views on the lessons and understanding coming from it. For each case has widened my perceptions by verifying things practically happening in their life, which were otherwise just considered stories and imaginations. Thus were first suspected and then rejected as it could not be proved and fathomed by mind's logical faculty.

I would request readers not to be judgmental and criticise the subject's revelations as one is narrating his/her reality. For having personal experience, one is most welcome to undergo sessions and see his reality for himself, rather than wasting time and energy in judging others. Anybody interested in historical validation of the facts is also welcome .But from the point of view of diagnosing the cause of suffering and healing the same and also gaining knowledge on this metaphysical subject, I am totally convinced.

For the better understanding of Mystic nature of life, a background understanding of changing faces of scientific theories , human energy system, healing, hypnosis, reincarnation is helpful .

The material produced in this book is a narration of communication between me and the subject regressed .To avoid repetition, I have framed Q -for questions I have asked the client in the regression session and A- for answers.

Kindly note- that when I ask a question, the 'I 'not only refers to the first person I with my intellectual knowledge of the subject by reading and hearing of people pursuing this field but also to my own observations of such experiences . Most importantly it is intuitive guidance from the Higher World helping in our healing session, guiding me to ask the questions in a manner so that certain facts about mystic mysteries are revealed. Same is with the subject, 'the person being regressed', his answer is not only the conscious interpretation of the fact but revelation influenced and projected from his subconscious access to the higher world in that session.

It can be confusing at times and is very important to discern the paradox in such revelations, as for few people conscious and subconscious does not hold clear demarcation as their perceptual window is open and both parts have merged into one. Yet they may not be ready to believe that their conscious thinking has subconscious access. Because their level of being is not matching with their level of knowledge. They have knowledge but have never applied this in their practical life .They are still prejudiced, judgmental and unhappy with their life. Same is with the person having strong faulty ideology conditioning his conscious mind that this wrong concept has filtered into his subconscious and accepted it as his truth. Fanaticism, lack of altruism, rigid attitude, and strong adherence to rituals and sticking to one philosophy throughout life are the outcome of such mind. They will impose their conscious point of view holding greater meaning and value thus reject the idea of breaking this cycle of continuity through healing or any such other Divine intervention. The success of any technique or idea lies in by being ready to break free from the mental barrier of judgment and conditioning of what one should be like and to accept the possibility of transformation to what one could be .

For better understanding, let us roughly divide consciousness into five stages –

1. Conscious– Physical awareness, interacting the world through physical senses
2. Semiconscious–Access to an emotional blueprint of past and the imprints of others .
3.Subconscious – Intellectual beliefs, dogmas, religion, and philosophy, not only of this life but of prior lifetimes.
4. Super conscious – Pure spiritual dimension,
5. Unconscious – Unknown. It cannot be known intellectually.

The stages of Soul Consciousness:

1. Physical pain or Injury as a disease or accident when it is experienced by the conscious mind.
2. Emotional Wounds – The memory of getting wounded in the mind, it has some story element in it. Semiconscious state.
3. Contract /Causal/Subconscious – The stage where one entered in a contract with the event or the other person because of intellectual beliefs, philosophy, religious dogmas is filtered into Subconscious mind.
4. Grace – The Divine part of us which is always whole. Pure Spiritual Dimension, our Source.
5. Gifts – With every pain, there comes some gain, some gift, and talent. Making it evident that there is nothing to frighten, destroy or simply trouble us. All good and bad, success and failures are included in the Divine Plan.

Language of soul

The body is controlled by the mind; mind speaks in the language of words, Mantras, affirmations, guided visualizations, Meditations. The mind is controlled by the soul .Which speaks in signs and symbols. These symbols have to be initiated/anchored and activated in our body parts through intension and repetitive practice.

The soul is under Spirit, the All That is, which speaks in the language of Energy and vibration.

1. Our body is an on-going process; Our body is an informational energy field.

2 .We can change our relationship to time and events with deeper understanding and conscious choice making.

3. We can change genes. Genes are memory records /Karma, either our own, our ancestors, our group or even animals or microbes.

4. Awareness is the key, through healing, Meditation, and Self-Reflection on who am I?

Why healing is needed- Why healing takes so much time? Summing up my learning and experiences in healing through various modalities.

Everything is Energy. LIFE is a process of learning to magnify, manipulate and manifest this life force energy for our highest good in our everyday life. Negativity is a byo product of the process of growing up through trial and error. We may give any names to this negativity – darkness ,Devil ,delusion , Depression , disconnection , disease or death, created by Past life imprints, Karma , Destiny ,Lessons, Ego, Self-Sabotaging beliefs, conditioning , psychic attacks, black magic, soul possessions,Vows and Curses, Crossing names, Decree , Soul contracts .

These things literally take different forms in our subtle layers of Aura, like disempowering Demons and dark entities, Spirit Intrusions,Unconscious Elementals, Nonsentient Implants ,Parasites, Insects ,Bugs, Bacteria, Virus, Vampires , Negative Ancestors, heavy thought forms, Disempowering Ideology of Individual or group Influences. These are like invisible seeds, entangled cords, stabs, pins, piercing of knife ,sword, creating confusion and short circuit or sucking our emotions and, draining our body of this vital life force.

At times, these appear on the body as different diseases ,accidents, even leading to death or may affect mind invisibly by creating circumstances suiting to support these entities like mental illnesses, fears, addictions, victim or criminal mentality ,guilt ,blame ,shame, selfish or self-sacrificing attitude .

Healing is like a cleansing our vessel (physical Body),servicing our vehicle (mind), renovating our house (temple of our soul) washing our clothes (Aura), Mending our wear and tear from our Energy bodies. Healing is seeking our re-connection to walk way back our real home.

Without being fully healed one cannot merge,back, seek union with holies of Holy, Our Father, Our Source .

Chapter Two: Intriguing Beginning

✣ ❋ ✣

This life is only a preparation

My beginning has been planned from the higher dimension, as coincidences are God's way of remaining anonymous. All my clients have revealed different aspects of continuity of life in such a way that I would get the satisfactory answer to the queries I had in mind about the mystic working of Life. I had already got proofs of it in the form of few visions and guiding dreams. I still cannot say with surety whether I am benefited more with each person viewing his realty through healing session or the person himself. Because there are people who do not learn from their mistakes nor do they feel happy about their achievements. They are controlled by physical senses and not ready to learn to believe their own visions and their own perceptions .That is why they are taking directions from the outside world , what is right and what is wrong ,what needs to be done and what not. They don't have this awareness that journey of life is more of inward than outward and we need to take direction by turning inside to our inner self. But I have tried to take home a lesson from each session as if each one is coming to me for healing, have agreed to become a model for my sake. I am showing gratitude by sharing my learning to both , the spiritual guides who arranged for our meeting on this earth plane and physical beings who agreed to open the windows of their heart and allowed me to peep through and dig out the hidden truth ,which was shrouded in mystery and depicted only in scriptures and fictions .

From the beginning I had mixed clientele coming to me for their healing sessions, Adults to old ones and young children to teenagers. Younger lot is at the threshold from where it is easy to slide both sides, backward to their past life and forward to the probable future. Yet there was the contradiction in this occurrence as there were many young people who did not see any of their past lives and there were some adults and old people quickly slipping to view their inner world .Being novice, in the beginning, at times I had doubted such people easily describing events as if they are consciously repeating some events of this life or interpreting some fanciful imaginative idea. Gradually I was learning to discern the difference and reached a state where I had no doubt in my mind that each case has been sent to me for experiencing diversities and paradoxes by dealing with all sorts of versatile cases. So that I do not take things for granted and form a fixed opinion of any occurrence .I do not boast of overconfidence in my ability and keep myself grounded.

Regression requires a tremendous amount of courage and faith. The main reason for this field to be left unveiled is that people lack this courage and faith. It is not an easy job both for the therapist as well as for the client, to bare open one's inner realities, of which none is aware, what might come up. The therapist is required to rise above the judgment of good and bad and fear of unknown .The client needs to be ready to accept himself for what all he has created in his life, and be prepared to forgive even dreaded enemy. Even though some people are curious to know about their past life but are not daring enough to face the truth of their life to experience it themselves through their sessions. Another observation about such people is that they are completely conditioned to think and judge present life to be the only reality. They judge themselves as per present life's achievements and status, thus cannot accept them to be the doer of some deeds which may not be yielding favorable results in the present. The blame is put on God, destiny and circumstances, which are always hidden from our conscious mind. They are also fearful if some unavoidable occurrence surfaces from the past and put them in danger, or are fearful if they get caught in some fanciful past situation. People judge these sessions to be organized on a worldly level .They don't understand that these experiences are being organized by some higher power.

It is an agreement at the soul level. Nothing is revealed that cannot be handled by the therapist and accepted by the client . What needs to be known at present will be unfolded, not necessary what one consciously think is important. It is like going to hospital with some problem but through investigation doctor diagnoses another more significant problem and insists on treating the diagnosed problem first. If we do not have faith in the doctor, we may not accept his diagnosis to be correct and may not agree with the advised treatment. On healing level, I would say that their time has not come, they have not awakened as yet to the fact that we are here to rectify our past mistakes, we can modify the past by healing our present, which will automatically transform our future. There is no God to punish and make us suffer. In fact, there is always help available if only we wish to help ourselves.

My understanding of the past, present and future is that everything is probable ,there is no absolute time, time is relative .Many of us view their past lives as if these are happening right now and are creating our future as per our attitude and capability to deal with the life here and now. This also makes it possible the effects of past experiences moving towards future lives, if issues are not resolved in the present. We can change, modify and heal our past here and now. This understanding itself is an evolutionary leap .There are people who are stuck with the thinking that only God can help them or they are destined to suffer .They are not even ready to listen and be ready to give it a try to change their destiny .They are stuck in that situation not believing in this simple proverb that God helps those who helps themselves .There may be others who are evolving and trying to grasp the foothold of their destiny in their hands. That is why two people will see their past and future differently because they move with the different velocities relative to the observed event because time is merely an element to describe a phenomenon. (Theory of relativity) the main reason for skepticism and disbelief in such revelations.

This is a very important observation from the point of our supersensory experiences. In order to validate the psychic flash of some incident, when we get a negative response to it, we feel it's our imagination playing the trick on us. This is Newtonian thinking as time and space are so basic to our description of the natural phenomenon. What we saw was real, since time is not linear, it may have already occurred, or may occur in future. It may even be a probable occurrence that may never manifest itself. Just because it didn't happen when we tried to correlate it, by no means proves that our insight about the possibility of occurrence was wrong.

This life is only a preparation; not real at all. Had it been real, there would have been clear instructions, where to go and what to do next. Future is only a path leading towards fulfilling the real purpose of one's life .The journey of life continues to perfect few virtues and win over some vices. As there can be many paths leading to one single destination (Source of our origin, our real Home) depending upon the location one has already arrived at and the means of transport one is using as per his capability and awareness. Same way there can be many approaches to life's path. There can be milestones, important landmarks on the way. That is why we try to validate from astrologers, fate readers, and the likes. They can guide us according to their knowledge and understanding of the subject .We may come across some mile stones and fly past others if we happen to change the velocity and direction of our journey. Most of us follow the extreme path. Some rely totally on such revelations leaving control of their life and do not exercise free will, they become fatalist. Such mile stones or predictions are not the final verdict from the lord but only guidelines to take clues as to which direction to take further and what measure to take to safeguard the best interest in this journey .There are others who prefer to completely close for any such possibilities and are walking the path in darkness without any inner or higher guidance.

But life is a bit of everything. One bit cannot be everything. Every subject has some truth to offer but not everything. Trying to ascertain our future through various such means is like buying a road map, marking the milestones to reach our desired destination. It could be like buying a syllabus book, guide book and marking important notes of the subject as preparation for the test. Knowing which question is going to come up for the examination is not going to help us pass the exam. We need to understand the topic thoroughly and practically exercise in our everyday life .Same way marking the landmarks and knowing which station is arriving next is not going to fulfill the purpose . We will have to really start walking through all those places, which we have marked on the map.

Life metaphorically is, a soul attired in uniform in the form of physical body attending school 'earthly existence'. We study different subjects in the school to expand our knowledge, to lead happy and more fulfilling life. No situation is to victimize or terrify us, circumstances and obstacles are created to expand our understanding of the subject of Life, enriching through various experiences. Good ideas are not adopted automatically; they must be driven into practice with courageous patience, these aren't learned overnight. Many factors must come into play before we ascend our path into next stage of evolution. Success and failures are not measured in terms of material gain and losses. Spiritually, Failure indicates that there is something more which we haven't understood yet. It's universe's way of opening up to new opportunities and other possibilities.

1st Case

And The God Says, 'I Give You the Choice'.

People call Him Different Names, name doesn't matter

Kriti 2nd December 2005

My first significant case was Kriti, an eighteen-year-old girl from Kangra in Himachal Pradesh. She came to know about my work in past life therapy from my son whom I had regressed recently and the information we had got was overwhelming. His case will be described later because he had so many problems and many sessions. It was Kriti's 18th birthday on 2nd December 2006 and she had one long session with me, which was self-guided in the sense that I did not have to ask her more, she was revealing it on her own.

History -She is very intelligent but lacks expression and communication. She would know the answer but she just cannot speak a word in the class or in any interview.

Session – After asking her to relax, she immediately slipped back to her childhood in this life. She continued describing her vision and feelings of her inner world.

Present life -She was seeing herself in her school in the 1st class, when Christmas is being celebrated. Whole classroom is decorated. All are dancing and making merry but she is standing alone in one corner. She said,' I am hesitant as I feel I might not be able to dance well like my classmates'.

'I am in the 3rd class, she went on describing, 'and the teacher is selecting three girls for the play. Teacher has not selected me though I am better looking and can perform better than the chosen girls. I am feeling left out and very low self esteem .'.

'I am in 9th class and its basketball selection match, I am a good player, but during selection game, ball slips down from my hand and again I am not selected. I am feeling very bad. The other girl plays well too, so during the match I am praying that our team should win. I am not jealous of the selected girl but the only bad feeling is ,why I am not in the team?

I am trying to catch the school bus to go back home but cannot touch it as the bus seems to run ahead of me. Suddenly the roads are broader like Delhi, even becoming more and more broad that the tall buildings which look smaller in front of those broader roads. And here she was going into her future but not realizing this at that moment, I asked her to go back to the time from where the cause of problems of her present life is originating.?

Past life -She said, 'I see a desert land, one man with the long robe and round spectacles is entering one palace. He is descending down the stairs of one big building (like a palace) and walking through the corridor and has reached one store house 'kothri'.There are many boxes in this store and he is opening them one by one and seeing each one filled with shinning jewels . There is a spark of happiness in his eyes and he comes up the stairs, he is wearing spectacles. She cannot recognize this man any one from this life yet she seems to know his name also but cannot pronounce it as it is very different and difficult to pronounce.

The man is going towards one hut, which is on one small hillock 'teela'. The locality looks desert like, Iraq or Afghanistan where there has been some war recently. His mother is waiting for him along with one little girl, maybe she is his sister. His mother is showing him with action, there is nothing to eat and asking him to bring something to eat. He says, 'from where can I bring? He looks very upset.'

He had spectacles when he entered the room

He got out from the house and is thinking something. As he is walking,he is seeing one fair, good looking girl, wearing big gold nose ring 'nathani and teeka' and a shiny bordered spread 'gota lagi chunnery.' She is descending down the stairs and he is following her quietly. He doesn't know this girl and the girl has come to the same store house. She is taking out ornaments from the boxes and trying them on her body. He is watching her from outside, the round spectacles are on his eyes, it looks as if the treasure belongs to this girl. As the girl leaves the place and he stealthily enters the room. He is feeling happy to see the treasure and raises his hands. He is praying to God 'Allah', now he is bending down and saying 'Namaz'(Muslim prayer). He gets up from the prayer but he is not taking anything from there and leaves the place. Now there are no spectacles on his eyes.

Note (I think his spectacles are symbolic of his distorted vision, he is in search of material wealth and is very happy to find it. But after praying to Allah to show his gratitude, some realization dawns upon him and his vision is corrected. (May be he has won over his temptation as he does not take anything with him). When her session was going on , she was describing on her own that he is wearing spectacles when he entered the palace and when he was coming up from the store house he was without it. I did not pay much attention to it at that time but later when I was going through it again, it suddenly struck me the relevance of spectacles, as afterwards I came across many such symbolic gestures and guidance in other cases.

A fakir

Now he is roaming lonely in this deserted place. He has some duck type toys on his head in a basket. He has left home in search of God. 'dar dar bhatak raha hai'. He looks like a Fakir (Muslim seeker). He has something like a kettle in his hand from which at times he drinks water . He has come to one house and the woman there is asking him, 'where have you come from?'He says, 'I am very hungry'. She asked him to come up to the first floor of her house. She is boiling eggs in one pan. Her husband is sitting down stairs. He seems to be suspecting her as she is talking to a stranger .The husband is telling her something. This fakir is feeling bad that this man is misunderstanding him and leaves the place without eating anything.

His search for God continues, now he seems to have travelled very far from the desert . He has crossed over to green area with hills. He is climbing on very steep and high mountains and looks like as if he has arrived in Himachal. There is only a kettle with him from which sometimes he drinks water. He is climbing higher and higher and has reached the snow clad White Mountains. Now he has grown very old, his beard has turned white and he can barely walk.

Now he looks very weak and feeble as if he cannot walk any further. The kettle fell down from his hand and tumbled down the hill. He is also trembling and falling on the steep hill and tumbling down from White Mountains to green ones. He is dead and has left his body; the body is now lying on the green hill.

She herself was this old fakir

After Death- He is coming higher up in the sky and is trying to touch God .The God is not allowing him to touch .God is saying, 'no, you can't touch me now, if you touch me, you will not be born again.' He is crying, pleading, 'please God, I left everything for you, I wanted to find You, I don't want to be born again and he is crying inconsolably'. And the tears were rolling down this girl's eyes like a stream of water.(She was feeling the pain of this old fakir as she was herself this old fakir).She continued, 'God is lovingly explaining to him, ' I know you are a noble person, you are not greedy, you were not tempted by the wealth even though you and your family were starving. Yet you have done a small mistake, you have pained your mother's heart, you did not look after your mother. Thus you have to be born once again and undo this by looking after your parents. This is the purpose of your this life and I am always there with you. And the God says, 'I give you the choice, where ever and who so ever you want to be born'.

At this point, I asked her, 'how does God look like and what is His name?' She replied, 'sometimes He has three faces, sometimes four, people call Him by different names, and all this doesn't matter'.

Preparation for rebirth-She continued, 'I have carefully chosen my parents. They were very sad, their one child had died, and another one is not very healthy. Looks like as if I am being born again after a long time.'

In the womb- I am in my mother's womb; mummy is gently stroking her hand on me and loving me. Papa is saying, 'son or a daughter, this child is going to make us very proud'. Papa is in the Army and posted at Leh , he is on leave at this time ..

Birth- I am born at Sidhbari in my ancestral home, my great-grandmother, and one maid are there at the time of my birth. I am two days old and I keep lying quietly and looking around. Mummy is very happy, she is telling papa, 'this child is so nice, she doesn't trouble at all'. 'On the sixth day of my birth, I am watching out from the window, there is a feast outside. Everybody is very happy and it is for the first time that a daughter's birth is being celebrated.' 'It is my naming ceremony and my great granny is telling, there has been a creation of our family and I have been named 'Kriti'.

At three years of age, we are in Srinagar, in Army quarters. I am sick. Mummy asked one neighbor aunt to bring medicine from another room .She is illiterate and cannot read the label on the medicine bottle. She brought some wrong medicine and I have been given that. I am very serious; my whole body has turned black. No voice is coming out from my throat, everybody has crowded around. Doctor says,' this is the drug reaction, she is very serious ' he is treating me, and I have survived at last'.

In my neighborhood one Sikh man is beating his wife. I am feeling very upset, I feel so bad for her but I am very small and cannot do anything for her. I am praying to God,' God please help her'. God is assuring me, 'I can help you but not her because it is her doings and she has to bear it.'

I am studying in the Army school and my aunt 'bua' is telling me, why should you play with officers' children? I am telling her, 'I am studying with them in the school, so why can't I play with them?'

My maternal uncle 'mama' is asking, we three cousins to write 'c', I have written very well but mama is praising my other cousin. I am arguing with him, 'mamaji, how can you be partial towards her. I am feeling neglected.

In a 9th class in half yearly exams, I had secured 85% and in final, I have got 75%. My mother is happy with this, so am I. I am kissing my younger brother and he is getting irritated. I am telling him, look, you are my brother that is why I love you. He is teaching me to play cricket. We are laughing and are very happy.

After her childhood, she automatically moved to her future and was surprised to see herself in a different setting. In her past life, she was not really relating herself to the person or situation. She felt as if she is watching somebody else. But she could recognize herself in her future.

Future: I have got this much salary

"My hair is shorter than what it is now and I am sitting in a big car, someone is sitting and driving. I feel he is my husband, there are two small children sitting in the back seat, I think they are my children. I am sure this is some foreign country, broad roads, very big buildings. We are going to some party; I have a big gift packet in my hand.

I am telling my husband, "you have a special place in my life, but my parents have their own importance'. I am discussing with him that this month I have got this much salary, I have to send two lakh rupees to my mother. He is replying, "What problem can I have with this, it's your salary and you are free to decide how you want to spend. He is so supportive in anything I want to do.(She is very happy and helping her parents financially due to her love and commitment for them". Her husband is so supportive that he has given her the freedom to spend her earning, which is so much that right now she can't even count 'beyond her imagination and expectation'. By now she was feeling tired and I brought her back to the present.)

After the session, She was partly surprised, partly accepting this possibility that she was this old Afghan fakir and she has seen her future. She said, 'I feel as if I have been very far and walked a long distance and still feeling tired. I feel nice to see my past and future .But 'when I was thinking of sending money to my parents, same time I felt as if I owe somebody ten thousand rupees but I don't remember whom'.

Note– I have to make a confession here. I had already opened up a holistic healing center but this case happened in the initial stage of my Past Life Therapy course learning itself. It was appropriate on my part to charge from people undergoing these sessions. But I never bothered whether some body is paying me or not. Whenever one was ready, I was too eager to have such session .Though I had to break my ego of not being able to tell others that there is nothing free in this world and one has to earn and pay whenever it may be. Sooner, the better it is. That is why the circumstances of my life had been such at that time that I was in need of money to progress professionally in healing... Kritika being a student and my son's friend, the thought of asking for fee never entered my mind. But when she was viewing her past and future life, the thought of asking her to pay my fee when she would achieve that place in future did cross my mind which got conveyed to her at that time that she owes some money to someone but cannot recollect whom.

Lesson

1. We all are paying debts of past. That is what she was doing and she was being warned by her soul not to keep anything pending. I did tell her about this, whether she follows it or not, that is for the time to see.

2. I learned my lesson that in the subconscious level how we are connected, the other person will immediately catch my thought and I have to be as clear as possible. Though at that time I did not think it that important but later as I got more proofs of this, I also got more help in healing.

3. It also symbolizes soul's migration from far off places to experience life in different land and culture to complete its learning of multifaceted dimensions of life.

4. As we talk of children sensing mothers feeling in the womb, it has been proved to be true.

5. The most important lesson was to break the myth that if we devote our life in search of God in mountains and monasteries, we get liberated, never to be born again. This search for God is one class, one lesson, which does not complete the other experiences. We have to learn to fulfill all our other relationships; only searching for God is not an end in itself. This was proved later by many other people in their sessions.

6. Was this a warning to me? As at times in helplessness, I felt giving up everything and just seek solace in seeking higher goal and God.

7. Was it an answer to my quest as I wanted to know that how one can achieve ultimate goal and happiness within? Not merely seeking God but by perfecting relationships with each other, doing something meaning full to God's children to help them evolve further.

2ND Case

My Last Rites are not done.

My body is buried under the snow.

Ayan December 2005

Sometimes the bucket is so empty that it takes so much time and effort to fill it that people feel frustrated and loose hope and belief in healing '

My second important case was my son Ayan. He was turning eighteen years in Jan 2006 and during that time his sessions were happening .As everything has a purpose, with time and patience everything is revealed. Now I realize that he has been my biggest obstacle, my greatest opportunity and my first lesson from the universe. He was a happy and healthy child but started having many problems from the age of fifteen .Obesity, chronic cold, leg pain on exertion, unsatisfied with life, depression and laziness.

Though it might be a bit confusing for the readers to understand, but I don't want to edit any occurrence just to maintain the authenticity of the session as much as possible. Thus I am describing it in the sequence as it happened .Mind slowly slides back, first, this life's memories are relayed, then only one can reach back to the past life. That is why it is a bit difficult for grownups to reach back to the causes in the past life as this life's experiences, memory and conditioning make it a hard work to break free, both for the client and the therapist.

First session- I was slowly guiding him back to the cause of his problems one by one .He had key moments flashing in his mind which were not in sequence but were mixed up. (Fragmented memory is due to the fact that I was already healing him through Reiki and many problems were on the way to its completion).

He said, 'I am seeing light coming through one hole in one dark room as if I was imprisoned in this room. I feel as if I am banging the door and screaming, 'mama opens the door' and finally I evaporate through that hole up in the sky and merge with the clouds'. Whenever he had a session, he felt very restless and pain of past experiences became evident in his present body.

Present life -He had few key glimpses of this life. He said, 'I am looking six /seven years old. I feel I am sitting on both sides of the beds divided into two halves as if half this side half that side .Now I am passing in between these two selves and joining to become one. It is a bit frightening to see myself like that. It means I am half good and half bad. (The positive side of younger lot is that their mind is not much conditioned and they sound verdict from higher perspective without hesitation of judgment of good or bad.)

Obesity -He said, "I keep sitting in front of the TV and eating buns at nine/ ten years of age because there is nothing else to do".

"I feel as if I am falling from a trolley type thing coming down with jerks. I can feel air touching my legs and after a long time landing on a dark sandy ground. It looks when one reaches at Kalka from Shimla by night train and light becomes visible at a faraway place. (This shows the impact of physical senses have on him, that in that regression (trance) state also he can feel the touch of the environment on his physical body) . I asked him to call his guide; he said my guide looks like 'nanaji'maternal grandfather, who was alive at that time ..(He left for his heavenly abode in October 2015)

Past life-My name is Rana, written on my name plate.

On 19th December, I regressed him for obesity. As he was ready to sink back in his mind to his past life ,I guided him to reach in one garden, and as he reached there, he said, 'it is snowing in that garden and now there was no garden at all but in the ground there is hut and a tier hanging in front of it. There was also a barren tree on that ground. Now I have reached by a river side below a hill where I am standing with brown colour shoes in my hands and socks in my feet. One binocular is in my hand; I am feeling breathless and cannot walk further. I am 27 years old. I am wearing army jacket and on the name plate my name ' Rana' is written.

On regressing further back, he said, 'I have reached a road, it looks like some small city of UP (Uttar Pradesh) with few white houses. I don't like the place as this is not my home town but a place of posting. I am walking along the road, there are many people but nobody is known to me. I am wearing an Army uniform and shirt is out from the pants.

I have reached one park, which looks like the Basantar Park of Mathura cantt but very big in size .There are flowers, swings, children playing; I have come here to see the tank. Some people are inside this tank and are banging to open the tank. I can watch them across through and through, though I am on the top of it and it is dark around.

I am wearing a PT dress, white shoes and I am at the basket ball court. Other people are calling out my name but I can't hear it clearly.

I am in my unit location , standing in front of a mirror, on which it is written with red colour, 'how do I look?' My unit tac no is 407, and in front of the office, one slogan is written 'ma teri raksha mai'mother in your defense.

Going further backward in time to his childhood, he said, 'I look eighteen years of age, in a small place like Dharamshala or Dari of HP hill station , There are some small shops with packets of Maggie and chips hanging out .I am coming down the road in a valley, wearing red T shirt and jeans . There is one card in my pocket with 'Agyaat' 'unknown' written on it. I feel very familiar to this place. This is my home town. But I am not going home because there is no body at home.(These were a few key moments from his past life) (In this life he has been to these places that is why he could name and identify , but this was not surely from this life as he has been in these places much younger, what he feels he is now seeing himself there in different body and looks)

(Though he had been a healthy and cheerful child so far, but in his present life, his sixteenth birthday wasn't celebrated because his mother was not at home with him. He was feeling very depressed and he started having frequent bouts of common cold and congestion in his nasal passage as he already had deviated nasal septum, 'displaced nasal bone' since childhood.

A card with Agyaat written on it is in my pocket

C**old and congestion**--I regressed him to his sixteenth birthday in his past life. He said, 'I am sitting in a bus, I am wearing a red T shirt and jeans .A girl is sitting next to me, I also know her in this life, she is my class mate. A sadhu 'Hindu fakir' is sitting to my right. A friend from front seat is looking back and asking me, 'Where are you going.'? I am replying him, 'to Dharamshala', a card with Agyaat(Unknown) written on it is in my pocket'. This seems the day time on his 16th birth day in his past life .

Regressed him back to see his home and family, he said, 'it is very dark, smoky, it's mid night. Suddenly I am feeling choked and suffocated as if my house has caught fire. My family should have been around but I cannot see any one in that darkness. My lungs are filled with smoke, I am feeling breathless and I am loosing conscious. Suddenly I feel I am on the roof top of Yol Cantonment Army quarters. (I think he lost conscious at that moment in his past life and felt at the roof top of the quarters where he was living, but he could not observe his family as he was too involved with his condition that even in his present body he felt discomfort. I had to stop the session and silently healed him at that point.)

Cause for leg pain-

(He likes to play basketball but he feels pain in the legs even if he plays a bit and then he ties crape bandage around his legs in the knees and calves. We keep telling him that such a young boy, why should you have pain in the legs, and if you cannot bear the pain then why do you play?

"I am lying unconscious, but I am standing at the head side of my body. –

Next session-He said, "I am 24 -25 years and am in a gym doing work outs. Suddenly one heavy weight falls on my legs and I am in severe pain. Two men come and pick me up and put me in an ambulance .I am in a vehicle, lying unconscious, but I am standing at the head side of my body.(out of body experience) I am looking down at my face, it looks red and sweating. Two men are touching and moving my hands and legs, placing their hands in front of my nose to see how am I? They are placing some ice on my face and chest. The moment they touched my arms, I am feeling extreme pain in my left shoulder. I am not able to move as my body is lying unconscious.

Vehicle comes to a halt in a lonely place and the door opens. One man is bending my left leg and then right leg and then brings me down and places my body below the road in a lonely place. They have gone, it seems as if they were taking me to some hospital but thinking that I am dead or in a serious condition, they got scared and fled away. I am lying there for a very long time; nobody sees me for a long time. I can see people moving on the road but they cannot see me. (Body was unconscious but his soul was wandering around that place for help)

Now some body has brought me to the hospital and my legs are plastered.It is army hospital, one sister is giving me injection .I am confined to a bed, reading some magazine.

I am back to my Army unit. All are in the playground , playing basketball, they are calling me by my name. I am watching them play, I like to play basketball but I cannot play as I am not fully healed of my injury.

Deviated nasal septum.

Blood is dribbling out from my nose and is falling on the snow

I asked him to see the cause for his deviated nasal septum .He continued, 'I am going on a posting to a new place looks like

Kashmir valley. I am in a convoy; it is taking very long time to reach my place of posting. Now I have reached my unit location. There is snow everywhere. I am away from my unit. Few other people are also around me. Suddenly blood is dribbling out from my nose and falling on the snow, colouring it red like ice cream with red sauce on it. I am wiping blood away , I am not telling other people about it.

I am wearing the uniform jacket and big army shoes, name plate is on my jacket, last word is Rana. There is this card in my pocket, 'Agyaat' written on it.

I am walking in a lonely place then I lie down on the ground for some time. Now I am walking again. I have lost the way back to my location. I am walking and feeling breathless and tired.

My last rites have not been performed. The card 'Agyaat' is lying nearby.

Death scene –Sun is shining, I cannot walk any further, now shoes are in my hand but I am wearing socks. I am tired so I lie down. It has started snowing around, and slowly my body is covering with snow, now my shoes are covered in snow . Snow has covered my full body till face. I cannot move. I remain there for a long long time. Face is looking up towards my detached soul. There is some struggle for some time and then silence prevails. It is February 1986, and I am 27 years old only .My body is completely covered with snow. It is still lying buried under the snow. No one finds my body; **my last rites are not performed**. The card 'Agyaat' is lying nearby.

Note -After the death scene as he said his body is still buried under the snow and last rites were not performed. I was deeply moved by these words .One can imagine being an initial case of my practice as a past life therapist and regressing my own son, who had so many memories troubling him from the past. Being from Army background, the information he was revealing was also making me a bit confused and bit wonder struck, whether it is his imagination or reality?. I was exclaiming! Oh God! What is this, is he telling the truth? But I got convinced by the depth of his pain and involvement during the session.

He performed his last rites.

I can feel the heat of the fire on my face even now. Ayan

For mind there is no time and place, mind only needs to bring a thought and action is already done .I guided him to search for the buried body, collect the wood. Here after he himself placed his body on pyre, which he had created and put on the fire and the pyre started burning .He said, 'I can feel the heat of the fire on my face even now.' The pyre is inside that hut on which tier was hanging and along with body the hut is also getting burnt and has vanished from my vision' .So this way he performed his last rites and felt relieved of the memory which was subconsciously making him depressed and become obese. His body had to go without food for many days and was buried under the snow, without any body noticing it and doing any last rites.

(It's my opinion ,the card with 'Agyaat'written on it was symbolic , as it was his destiny in that life to die an unknown death, as there was no body in his family and unit people didn't find his body and he was missing . I consider it our Guide's work to give me the clue to understand the situation. His mind was also wandering in search of his identity, as he felt in one session that he is in one park where there are Army tanks. There are some people trapped in that tank, which he can see through and through, he said, 'though I am standing on the top of the tank. (It's later I realize that all these symbolizes his life's state . Hut ,tier and barren tree because his body is placed inside the hut where tier is hanging . Tier symbolizes the wheel of karma mechanically running and hut is symbolic to his body meeting the fated end. After healing this memory from his mind which means now the brakes have been applied to the wheel and averted the fatal end which he would have repeated in this life too).

Heavenly experience-

I directed him to go up and meet some guide in the sky. 'I am high up in the sky, stars are flying around me. One white Angel in white robe is holding my hand. I asked him to find out from his

Guide ,what is the purpose of his present life and whether the purpose of that life is done? He replied, 'He is not answering anything but there is a smile on His face. After sometime he himself said, 'Purpose is to join army and to meet my parents. Now something is pushed in my body to make it swell and I am descending down through the golden path as if a film reel is rolling down and reaching at a place from where lights are visible.

Laziness and Irritation in the eyes. Ayan - Jan 2006

"**Jesus is saying, I am his very dear child** -As many of his problems started in his fifteenth, sixteenth years. It required many sessions .I even discussed his case with my teacher (Shamta Sirohi) and took valuable guidance from her. For obesity he had seen many lives where he was starved to death .This time I wanted him to see reason for laziness and irritation in the eyes.

Past life -I am a poor slave, I am tied to the wheels of oil machine (kolhu) I am so starved that ribs are visible on my chest , there is only a thin covering of skin ,no flesh at all. My eyes are read because of lack of sleep. I am a slave that is why they don't give me anything to eat, only water to drink in a wooden bowel. I continue pulling that machine in circular motion day in and out.

Death – After few days when there is no energy left in my body, I faint and die there tied to that oil machine itself. Two black, fat, top body naked men are coming; they pick my emaciated body and throw it in to the bushes. And again the last rites are not done. My body is lying there till it decays.' Again I made him do his last rites.

In the sky – he continued, 'I am up in the sky; some white saint in white robe saint is coming to receive me. He is Jesus. Yes, Jesus is saying I am his very dear child; I get whatever I want good or bad I also know why I did not get selected in AFMC because I was not very confident , when I will be confident , I will get what is good for me. But I have to work hard for that. And there is very less time, so I don't have to waste time. I was very close to Jesus when he was on earth'. Then he turned to me and said, 'people are not accepting you now, because you also did not accept Jesus when he was on earth.

This is that phase of your life. But it will be over, don't worry.' (I did not give much importance to his words as I thought he thinks that I am worried about the progress of my work).

" You killed me in one life"......Ayan

I was yet to receive another shock from his session- In one of his session , I askd him, 'what is your relation with your mother? Why are you born as my son'? As in his session he had said that purpose is to join Army and meet my parents .He shot back, ' you killed me in one life' I was shocked; it took me some time to gather the courage and ask him to clarify, 'what do you mean by it'? 'Yes, you had killed me '. He continued, 'I am a poor peasant and you are a Maratha sepoy. (He described the dress ,the Maratha people wore that time and wass directly addressing me as that person of that time) You are wearing turban, long frock shirt and payajama. I have been brought to you to undergo some punishment. I am biting hard on your hand. You are getting very angry at this and hit me so hard that I die there itself. (I just kept hearing all this and did not know what to make out of this. I thought there may be some misunderstanding in my hearing or in his observation. Slowly I mustered some courage to probe further, 'how can you say that I am that sepoy, how can you recognize me, he is a man and I am a woman'? He firmly replied, 'I can make out, it's you. Though you didn't mean to kill me, you only wanted to punish me hard. Now the sepoy is repenting'.

Healing -I wanted him to heal the memory by making him realize that he is not living in that body anymore which remembers as being killed by me . I asked him to see his cremation so that this painful memory is erased from his mind and does not interfere in our present relationship. I told him to make the funeral pyre ready and see that body is burning there along with all the memories and sufferings from that life which might have got projected in this life also. He said, 'the sepoy is so overcome by grief and repentance that he has collected the wood and put my body on it and putting the pyre on fire . He is watching it burn and meet with the dust. He said, 'But a snake comes from somewhere and bites the sepoy. He too dies there itself'.

Note -(Being his mother, I want to elaborate bit more about this. When I was expecting him, I had mixed emotions, though it was natural for me to feel very happy at the prospect of my motherhood. But this nagging feeling used to trouble me that I am happy for myself only , what about those people, whose family he/she is coming from, who knows whose father, mother or brother s/he may be? How will they bear the loss? My gain is some body's loss.

Another disturbing thought was of the fear that my child should not be handicapped or mentally retarded. And I used to pray for my child to be healthy. As my sister in law's five year old daughter was mentally retarded. I wasn't very spiritual at that time, nor was I reading any scripture. In fact I some time regret the fact that why wasn't I so spiritually inclined at that time? My praying, reading spiritual books, my knowledge and connection to such things would have affected my children's evolution. I had seen in Kriti's case that child senses all the emotions of the parents.

When he was 2 or3 years old, he was quite obedient, mature and always overgrown child. Sometimes I might be punishing him for some mischief. I remember having one dream few times that I am slapping him with my hands as I am very angry at him , but there is no strength in my hands and hence no effect of my slap on him . That night all those memories came flashing back . Was my soul trying to protect him and warn me that I should not commit the same mistake of hitting him hard in anger that past memory of dying with my hitting may come alive and leave the body? Aren't such cases happening where parents hit the child may be just to reprimand him and he dies , to keep them filled with this guilt throughout this life and repay back again in another life? This life's purpose remains unfulfilled.)

Having got a toy gun as a gift on his second or third birth day, he used to play (fauji) Army game , where he used to be a soldier and machine gun fire coming across and injuring him .His leg used to be injured first, lying quite for some time he would say , I am injured .Then slowly he would sweep his injured body, drag a little farther and then finally he would fall completely and say, I am completely dead now, pick up my body and drag it away from here. We presumed that time, that he is watching all this from the TV. But now I can contribute it to past life memory appearing on the surface and selecting parents who were in the army and seeking inspiration to join the army again in this life to complete past life's incomplete journey. 1. Meet the same fate in this life by creating accidental circumstances to leave the journey of life midway. 2. Or this could be the way of taking revenge from his parents for their past deeds by giving blow to their heart as dying young? Making his parents filled with remorse and repentance.

As he grew twelve thirteen years, when ever asked what do you want to become when you grow up, he had no other choice than simply be a soldier. He used to say , I will do anything but in the army.. Yet his obesity had some purpose. His DNS had some purpose. His body was using it as a defence. (Thereafter he did confide to me that he always imagined that he will join Army but what will happen after that as if there is nothing more interesting after that ,that's the end of this life).

Session cont-

After death - Now he said on his own, 'I am higher up in the sky. Guide, who resembles nanaji, is coming and holding me. I asked him to find out, 'if this is the truth,(i killd him in one life) then why are we together in this life'? He replied, 'You have to live together in one life, clear your grudges or revenges, love each other and help each other progress and grow further.'

You are being deceived -Ayan .... (Message for me)

After the shock there was also a message for me . He turned towards me and started speaking, 'you are being deceived, so much of your energy is being wasted. You will have to supervise everything yourself'. I asked him just as a matter of fact, 'how can I do everything myself, I need help from people? He replied confidently, 'You have to take responsibility', you will be able to manage everything.

Don't force people, who need your healing, they will come to you on their own. People are not listening to you because you also did not believe in Jesus, this is that phase of your life, and it will take two and half years to clear that and reach the success. By that time you will have eight followers and most of them will be ladies. Now you have only one follower, she too does not follow you fully.

'Grand ma 'is not receiving from you, but when she will fall very sick, then she will receive healing from you. Pisho (uncle) had received maximum healing from you and he even needs more healing. You have to heal his daughter and him together'. When he was revealing so much on his own, as he was being given clear vision of what was to be conveyed to me from the higher dimension, I understood the divine intervention and I felt tempted to ask him few more things. Q-Are my parents following my work? A-Now they don't understand, what you are doing, but once they will realize it, they will follow you. Papa is already following you, only for fear of ridicule, he doesn't do it openly, and I am already your follower. Simmi may be healed in two and a half years' time. 'Tussi', will live thirty five years.

Note -Universe was revealing to me the working of invisible energy world, but I wasn't only blind but deaf also. Ayan was describing whatever he was viewing internally, unintentionally. He could see as if a man is smiling wickedly and stabbing at my back. I did not take it seriously , I thought it is his imagination regarding my hard work and his biased attitude towards this person ,whom I think my well wisher but Ayan may not be feeling the same . Now I know that he was being given glimpse of the psychic attack on me by my apparently looking well-wisher but internally he was jealous of my sincerity and hard work.

1. Pisho is his uncle who had met with an accident one year back and was in coma .I had healed him through Reiki, without any feedback from him or his family or from mystic world.

2. Grand ma is his paternal grandmother who is blind due to glaucoma and suffers from obsessive compulsive disorder.

3. Simi was being healed by me for polio both legs . I taught her Reiki but after two months I lost contact with her.

3. Tussi is his cousin who is mentally challenged. I have tried to heal her from my side whenever guided to do so.) (Effect of healing on her and her father was also viewed by her sister and her step mother later in their sessions. Making me wonderstruck and become more responsible as I was given proofs that nothing is going waste)

Future.-He started seeing himself in the future. He said, "I have passed AFMC exam (Armed Forces Medical Entrance Exam) I am appearing for an interview, you and papa are also there. You are wearing blue colour suite and goggles. Papa is in uniform. I am keeping all my certificates before entering the interview. You are asking me, 'have you kept the Reiki Certificate? I am saying, 'yes' ,to this papa is saying what is the need of Reiki certificate here? Nothing much is being asked from me in the interview. I am selected. Papa is calling grand ma to inform about my selection. Papa looks very happy.

Now, I am in the class, its anatomy class. On the board, there is one diagram and teacher is teaching. I am very attentive and happy as my dream is full filled. In the campus, I also meet one of the senior students, who was my senior in Army School Yol (Kangra) .He is talking to me and assuring any help. I also feel nice to know that someone known to me is already here.

Now, I have come to my room in the hostel .Its dark there and I am not happy as if something is lacking in life. I don't like this darkness as its making me depressed. I do not want to live here.

(I thought probably he is externalizing feeling of homesickness as it will be for the first time he will be away from home at that time.)

He was feeling very restless and did not want to see anything more because he was sad. I wanted to make him cheerful by healing and making him think positive but still he resisted and said, "I do not want to go to that room"

(Future-it's my observation, there is no fixed future that is why we can heal, mould and change our future accordingly. He saw himself in AFMC. But he saw something negatively affecting him and making him depressed in the hostel room, that means there was something more to be healed.

Note- *I did not understand much significance of this future vision at that time because whatever he said never happened in his life. He wasn't selected in AFMC. So I had decided to just pen it down to maintain the authenticity of the case. In his session in August 2008, he had said, ' you will come to know everything when you will compile my case and later Shivali also told in her session in October 2008,'you have not yet written the book how it should have been written by explaining everything . So I want to explain about this future vision.*

I was healing him through Reiki for obesity and admission in AFMC. It was also his father's ambition. I had even taught him Reiki and still continued healing him. Though at times he would be so depressed and angry. His Papa would consider it a sort of challenge for me and say, 'why don't you do something for his admission in AFMC, if you have so much faith in Reiki? I used to feel upset. Not that I thought ultimate success for him is to get admission in AFMC .I had this much faith that my healing will bring the best for him, may be not that what we consciously desire. My pain was at those people who were not understanding the value of this divine power and my efforts, thus they were challenging me to be rewarded what we logically consider best for us.

I wanted to take his further sessions but he wasn't willing now .It is clear now because there was something fatal coming his way, which he did not want to see or probably I being his mother and immature at that time would have not been able to handle it. Later I got feedback through Shivali's session about all that probable fatal future. Had it not been healed through Reiki and by his direct sessions? (Everything is revealed when we are mature enough to handle the situation)

He would have got selected with his efforts and my healing, which would have made his papa very happy. But that would not have been in our best interest and Reiki does not give us what is not good for us in the long run. In his future vision, My asking him for Reiki certificate was to remind me of the importance of Reiki in his case. We may have got disheartened by his failure at that time .There was much more need to heal his grave causes. His own past lives memories of living short life and accidental deaths , his mother's cause described in this chapter , his father's causes , which his father himself saw ,when he had seen his past lives later . I now know that he was being healed step by step. First step was to heal his accidents and fatality. Then was his carrier and the obesity would be the last one.

Spirits in our ancestral house

March 2006 Ayan

He opened me to yet another reality .As the days were passing and he was attending coaching classes for seeking admission in the medical colleges. Once he did not do well in the class test, his dad was not pleased with his result. Though by now he had closed himself for my sessions because he needed some time to digest the bitter truth,I thought so. Seeing him depressed on that day, I suggested him healing session and he agreed. And the session went like this.

Session -I guided him to breathe out all the negative thoughts from his mind and breathe in positive energy. But he was feeling choked as if everything is dark and suffocating. I asked him to breathe ou that negative energy from his system. He said, 'my mind is clogged with dark thick clouds. Black colours handkerchiefs types are coming out from my mind'. After taking out that completely, I asked him to see the cause for this, from where are these things coming to your mind. ? He replied, 'whatever you people tell me, it pinches me and burdens my mind .It makes me feel helpless and frustrated..

(I concluded that this was psychic attack caused by us . Though we parents want to inculcate good sense by preaching and showing harsh reality to our children but when advice is not received positively or he is not able to cope up ,it can harm child making him feel frustrated ,insecure and incapable) It was obvious that he was very depressed. I wanted him to see our love and concern behind our reprimand and such preaching. Knowing what relationship he had with me in the past, I wanted to heal and fulfill my obligation of helping him.

I took him to see the time when he was born, so that he would be able to feel the love and happiness in everybody's heart and understand the positive side of the things. But he could not see anything and said 'I am very lonely, there is mesh type around me, it is dark.' I again insisted him to see at least your mother was always there with you, when you were born, you were never alone. He said, 'no I cannot see anybody, I am feeling there is very heavy air around me, as if something is flying in the air, making it dark to see anything. There are big photos hung on the walls in that house and this heaviness in the air is originating from these photos. (I felt bit upset that he could not feel the security and love given to him at the time of his birth. Thus I prod him further to find out what these floating things are?) He elaborated, 'some faces are peering out from those photos, now they are turning in to full figures. Looks like as if they are the people of that house. Yes, they are papa's grandparents, now they are sitting on those chairs', in between they float in the air'. I never expected him to even imagine such weird things; I asked him what are they doing there? "Haven't they died long back, much before even your father was born"? He replied, 'but they were tied down to this house by some force, as if somebody from the family did not want them to leave that house. Somehow they got tied down to this house, they could not move up'..

I started sending healing Light to get them released and help them to move up and merge in the Higher world .He saw that slowly they are getting covered in the white light projected on them and finally merging in it and evaporating up in the sky (Much later when I was able to regress my husband, I regressed him to see that time, he also saw the same thing. Though he had also not seen them when they were alive, living in that house but he could recognize them as his grandparents and one uncle from photos and listening about them in the family. Being a doctor and brought up in a modern Brahmo Bengali family, one can never expect such wild imaginations from him).

Note -It was a known fact that my father in law was very obedient and a possessive son. He had made a memorial in marble stone ,on which 'in memory of our dear father and mother 'was engraved .It had two holes keeping his parent's ashes in small silver containers. Grand parents' big big photos were hung on the walls of our ancestral house, where Ayan was born. The house got damaged in 1988 due to earth quake when Ayan was just six months old and we were forced to leave that place permanently. Thus it was not possible for him to consciously remember.. But his subconscious mind had access to the memory of any time and place and could relay it now because it had an adverse effect on him.)

This revelation by Ayan also made me dumb along with blind and deaf. I could not even think of speaking this truth to any one belonging to my family. They always called me insane and any such statement will make it foolproof. I still mustered the courage to speak to my mother in law and my husband. 'How is this possible? Our grandmother is supposed to be highly evolved soul' was all they said. But I do remember this talk in the family some time back that grandmother was around and she had said, 'nobody can harm my son till I am around'. This had been revealed through plan chit which is popular name for automatic writing which few people were practicing in that place .

Note –(Reflecting back on those days when Ayan was born. I have always said that, it was the black period of my life. Though I am broadminded optimist and was happily married to a loving, well to do Bengali Brahmo family. I should have been on cloud nine as now

I was also blessed with a son.. But I was depressed those days, though I tried to keep a brave front, but for the six months I stayed in that house, I used to cry every day, quietly without any apparent reason. I presumed it as post natal depression. After six months we were forced to leave that house because earth quake in that area damaged this house severely. And if mother's mental state affects the child, then that is what he was saying. I felt very sorry for him).

Obesity: This is the only hurdle

When he was seeing his ancestral home, the thought of his obesity due to genetic factor came to my mind, so I asked him, 'can you see what is your relation to this family because you have inherited obesity from them?' Opposing my opinion, he replied, 'no, I don't have any relation to this family in the past, I have a relation with nanaji, (mother's father) '. Nanaji is young ,in army uniform, smiling and telling me,'this is the only hurdle 'obesity'you have to clear it, everything will be all right then'

(I was reminded of the instance when my father had met my in laws family for the first time to settle the arrangements for our marriage. He confided to me that they all are very nice people except that everybody is so fat.' I lightly replied, 'how does it matter to us, they are fat by eating their food not ours'. My father seemed concerned and said, 'no ,it does matter to us ,as my grandchild will also become fat'. Afterwards I had narrated this incident to Ayan and he would say, 'I am fat because of nanaji's black tongue .Why he had to utter this prophecy for me? His younger brother Rohan is of normal weight.)Is anybody consciously speaking out at times or some unforeseen force unconsciously relaying our fear, which is going to come true?

Origin of obesity- He started, 'I am in a Muslim Ruler "Mughal "typesetting and dressed one like them , I am very fat , I keep sitting and eating only, there is nothing else to do, I am not allowed to move out of the house . Same as I have nowhere to go now a days, there is no creativity, only study, eat and sleep 'he was comparing those circumstances with his present life leading him to obesity.' Why he wasn't allowed to go out in that past life? He could not clarify, but he dies young in twenties only and feels relieved that there was nothing interesting happening in that life.(Was he mentally challenged in that life? It's my own interpretation as he was rich and obese but was confined to one place as if imprisoned and doesn't understand anything of that life time why and what is happening to him. He is happy to be released from that body once he dies)

After death -He became very restless. He said, "I am standing as a five year old boy in an island. I told him to move ahead but he refused, 'I cannot move further, I can't go anywhere. I don't want to move, I am tired'.

Future- Realizing the depth of his problem and his negative attitude. I wanted to heal him by taking him to some positive happy event .So that he can feel optimistic and consider our reprimand a signal to encourage him to reach his bright future. I asked him to see his probable future. He said, "I am sitting in a train. Papa has placed one black box with me. I am going to a very far off place from where I do not want to come back. And I never come back home again". I thought because he is depressed at this moment ,so he is expressing his frustration and anger at us, threatening us that once he leaves for higher studies to far of place , he would never want to be back. I consoled him and requested him not to talk like this. But he insisted, "no, I do not come back"'. He was reluctant to listen to any advice. (But now I know that he was seeing a symbolic journey to his destination from where he wouldn't come back .He was depressed because he could not finish working out his past karma .Black trunk symbolizes carrying forward his karma)

The truth he was revealing was beyond my comprehension at that time .He was finding it difficult to digest so much bitter truth, I wanted him to see any happy life he must have lived in the past , so that he can enjoy his session feeling hopeful that there are also good things in life . Yet he had become so closed and did not want to undergo any further sessions. I was under tremendous pressure to see him healed and his unwillingness for further sessions. I was giving him distant Reiki and a stage came in between when he just stopped talking to me. I was also turning bitter because in spite of doing so much for him he is not improving. This time my husband who was totally closed to any belief in my work, intervened and persuaded him to undergo a session.(In March 2006 Nadi Astrology (An ancient form of prediction in India) had made him reflect on some truth in the circumstances of our life and must have started realizing some importance of my healing work. So far being an orthodox Army doctor he wouldn't give it a second thought.)

Psychic Attack on My Parental Family

You are putting salt on my wounds........Ayan

His every session had been hitting me like a bolt from the blue and I don't know from where I gathered so much courage to withstand unexpected and unbearable revelations made by him. How many times I have had a lump in my throat and my eyes filled with tears even now, whenever I read or reminisce those sessions. Whether it is my grate fullness to the higher world for making my house the laboratory and my family my experiments or for the sufferings my family was enduring or the courage I was displaying or for all in one . Was my fear erased by my prayers and had the healing done through Reiki infused me with courage? I also know that all these things were being revealed to me because I had wanted to know and had the courage to accept the harsh realities of life. I had taken up the responsibility of healing all these intricacies .I was ready to withstand the truth, not to get crumpled down by fear, anger or blame. I was not to feel revengeful towards people who had done something negative towards me. How could I blame others when I had accepted his revelation of I being culprit of killing him in one life?

Session- I made him relaxed and gave him Reiki by touching him. I told him to visualize the healing Light soothing him but he became very restless. I asked him, 'what is troubling you'? He shot back, 'my body is burning, as you are pouring salt on my raw wounds in my body '. I assured him, why should I do this to you?

'You are my son; even to any enemy I cannot imagine to do such a thing'. Still troubled by the burning in his body, he replied, 'but I am feeling so'. I was taken back for a moment and did not know how to convince him and relieve him of pain. I thought the memory of that life is still haunting him where I must have killed him . So I asked him to see that life again whether the cause for his present pain is originating from that life? He answered, 'no that part is healed, it is coming from somewhere else, from your home in Palvi (Shimla). I asked him to elaborate and I was gasping for my breath at his narration and at perfect divine plan, where my own son has been the channel to convey to me everything I needed to know to progress in this field. Having broad outlook myself, I had never ever imagined all these things remotely affecting our lives (I had learnt in my past life course that it is not possible to regress and heal your own family members and close friends because of familiarity, your instructions are not heard sincerely and one cannot seep deeper in to mind. Contrary to that my own son and later my husband had revealed to me so much by becoming my experiments)

Continuing the session, he reached back to his child hood and started narrating an incident , 'I am three/ four years old and some body is cutting my hair outside the house in Palvi Simla(his maternal grandparents home).Some hair are lying there itself. We have come inside our house. Somebody is picking up hair from there and offering it in the fire in one small temple. And the burning of that hair is causing this reaction in me, as if you are putting salt on my raw wounds. I asked him to find out, who is this person, who is offering his hair in the fire. ? Is it the person who cut your hair? He answered, 'No, he is not Palta nana(our family barber) because I know him, he is somebody from your village, whom I had never seen in reality thus I don't know him. But he knows your family and you also know him. Then he started seeing when I had met him last and continued describing , ' three/ four years back, he came there and you are talking to him from the verandah of your house, while he is on the ground floor, going somewhere else. He has also put something negative in your two cousins' house there. But one of your cousins does not like him and does not allow him to be near his house, so he could not do anything to him. He has given some Prasad (portion of sweets offered in the temple) to eat to Nakul (Ayan's cousin) with the intension that he should not concentrate in studies. He has also done negative to younger mama (his uncle) with the motive that he should not do well in life. I asked him why younger mama, why not elder one? A- Because he is more educated and could progress more, which he wants to prevent.

I think he was sensing my disbelief and to give more proof, he started narrating yet another remote incident. 'When younger mama was three four years old, he is even causing his finger to get crushed in the door'. I asked him, 'how did he do that? Was he there to push him towards the door? 'No, he wasn't there at that moment, but had been there two days ago ,when children were playing. This man is coming forward and pointing the door to mama and saying, your finger will get crushed in it. And two days later it really happened. Mama was two three years old and wearing check colour shirt and you are also there at that time.'

He was being given the vision of that incident-He was describing everything of the surrounding when this accident had happened many years ago.(This serious accident had really taken place in front of me when I was about twelve years old but do not remember the details, which colour clothes we were wearing or who had come two days ago or did he create this accident by pointing out at the door to my younger brother .All I remember is that his left hand little finger had almost cut midway and there after I had been reprimanded badly by my mother for not taking care of my younger brother. He had a permanent disfigurement in it.)

He continued, 'He had even given you something to eat when you are five six years old ,coming back from school. He is placing his hand on your head and telling you to eat it as it is Prasad'. I told him, 'but I don't remember any body giving me any Prasad on my way back from school'. Not getting distracted by my rejection of his revelations, Ayan further described this person's background, 'earlier he used to rear sheep and now he cuts trees in the jungle for making houses'. Ayan could even see what work he did for his living. He continued, 'he has even kept your photograph in that small temple, you are wearing a pink sweater and your hair are tied up in two pleats'. I asked him from where did he get this photo and what he wants to do with that ? He replied, 'he is in your house and while watching photo album, he has stealthily taken away your photo.' 'He wants to harm you' because you are very bright. I asked, 'Isn't my mediation and healing protecting me from his influences? That is what happens, actually he cannot harm you, because of your power of healing but then he can influence your people negatively about you, they don't understand your viewpoint and don't listen to you and then you feel very frustrated.

I wasn't taking it seriously but was wondering why is he going on narrating in which I don't have any belief and interest .

This man had even caused my papa's accident, He continued, 'apparently he is very friendly with Nana ji, few years back ,they both met somewhere on the way and nanaji was telling him about papa's promotion. He went home and started doing puja in that temple and after few days papa met with an accident but did not harm much because you were already healing him. (This had really happened in 2000 when we were at Mathura. Everybody who saw the vehicle which met with an accident ,were presuming that the victims must have been brutally injured but to everybody's surprise both driver and his father did not have any serious injury only had slight backache for few days) .I asked Ayan ,' if he is friendly with nanaji, then why does he do all this to us ? Ayan replied, 'he is saying in revenge,I will not leave you. He is cursing nanaji and it makes nanaji so helpless, so frustrated that snakes types are coming out from his mind'. I understood this to be past karma making my father suffer this way and that person is causing suffering to my father like the poisonous snakes rolling in his mind. I further inquired him, 'hadn't he done anything to other people in my house then? He said, 'no, others are suffering because of their own doings, elder uncle (mama) had been possessed by one spirit, few years back. So had been Aunt massi.(His Maternal Aunt) Mamiji (his uncle's wife) is suffering because one family in her neighbour in her hometown is jealous of her for being married in your family'.

This was about negative influences in my parental family , which I never ever wildly imagined and when I told my people about all these things , they simply would not listen to any of this, saying that, 'no, we don't have any enemy ,so nobody will do anything to us. And we don't suspect anybody doing some whitch craft on us .No one has ever heard of anyone doing such in our place '. I did not probe further for I was happy to see their positive attitude. But the question was always haunting in my mind, why it should occur to Ayan such weird experience? Soon I was getting feedback for such things happening with many people irrespective of their belief or any suspicion on their part.

Thrombophlebitis Right Arm Aug 2008

My hand is blown up in a powerful explosion

Past life-Though this session happened two years later, I had to put it up here because he had similar circumstances triggering pain in his right arm. The day he visited Drass War Memorial in Leh Ladakh Region ,for the first time on 28 August 2008, he suddenly started having pain in his right arm. We were there on a pleasure trip but he could not continue enjoying as he was in severe pain and discomfort thereafter.

This was my second visit to this war memorial, this time simply to show him around as he had not been able to visit it earlier. I had sensed the purpose of my visit to this place in my first trip one year back and had started healing such places but this time I had strong emotions that I could not control my tears . I was continuously praying for all those who sacrificed their lives and also for their families to be able to accept the loss of their loved ones. As I saw the photographs of bodies of two enemies blown in to pieces, I placed my hands on it and started praying intently. Knowing how the soul must be suffering in another life because their bodies had experienced such powerful blow and strewn in pieces.

On reaching our place in Kargil, Doctors diagnosed his case as thrombophlebitis, a very common ailment in this high altitude area, and symptomatic treatment was offered. Seeing him in discomfort I started healing him and suggested him direct healing which he agreed to. Following are the details of the proceeds.

Session- Mind was clogged with pain and clouds. He said, 'touch of your hand also hurts me, touch me lightly '.Healing his mind of those clouds and congestion, I asked him to breathe out deeply and intend feeling lighter and healthier. As he has had so many sessions with me by now, I did not have to spend more time to make him focused. He started feeling warmth and then light entering in his pain full area in his right arm. Slowly he was reaching back in mind to the subtle cause of his pain suddenly coming to surface beyond commonly believed excuse of high altitude effects and all that.

He said, 'I feel my right hand is blown up in a powerful explosion.' My arm is lying separated far from the body. Though my body is not visible but I feel I am lying on the ground. The place looks similar as we had visited today but as if this is happening in a very old time. People are running here and there. There are many people injured and scattered on the ground. Nobody bothers to help me; rather nobody has time for anyone .I keep lying there, writhing in pain and helplessness. Slowly my body gets buried in the soil. Q- What time of the era it must be? A- I am not very sure but it does not look very recent time of Kargil war (1999) Q -That means you had been in the Army many past lives as the one recent past life has ended in 1986. ? A- Could be. I cannot see my body clearly but I can see my arm and feel pain in it. (Because by now with so much of healing his body was healed .This sudden pain in such a young boy of twenty years was either to show us that one life again he had been in the army and met the fatal end and his body was buried in the soil .By visiting that place the memory and pain of that past incident came to the surface .Or was it to show the reason that why he was left handed ? could be that subconsciously his right arm is weak as it carries the memory of lying separated from the body after that powerful blast)

Healing- I was continuously healing him and he saw as a result of that there are beautiful flowers grown on that soil. Now these have become like a bunch of flowers. With this process now his arm is also getting united with his body. I was reminded of the beautiful flowers grown in that memorial area. I thought, is healing aiding in this way ? I was also reminded of my emotional outburst in the war memorial during my visit there. So I asked him, "What was happening, when I was healing those souls there"? He said, "They are saying thank you, for walking our path. They are released now but they come back when remembered '(because I was selflessly healing enemy and friends both, was it my reward that my son has been the channel to reveal to me all that mysteriously happening there.)

Healing in higher dimension- I asked him to see his healing happening in higher dimension. He said, "I am in the sky somewhere higher up. My right hand is plastered; rest of my body looks transparent or invisible.

Next day after healing him again I asked him to see healing in higher dimension. He said, "Now the hand is opened from the plaster but looks fragile and uneven and some voice is coming that I have to give it some rest". He was cured completely within three four days that he could even drive down from Chandigarh to Delhi.

Finally I had a dream after one and half year that I am hugging Ayan who is looking slim and smart. I am also happily introducing him to my friends. I am sure now slowly his body will start releasing excess fat after all his fatal causes are healed and he will be healthy and slim trim.

Feedback on Ayan's Healing

I have verified all these facts from various other people researching this reality, I can elaborate further about the feedback on Ayan's healing. Kindly note that our relation in the past was of antagonist and we would have carried forward those traits subconsciously and something untoward could happen in this life or we would be the worst of enemy to each other .But since we were together to make amends, to accept each other, heal the past to transform our life for better future. Bewildered at the revelation that he holds me responsible for his death in one life,I had asked his subconscious, why are we together in this life? The answer was, 'to forgive and learn to love and help each other grow further. I accepted the bitter truth and forgave myself for whatever I must have done and was ready to heal and transform life, by erasing that blame from his mind, we became best supporters to each other. He had been made channel from the higher dimension to reveal the secrets to me that I needed to know and I became his healer.

Ayan had gone away to Dental College in Bangalore. He met with a small accident and felt shaky after that to cross the road. Now he wanted to have session with me so that he can get rid of the phobia. This was not possible because when he came home on his first leave, I had been away in Air Force Station in Bhuj for my first outdoor camp organized by Mrs Ghotia. I had considered this opportunity provided to me as my test to see how serious I am in my mission of spreading healing and awareness about our Spiritual connection. I did not care for my son's first home visit from hostel but attended to my inner call.

I was well rewarded for this as I got feedback for his healing and further progress through somebody else's session

Shivali became a channel to view Ayan's healing in October 2006

This is a note from her.

"Regression was done to know the cause of my failures in the examination. It started with my future if I would have cleared them all and got the admission in AFMC...it would not have made much difference to me because I lost my best friend (AYAN)..The cause of his death would have been the operation of his nasal septum. I would have completed my MBBS and joined defence but I could not accept Ayan's death ...the person who was the support in every stage of my life, from the time I knew him, was not with me anymore was painful. Now when I look at it presently I really thank god for saving me from such a disaster.....

I have learnt only one lesson that "WHATEVER HAPPENS IT HAPPENS FOR GOOD".......

.There is one more thing I saw but I could not connect it to anything. I saw Ayan's dad crying alone because his family is blaming him for Ayan's death and has left him alone....

Thank you very much.

Regards, Shivali

Note -I must elaborate this session in detail .They both had been course mates in their coaching classes in Delhi while preparing for medical entrance test in 2005-06. Both had first preference for AFMC as both were keen to join Army. In spite of their best effort and our Reiki healing they both did not get through. Thus they were depressed. Shivali had taken Hotel Management and Ayan had opted for Dental degree. She knew about Ayan's recent phobia and his desire to have a session with me this time. This was not possible. She too wanted a healing session; she was also keen to know why she did not get selected in AFMC. She willingly approached me for doing Ayan's healing through her. Her first session about a year back had to be discontinued mid-way as she became very emotional after breaking down in tears. (I think there was something at that moment which she would not have been able to bear or I being amateur would not have been able to handle. This I realize now when I have gained quite a bit experiences in dealing with future fatal accidents)

Shivali's Session– In the beginning she saw Ayan's Dad as her guide, who is standing in the lawn of his house in Delhi .There are some flowers around in the garden .She again became emotional as she felt guilty and failure of not being able to achieve and felt she had let down her father. She wanted to know the cause for her failure. Also she had been very negative and depressed while doing coaching in Delhi.

First I took her to the cause of her failure and depression at that time. She saw she was feeling very weak and lethargic because there was some smoke emanating from her kitchen gas stove towards her food being cooked; which in turn was filling her up with negativity. I was confused, the food should give her energy and strength but instead it was making her lethargic and negative .On probing further I got to know the positioning of the gas and water sink was creating vastu defect. Same way in one of the bed room the electric wires were frequently creating short circuit and making electrical appliances out of order due to vastu defects. In her room, books and papers were sending her negative energy making her burdened with heaviness and unable to cope with the studies.

Proof of healing- She saw that black smoke and heaviness gradually rushing down through the floor as her mother was doing her healing and that of the house. As by this time her mother (Mrs Nirmala Ghotia) had learnt Reiki and was doing healing for self and others. So all the defect's creating negativity was gradually getting cleared of negative energy. I was pleasantly surprised that she could see the healing effects and asked her, 'then why did you not succeeded in getting into AFMC? She replied, 'because it wouldn't have made me happy in life'. Q- 'Why you wouldn't have been happy? After all your ambition was to become a doctor and join Army .That is why you were slogging and are unhappy now because you could not succeed in it? A- 'I would have got selected and joined the Army. I don't know what to make out of this'. She paused for some time and looked confused and hesitant. On probing ,she began describing her feelings and visions, 'I see a newspaper in which there is a news about my suicide .I am in the Army and posted somewhere in a remote place. I feel very lonely, I am very sad as my friend Ayan is no more'. She was trembling with emotions and tears were rushing down her cheeks. Then she herself started giving clarification for the action which as if she had done or would have done in future. 'We both had decided to be together in the Army and if he is not there, I don't feel any purpose being in the Army or in life itself.' She went on to narrate what she was viewing. Then as if she is coming out of that horrid future and she is feeling relieved. 'Now I am happier as I understand that it has been for my good that I did not join the Army but took up some other course.

Psychic attack –She saw one known person, who claimed to be very spiritual that is why he was friendly with me. But internally she saw him sending negative vibes to our house. She explained, 'Ayan is acting as a protecting shield between his family and the negativity sent by this man. Ayan is tied with ropes and this man is telling him, I will not leave you, your mother has caused much harm to me, that is why Ayan is becoming negative , depressed and his relationship with his mother is not good. As if there is no communication between both of you. This time also he wanted to talk to you, take your help in erasing his fear of crossing the road, but he could not convey it. Neither had you given any importance to his problem.

Channelled healing -Now she was seeing Ayan standing and directly talking to me, 'why you had to go to Bhuj now only, you could have gone some other time? I was also directly communicating to his subconscious through her as we do while healing somebody distantly. I asked forgiveness from him, if he felt hurt. I also stressed. It was my test and you being my son will understand my yearning and need to attend to my soul's calling. And if you are asking for healing, for that there is no distance, I am healing you right now from your phobia. I healed him through her, she saw healing Light fall on him, slowly releasing those ropes in which he was tied. He was feeling lighter and happier. As if now understanding everything, my predicament, his willingness to protect his family from any harm. She also saw that he is in the train at this time and going back to his college to Bangalore. When he was in sleep in the train the negativity had affected him because his subconscious had been open then. Whatever negativity was sent by this gentleman towards your family was received by Ayan. I wanted to know why and how is Ayan protecting his family? She replied, 'there is some protective shield around him, this gives him the strength to withstand the negative effect, which others could not have with stood. What is this shield and why it is around him only? I asked her, 'this was earned by him in some life by helping people.' was all she said.

(At that time I had not thought seriously about what shield she is talking about , gradually as I am going through his case everything is becoming more clear . Was this the shield he described, 'the guide had pushed something in me to make me swell? That is why only he had described to me about psychic attack done by some man in our village, whom neither he knew personally nor I could trace his identity. He had even described about this known gentleman's negative intension on my work but I had not taken his revelations seriously ,thinking it Ayan's conscious interpretations of his biased opinion towards this gentleman, whom he may not be liking for some reason. In both cases Ayan had nothing to do with these two people. Was he protecting me by being victim to their negative projection towards me and others in the family? That means it is true that we have to pay back the debts for our ancestors' deeds. Because the man in my village had something to take revenge with my father, and this friend of mine had professional jealousy with me)

Healing fatal future– Realizing some significance of what all she was revealing, I got curious to know what all had been healed in Ayan's life? I asked her, 'what would have happened to our life had I not been doing healing? She started seeing as if another life we would be leading .She said, 'you all are very sad rather miserable. Ayan is no more alive and you are blaming his dad for it. He is also feeling guilty for Ayan's death; there is also some court case going against him.' She went on to narrate further in detail. In between she would get confused and question herself, how is this possible? Every incident was different from what it is now. She started describing in detail the circumstances leading to Ayan's death, 'Ayan's nose is being operated, he is on the operation table .He is bleeding excessively, its emergency, everybody is tense .Suddenly she exclaimed, Oh God! He is dead on the operation table. How is this possible?

She was again filled with intense emotions and pain. She turned towards me and said empathically, 'you did not want him to get operated; his dad took this firm decision as he wanted him to be medically fit to join the Army. Ayan's Dad is feeling very guilty as you all are blaming him for Ayan's death , because of this operation. All of you are very sad and separated from each other.

"Ayan's dad is doing some operation on a patient'. Again she was seeing things and self-criticizing, "How can he give anesthesia, he is not anesthesiologist? "Because of this the patient is paralyzed. He has been sued in the court for this negligence. But it's not Delhi. He is somewhere far from Delhi"(as at that time Ayan's dad was posted in Delhi , she was trying to co-relate the events with present time and what she was seeing internally . She was confused and also surprised why she was seeing something which isn't true at that moment? Like Ayan's death on the operation table, his dad not anesthesiologist, then why is he giving anesthesia, which is causing him a court case. He is posted in Delhi but this case is happening somewhere else).

(It was natural for her to feel confused and unsure of what she was seeing because she was seeing something which was probable but may not happen as things were being healed gradually)

(After the session was over, surprisingly she described many things, which she could not explain during the session, either she could not understand or had no time to narrate while in the session .She said, 'I am a bridge between you and your son. I will help you both break the barrier of misunderstanding. I also saw that I have become a Reiki Master much later in my life, when you are not there anymore .'(meaning when I would not be alive)

What has Reiki given us? The universe was revealing what healing has done for our family. I was too happy to have received recognition from my Reiki Gurus in the form of' Best Reiki Master's and Best Reiki Grand Master's' award in the year 2005 and 2006. This was more than enough to encourage and give me confidence that there is someone watching up there and appreciating my actions

.My mother in law became my teacher at this time and always taunted on my excessive involvement with healing and questioned ,what has Reiki given to our home ? I had felt pained at that time because I never expected anything in return. I was content that I was getting some inner peace and stability in me while pursuing healing .Though I always had a feeling that Reiki has been giving us something invaluable, but what it was, I had no idea? I could not expect or even imagine that I could get direct feedback like this. My logical mind's conditioning of considering myself limited and separated had not yet broken completely (This is the problem with our logical mind, which considers itself very honest, weighing and measuring everything judiciously. But it still has got limited capacity to keep account of everything. The universal mind has got more fitting account which can never misinterpret and waver in its reward)

Why would Divinity shy away from rewarding me for my selfless actions?

Was this revelation a reward for my dedication without any expectations or feed back of my efforts in healing or an answer to the question 'what has Reiki given us'? My throat chocked with emotions for some time and then followed uncontrolled tears rolling down my face. Tears of gratitude to the higher world that this is what it had to teach me, tears of pain for what we had in store for us and we would have to go through it in the future, tears of relief that all this will not happen now.(I also knew there is something negative about Ayan when in one of his session he saw himself in AFMC hostel room but the darkness in the room was making him uncomfortable and sad) I had been healing him for obesity, and for seeking admission in medical course in AFMC. Sometimes he would be so upset and annoyed with me that out of frustration he would shout ,you are mad ,so is your Reiki. I was novice at that time, so I had asked Sunita (Manager Reiki Healing Foundation) for his this outburst .Her answer very aptly fits with my experiences now. She said, 'sometimes the bucket is so empty and it takes so much time and efforts to fill it that people feel frustrated and lose hope and belief in healing '. Now I have seen it myself that sometimes when there is so much and many life times to be healed, the person is not able to tolerate high healing energy. They feel very restless while healing as if the bright light falling on them is making them close their eyes and they are avoiding opening it for fear of getting hurt by this Light. That is why healing does not depend totally on the healer. The amount of energy a person to be healed can tolerate is being transmitted and transfused. Everybody is unique with varying capacity to integrate this Divine energy ,that is why things cannot be rushed but has to be waited with hope, faith and courageous patience.

There are no failures in healing; there can never be any harm.

Healing is a mercy, descending through healing hands in response to a plea sent to the Divine by a suffering soul .Healing is our reconnection back to our Origin. One is not to demand the result but to surrender to the Divine will, learn to have patience and accept the outcome optimistically. As everything is happening according to Higher Will. As in any venture there are two types of goals, long term and short term goals. Sometimes the short term goals have to be sacrificed for long term goal but nothing goes waste. Can we call an activity like preparing the soil, implanting a seed and then watering it, protecting it from harsh surrounding, a waste of time and energy, as so far no result is visible yet. ? Without this basic preparation no long lasting plant can bear the fruit. Same is with healing, if we are doing it unconditionally and yet there is no visible result, be assured that the basic foundation is getting strengthened. We may become impatient and view things in terms of success and failure in worldly sense and feel frustrated as our short term goal has not materialized. But in spiritual terms, healing is about releasing our negative karma, healing our past, present and future. Because past, present and future are not compartmentalized, these are running simultaneously. Healing is about digging the thorny seeds,(causes of the present life problems originating in the past ,dissolving these and clearing the soil from ill effects of these thorns and then planting flowers(healthy and progressive seeds) At this stage only we can become interior decorator of our own house, our body vessel. We can avail benefit of free will.

Lesson from Ayan's sessions –

Everything I would come across later was being revealed to me through him from the higher dimension.

Crushed my ego of thinking myself very noble and humble at the outset by telling me that I had killed him in one life. This helped me become non-judgmental as how can I become a moral guardian and judge others when I myself had been declared culprit by my own son.

Nobody is greater or smaller -He was very close to Jesus when Jesus was on earth and I was the one who did not accept Jesus at that time. Making it clear that not necessary those who are spiritual today, have been always so. We all have been good and bad both in the past and even now also. Just like a child may not have been serious in one class but improved in the next class. So nobody is smaller or greater.

Guides are present in human form -He also aquatinted me that not only the God form or spiritual Beings can be our guides but any living person can be our guide. Apart from his grandfather, once his father had come as his guide. Once his guide had resembled one of his distant uncles. If Guides are our teachers, so our near dear ones are the best teacher, teaching us through direct interaction, relationships and experiences.

Messages from higher dimension inculcated hope and faith in the higher plan of things thus making me ready to become responsible and confident to start doing things independently.

Distance healing– He gave me feedback on distance healing done by me on him and some other people, who were not even aware of anything being done to them by me. I did not possess any intuitive powers and experiences at that time ,so I was also not sure whether my healing is really doing anything to them because of lack of feedback from them or from any other source. I felt reassured that I am not wasting my efforts, my action is being watched and I am on the right direction.

Psychic attack and black magic –Though, initially I could not believe in his revelations of such things because like others I was blocked to accept any such possibility, for the obvious reasons. Probably now I had arrived at the mile stone where this truth is revealed and experienced .It was revealed to me for the first time by him and I had taken notice of it as I could not deny the authenticity of his experience and later others verified this fact.

Soul's possessing living people- Even my pet dog, who used to bite people was possessed by some spirit, that is why it did not want positive people to touch it, because the negativity will have to be dissolved, which the possessing entity wanted to prevent .The dog was so cute and loving and was attracted to us naturally but the moment we touched it with love and pampering, it used to bite unconsciously.

Assessing subtle energy around us:

Negative energy- I asked him about negativity affecting our house, and he had been able to see exactly the objects in the house emanating negative energy, like crystals used in the car were lying in a tray without cleaning. Peacock feather lying in the corner of the room had collected negative energy on the way from where it was brought. The same negative energy was spreading in the house like thin layer of smoke.

In my room,I was using a black cloth for crystal ball gazing, it was absorbing all the negativity from the surrounding but was also absorbing positive energy from me. In that altered state of consciousness he advised me to use yellow colour cloth instead.

Positive energy –

Effect of healing -He explained to me how healing converts negative thoughts into positivity , if the mind is thinking and moving in the negative direction and while healing him through Reiki midway it changes into positive direction.

Power of crystal- How the crystal is getting broken by excessive negative energy unable to bear it ?By charging the crystals how these are spreading positive energy.

Conduit for channelled healing- He was also instrumental in giving me a hint at substitute or channelled healing for others. He became a channel to know about his Grandmother's eyes problem as if she had knowingly tied a black ribbon tightly around her eyes. Which she was expecting we should remove it .He saw his father's chakra full of blockages .I also healed his father and grandmother through him and the result was that his father also became open to experience my healing sessions.

He had stopped going to past life for seeing any cause from the time when in one of the session he had said I am my own guide from now onwards. That was the time his past life was healed, which would have resulted in ending this life midway as has been happening in the past many lives by creating similar circumstances. For further healing and progress he required time and surrender to higher will (patience). And it was for this reason that he was sent far away from me as I might become impatient and feel disappointed that in spite of my sincere efforts his obese body is not reducing in size .

Once in a while whenever he came home ,he always had some or the other minor problem and was always willing for healing.

Internal vision- He started seeing his problems in his ethereal body, the physical twin (the blue print of our physical body).

His nasal septum looked curved and obstructing the passage, His bronchus is displaced from his trachea thus he feels much suffocated and has breathing problems and frequent cold. In subsequent sessions he saw it being healed and assuming its proper place. His chronic cold had subsided by now but over weight still persisted.

Obesity- He saw his mind is not detached from his abdomen that is why he functions from his gut. His abdominal area (in ethereal body) is full of nerves and these multiple nerves cause excessive hunger in him. He cannot think of anything else but about fulfilling his hunger. When he is disappointed he cannot think of anything else to erase his depression other than eating. I detached his mind from his gut. So that his mind can function independently and sealed those extra nerves (nadis) so that the supply to extra area is cut off.

Why his body is still fat? In another session he saw the nerves are less in numbers but knots type making it difficult to filter the fat from them and thus the fat gets deposited in his body. By directing healing light, these knots were dissolved and excess fat is getting burnt. But then he saw that his body looked very emaciated and thin with holes and fissures init. Thus, this fat was protecting these weak points in his body. When healed further his body looked white astral and started stretching and strengthening. Making it look taut and slim trim. Making it clear to me that his weight loss will have to be slow and gradual as the fat is protecting his weak points, where there is memory of some wear and tears and energy leaks in his body, the vital force might leak out from these weak points, if he reduces weight before these weak points are healed. Every point has been caused by some negative experience. Which would again resurface creating similar experience, fatal and painful . Thus, these are needed to be healed to erase such memory and seal the fissures.

Nothing is wasted-He also gave me feedback that everything is happening but we need to have patience. As many life times are being healed. Everybody is unique, and there is paradox in nature. There is a very thin line of demarcation what is right and what is not. We have to work hard to achieve what we desire, yet surrender to the Higher Will which has to be fulfilled first. Material desires also have some purpose because when we intend to heal these desires, if it has not succeeded in fulfilling that material desires then something grave is being healed from our memory.

Was his obesity a protection provided from higher dimension as he has fallen into the habit of compulsive victimization of meeting fatal end in many lives? This mechanical cycle needed to be broken by bringing the past experiences in to the surface and erasing altogether .Healing is the energy, the awareness which apply break to this mechanical cycle .Thus by creating desires in him , it was creating circumstances where more and more healing light is projected in him.

By now he had started feeling the importance of healing. He confined in me, 'whenever I am upset over something I always heal by doing Reiki'. I was also healing him for obesity and whenever he requested me for any other reason. I was more than willing to do Reiki for him , as in my family he was the one who had so much experiences in past life and Reiki healing.

Why he has been the victim in many lives?

When I saw so much maturity in him, I asked him to see what is the root cause of his suffering? He said, I don't know, I can only see that I am chopping off the flesh from a big whale and probably selling it to people to earn a living. I asked him to ask forgiveness from that whale because wherever that whale is, it has not forgiven him or his own soul has not forgiven him that is why he has been suffering in many past lives. He replied, 'yes, it is in the sky, now not as a whale but in some other form and it is willing to forgive me.

My teeth problem -I also got tempted to ask him about my teeth problem, which has been from my childhood and till now I have to keep visiting the dental department for filling and extraction. I asked, 'can you tell why I have weak teeth? He said, 'yes, I can see, you are pulling out the teeth of an elephant. For the purpose of healing, I asked him to ask for forgiveness from my side for causing it so much pain knowingly or unknowingly. He said in astonishment, 'it is papa in that elephant form and is forgiving you now. But he says what damage has been done cannot be undone but he forgives you now. I said, 'thanks for forgiving me now at least'.

Purpose of healing him-After learning from Ayan that I was his culprit , I always had this thought in mind that the victim and culprit have to work out their karma together, one by suffering and other by being his close relation and enduring his suffering by watching him go through that suffering. Because subconsciously, one is guilty and other one is revengeful. Though consciously both may be suffering and wanting remedial measure. I was convinced earlier also and now he gave me the proof that I must have pulled somebody's teeth causing teeth problem in me.

Teaching for me-When I asked him what is the purpose of your so many problems and my healing you this way? He replied, 'when you will compile all your experiences in your book, you will come to know everything'. I was coming to know in bits and pieces from the beginning; initially it was just assumption and presumption which were slowly becoming fool proof. When he said this, I was reminded of the dreams which Sushila had described to me in January and Samira in February 2008. Why I am compiling everything here? Because he told me that I will come to know everything when I will compile his case. I was analysing dreams and understood that dream gives some message to the dreamer. But by now I had grasped this insight that if I am sharing my experiences and learning with others ,so that at least some one might become aware to take some message home from it ,so are others' experiences and dreams for me to take meanings from it .

Now, I understand the meaning conveyed through Sushila's dream.. That time I also did not think its meaning can be applied universally.

Sushila –February 2008- Dream.

Two children are playing happily, but when the time came to leave the school, they started crying and bleeding as if they are injured .Though they seemed to be children of her relatives' but she could not recognize who they actually are? When their father came to take them, seeing him, she is wondering as the father looks very wicked and frightening. She is trying to pacify them and is also thinking, till now they were playing happily and when the time came to go home, why did they start crying?

Analysis –This was a symbolic dream .These two children were her relatives and they were busy playing in the world (school) But were destined to leave for our Home early (cut life short) When they are in this life (school) they are busy playing and had forgotten their (destiny/ Kaal/ father) but when their school time is up, their pain and suffering is reminding them of their dreaded fate (kaal / father). She had no alternative but to hand them over to their father .Short life is the destiny to cut life mid-way (This was also a message for her that in such situation, she will have to hand them over to destiny. The dreaded father is loving father now because the child has endured much suffering and while healing he has understood the cause for his sufferings.

Samira's Dream- March 2008- (these both ladies Has sessions with me in 2008) Samira dreamt that a lady is sitting on the ground with her child, whose legs are plastered and right hand is cut and lying separated from his body. His devil looking father had chopped it from his body. Mother is very patiently nursing the child. But Samira is filled with rage and asking the mother in astonishment, 'how can you be so cool and tolerate such violent man to be his father? The mother is calmly explaining to her, 'don't worry, it will also get healed. See how his legs are healed'. She can see that the legs are healed and mother is trying to heal that right arm by bringing it closer to the body and plastering it together. Samira is filled with hatred towards such dreaded father and is astonished at the mother's patience.

Analysis-Till now I thought the dream was for her but now I could not help but reflect the meaning it had wanted to convey to me .I thought am I the mother who has to nurse her child unconditionally irrespective of who does it to him. Destiny or Kaal is included in the divine plan until we put effort to heal, become aware and exercise free will to change the outcome for our higher growth. We have created our own destiny ignorantly/ unknowing or knowingly by defying the laws of nature. Our father (kaal) is only teaching us by making us undergo experiences, what we have done to others. Is the victim like an innocent child, who has angered his devil looking father(kaal)? Or is victim a naughty child who has harmed others just for fun? No one can convincingly answer such questions until person arrives at his own understanding. That is why it is said, 'When we have arrived at the destination, we may realize that the journey has been from myself to Self.'

What is the Root cause? When was the actual beginning?

Once Ayan had asked me, 'how an action becomes a karma? If you killed me, that was my karma, I understand I must have done something. But when and why was I forced to do that something which caused fatal action by you .I mean when was the actual beginning? I had tried to explain to him with whatever little understanding I had. But this has helped me in accepting that nobody is greater and no one is smaller .I am his mother, his healer and I call myself seeker. He is a child and victim but he is asking me a question which I still had not dared to ask anybody because I don't think I have matured enough to understand the complex explanation? I don't want to search philosophical answer but whatever practically is offered to me.

It is very difficult to fathom the working of Karma. People do same action and reap different rewards. Though it is said that it is not the action but the intension behind it and in thinking doer of the action. But then action done in ignorance also causes reaction. Nobody is excused for an ignorant action. That is why ignorance is a curse. Whenever we are judging some body or some incident from the history, we are also becoming partner in that action, and thus we have to become the victims to same circumstances. (This verifies group karma, where many people meet same fate like accidents or natural calamities). In my opinion we are not only paying back for our actual deeds , in many cases we may not be actual perpetrator of the action but we might be facing victimization for judging actions done by others to be wrong. I on my part am not judging anybody or anything and collect more karma, where ever I have quoted something, it is just to draw inference and conclusion not to criticize or reject any happening or a person.

How can we judge? And why should we judge?

Is once culprit, now being victim to same circumstances where he must have been perpetrator of the action? Where is the beginning, where is an end? Is birth a beginning and death an end or death a new beginning? I am writing this to clarify my stand that just by doing few sessions in past life; I cannot judge somebody's action to be good or bad. Since I am a healer and my intension is to heal a person from the sufferings, erase the illusion of separation and bring in him transformation by enlightening him to accept the cause displayed by the subconscious to be the cause of his present life problem .The memory in subconscious is like a virus in the computer. Healing means to erase that faulty memory of holding somebody else responsible for our life or holding ourselves guilty for others' miseries. Replacing it with higher understanding or universal knowledge. That nobody is punishing others, nobody is rewarding anybody. Reach at this understanding that we are creating everything according to our thoughts, words and deeds.

This life is a school –A child cannot be judged a failure based on one subject. He simply needs to be made understand his weak points .Tomorrow the same child may excel in his weaker subject or in another field even making his teacher feel proud of having had the opportunity to teach him once.

This life is a stage and each one is acting their part to the perfection..Like an excellent actor what if he gets personified and typecast with the same character.

Getting stuck is also a part of the growing up process, no activity is waste, no experience is to harm. Everything is included in the overall plan. Evolution and Enlightenment is slow and arduous process .It is perfectly fine to rest now and then. It means the actor is tired or having some difficulty in accepting another role.

Who is the villain, who is the hero? Has villain come from some other Creator? This is the same question like who created the creation and who created the creator of the creation. The whole fight and conflict in different religious faith is because of this ambiguity. Creation is because of duality.

Negative and positive are like two charge of an atom that can create current, some movement. Shiva or just pure consciousness is motionless or calm in itself. It is Shakti /Creation which brings motions, life in to this calmness. The negative character or negative experience is the contrast background on the canvas to make scenery shine forth .Negativity offers resistance by creating obstacles, because this life is not a race to be won over .We must listen to the music before the song is over.

Some after thought -

If Life is a Mystery, then yes, our life was also shrouded with mystery. We could have never imagined the events in Ayan's life taking turn in this way. Life is kept a mystery to protect us from carrying unnecessary burden all the time. Because we have learnt certain moral values and we try to fit in conventional mould of goodness. We judge ourselves according to present status and circumstances, forgetting that we are journeying since ages for gaining various experiences. We don't want to face the truth and unpleasant experiences. Thus till the time is ripe everything is kept under the wrap (maya ka parda),gradually enfolding incidents and circumstances . .

If life is an open book, it is so. We wish for best of everything, yet we are filled with fear of uncertainity There are always hidden clues giving hunches . What we fear may come true and what we resist will persist. Following guiding hunches and clues were present in his case.

-My mental state at the time of his birth. Empathizing more with his previous family . Was it hidden guilt from the past, which subconsciously, I would have to deal in this life? (Future is probable occurrence so anything could have happened. A- Why we empathize with the parents who go through pain and guilt when child dies after being hit by his parents over a trifle matter or vice versa ? We know that every parent bring up their children by giving their flesh and blood. As past memory of such fatal event becomes alive and victim easily leave the body. B. Why does a child give heartache to his parents by dying young? C .Why parents' regret having born such worthless child who is giving them heartaches and destroying his own life by falling in bad company or crime , in drugs or addiction ? We are all culprits of same circumstances and we might have to be victims any time)

Why did I get hold of some words spoken by Bapu Asha Ram ji in one of his discourses in 1999?

1. Don't become a mother simply to wish for material riches and worldly pleasure for your child. Be a mother to help him free from coming to womb again and again. I would wonder, is it possible to wish and accomplish such higher things for our loved ones?

2. Who knows your child born to you is which life's enemy, friend or a servant? He will either take revenge or be a friend or serve you according to his past memory.

3. Wasn't my dream warning me not to be very harsh on him? So that past mistake is not repeated.

4. His imaginative play of a soldier game, his ambition to join Army was taking him in the pre destined direction..

5. His laziness and obesity making it obvious that he had overtired and starved his body.

6. His desire to own a vehicle but not getting fulfilled because of his father's fear of accident and financial constraints were protecting him from meeting accidents, all because of healing.

Life is uncertain

Whether we believe in it or not, we are drawn towards fortune reading, astrology, and other such predictions. We somehow want guidance and assurance because we are uncertain what may come up .

There are some who even criticize fortune readers for predicting bad future, some argue of inaccuracy in prediction. If there is a bad event, it will happen unnoticed and unprepared. Above all future is predicted as much as one is mature enough to handle it . If something predicted didn't come true, it might have changed to some better or worse attainment depending on our effort and attitude in life.

Predictions in his horoscope

His first horoscope from Simla (palvi) by one God gifted astrologer had two significant predictions in it ,which were ridiculed and rejected then and there. It said, "(He will be wheatish in complexion). Like most children, he was quite fair when he was born . Second one was that his mother will be a great devotee (bhakt) and he will be very obedient and her admirer). At that time I wasn't anywhere near considering myself Devotee in the conventional sense .Though everybody desires to have obedient children yet I could not think myself that fortunate that my son will be very obedient and my admirer. I could not imagine I would develop so much faith and feel so connected that I will be able to have glimpse of truth behind superficial nature of our life. I am seeking and devoted to the supreme Source through healing (Sadhna) . Ayan has accepted to be recipient of this Divine Grace (Healing) that itself means he is obedient and admirer of my work. I asked him, 'how much you do believe in healing? He replied, I cannot quantify how much, but I know there is a basis for every physical phenomenon in the mystic world , I am having a glimpse of it in every healing session. I am also using Reiki whenever I am disturbed over something. Recently there was an article about past life case in the newspaper and unlike others, I have not read it just like another vague research and forgot it. I know there is truth in it as I can relate to it with my personal experiences".

One of the significant predictions have been through Nadi astrology readings in January 2008 .It says, at present he is under the influence of ' Kaal serp dosh 'a very grave and grim period, where nothing will fall in place. Depression, obstacles and failures in pursuing his desired course in study , fatal accidents, monetary loss, not able to keep his promise all truly indicated his present circumstances.

There is always something lacking, physical discomfort, some unfulfilled desire, feeling lonely and out of place due to biased attitude of people from different culture in that part of the country .

Isn't it because of healing that he completed his dentistry course from Bangalore? He had serious accident but did not have irreparable loss of body parts , monetary loss or failure in study . He could have a successful career in the Army,,other wise there are infinite possibilities waiting for him, as he can avail an option of free Will now. Place or position doesn't matter. He is happy in his professional life.

Courage Is a Fear That Has Said Its Prayer

Fear is the darker side of the thing without knowing what is there

It is not that I could fully accept the revelations made by Ayan during his sessions. But I could not reject either. Every time I thought I am nearing the truth, I felt higher truth replacing the one below it. I was ready to face any harsh reality simply because of confidence that Healing Energy will protect its user because I am simply a representative of God , my intention is pure and I have surrendered to the Higher Will to manifest the best for me.

I was like a fool without fear who is better than an Angel with fear. I knew courage is a fear that has said its prayer. Simultaneously all sorts of self-dialogue were going on in my mind. If it is true then why don't people know and accept this reality, if it is simply his imagination, then what is the source of his imaginations? He wouldn't have even read such fictitious stories or watched any such movies. As far as his family background was concerned, there was nothing to give him such information.

Slowly other people were coming to me for healing and surprisingly revealing similar and much more such facts. As I started opening up to accept some truth in this, I was also seeking some proofs for it by various other people researching this reality. Past life therapy work has not revealed much on this sort of information .My teacher had apprised us of the risk of spirits coming up during Regression sessions which would sometimes prove to be quite annoying and stubborn and may fill up the therapist with negativity. After few months, my qualified and experienced teacher left this work on her Guru's advice as she was getting affected by such cases, besides her Guru was against healing and past life therapy because he believed that why should one play with higher energies ? If past life is kept a secret then ,why should we try to dig it up , God did not want us to know it,that is why we don't remember it? Why should we go against nature?

After getting verifications on such phenomenon I proceeded to write my first book 'Mystic Life Revealed'. I would request people to be more aware and enlightened to the fact that as a particular drug is required for a particular disease, same is applicable to such negative influences. Some people are blocked to accept such facts. They say if they haven't seen anything of this sort, then it does not exist. They are so hypnotized by the logical mind that they are ready to believe a person suffering from any bacterial or viral infection, though neither they have ever suffered nor they have seen the virus or bacteria and how it affects any individual. For which they are ready to believe others (doctors) but for people who are suffering because of negative influences (spirit, psychic attack, all mental sicknesses, past life influences creating this life's circumstances) they simply call them their imagination and having no existence at all. Because whatever science cannot explain, it simply refuses to believe and brushes it aside.

We have to learn to take responsibility, to heal such things .We cannot get away by calling a spade a spade. The issue has to be addressed sensitively and with good intension, both for the victim as well as to the source of negativity. Reiki healing and regression have proved to be effective in this type of negative influences .Slowly the dark patch of negative energy which may have any form ,may be a spirit possessing some body or some psychic attack projected on the victim or even Tantric work done by powerful tantric. All have been released effectively and safely. There is never any danger either to the healer or the victims as opposed to the people who are asked to perform frightening rituals along with Tantric and shamans himself ,to get rid of the negativity from the victim.

Tantrics do possess some power not only to eradicate something of this sort but also some control in spreading this negativity either with the intension to harm the victim or control others with his powers . One possibility could be that not having the proper understanding of the subject subtle energy world, they may be ignorantly spreading this negativity on to the face of the earth. (I have seen people without any knowledge trying plan-chit (automatic writing) and then getting possessed by earthly wandering negative spirits)

When I had started doing a course in past life therapy, I was so happy thinking that I can come to know the cause for everything and then healing will be spontaneous. During that time I had a dream in which I was in some big gathering and repeating these lines which are still fresh in my mind. " I was saying that when we started from home in the morning it was dark and now when we are back home, it is still dark. 'Ghar se chale the jab hum subah tab bhi andhera tha ,ab jab ghar pahunchen hain tab bhi andhera hai.' Which I concluded was giving me a message that if I think that I will come to know the cause for everything through past life therapy then I am still in the darkness because there was much more to come up subsequently.

(Now I understood the meaning of the dream. Whatever work on past life regression is done so far, is not all there is., I still have to open the new mysteries of the mystic world. After all, I had ventured into the depth of mind only after I had transformed brain object into mind energy through healing. Being energy it had no limitation of physical nature and could be connected to the universal mind and receive information on anything from anywhere. It is a natural evolutionary step .And in the beginning I was being given the preview of the depth, I would have to venture as everything is being recorded in the universal memory.

Here is the brief account of research done on the subject of mystic mysteries and verification of my information revealed to me through regression session.

Dolores Cannon through her research into hypnosis and past life therapy in her book "Conversation with a Spirit" describes the reality of ghosts, possessions, poltergeists and other negative entities influencing people in physical form. Also the existence of God, Guides, Angels positively helping one attuning to them through contemplation, meditation, dreams etc.

Karmic Facts &Fallacy by Ina Marx)
Psychic attack

Human Devolution' by Michael A Cremo .The Scientific explanation of Wandering Souls/spirit possessions /stagnant energy, Remote viewing Targ and Path Off p 607.
Astronomer Camille Flammarion. In his master piece "Death and Its Mystery"

Alfred R Wallace the scientist , who co-authored "The Theory Of Human Evolution" along with Darwin "Beyond Stones and Bones and The Spirit World" he writes.

In Mahabharata Lord Krishna had conferred the power to Sanjay to view the war between Korvas and Pandva in the battle field of Kurukshetra, what may be compared to the present time remote viewing.

In Bhagvad Geeta 11.15-1 describes these psychic abilities as mystic perception of yoga, acquired by yogi, who has conquered the breathing process and fixed his mind on me attains sidhi. One of which is (dura shrawana dura darshana) the ability to see and hear things at a distance. Chapter 15th deals with sidhis and how to attain these. Interesteringly enough the sidhis are considered obstacles for those on the path of complete spiritual perfection.

As one may get tempted to using these sidhis for selfish goal and acquire power, which may help ego boost.

No deed is spared but can be substituted-

Nobody is spared because we are a culprit, so we have to be victims sometimes and pay back in the same coin. Pinpointing fault with outside world, blaming others for our sufferings, we cannot escape the pain we have caused to others. Our deeds can be substituted with some softer ,less painful payback, provided we make amends , make our self-worth of seeking grace (healing) pray for mercy , try to ease or soothe somebody else of his pain selflessly. People blame God, destiny, and others for their miseries. They can cry , complain about the injustice meted to them by Fate , God, and system . They can show their physical bruises and medical bills, seek solace by taking marches against social malice and gain sympathy by showing their apparent sufferings. I had only my inner corner to turn to and pray, whenever such eventuality was knocking my door. Healing was my only weapon, the inner engineering technique to transform pain into learning.

I have experienced the Truth

I do not have to say that I believe because I have experienced it myself, the truth behind our life's superficial appearance. My life is most ordinary like million other people I may appear fairly happy, healthy and contented yet I had my shares of backlog of karma. I had faced obstacles and failure , physical pain, mental agony, material loss, relationship problems, uncertainty, changing values. Because nobody is blessed one partial to anyone. Oblivion to the fact I had shares of my past deeds to face. I had to tell lies to pay the fee for seeking this obscure knowledge (healing), being ridiculed on my enthusiasm at some amazing experience, faced criticism for my healing efficiency ,I have been judged for my knowledge and sincere efforts. Thank God, I was spared crucifixion because others before us had faced that challenge and paved the way for us to follow.

I wonder what others must be going through, who are faced with any of such situations or much more than this. Mentally retarded children, physical handicaps, fatal diseases, accidental deaths , relationship issues ,addiction and crimes .It is a whole lot of Mahabharata and Ram Ravana Yudh (war) ,crucifixion of Messiah and sacrifice of Mohammad going on in each one's life .

We can progress by being copy cat till we seek our uniqueness

I admire great work of Western scientists and I follow the simple preaching of Eastern Gurus. I am seeking my truth and presenting it to the world. Whether others take clues from my truth and start searching their life's truth or not, that's not my prerogative. Everybody has to search for his truth by taking guidance from those who have walked ahead of us. The World is there to teach us and we are also here to do our bit and leave a trail to teach through our life story to the world.

Though we may criticize, condemn and condone the word Copy Cat. But initially, we all learn by being copycat only. Today we may resist those who are trying to teach us or we may criticize and condemn those who are trying to copy , seek inspiration from their role models .One day we have to do the same thing ourselves. Because nobody invents anything new. The journey of life is to enfold the hidden possibilities in our genetic structure and accept this truth that as you sow so shall you reap .Apple seed cannot give papaya fruit or bitter guard cannot give mango. Yet greatest secret and contradiction of creativity is enfolding the possibility of transformation and transmutation by genetic engineering of above and much imaginative creative idea .

There is nothing new

The possibilities of seed are imprinted in its memory, in its genetic structure . So one cannot say, one is doing something new. Though as a young overenthusiastic child, we may become proud and egoistic with our new found achievements. That is why I call science a young age of evolution. It is not aware of the bigger, diverse overall

Divine plan . It is overwhelmed by small feats at the hand of nature. Just as a successful young man in his glorious years of his life forgets his parents' sacrifices to bring him up from a tiny little bundle to this strong capable person . He is aware only of the fragmented part of his life remembered by the logical mind. Because it cannot go beyond that ,thus he is negating and not giving any importance to his roots. When he reaches parental stage himself, he reminisces old incidents and verifies these with his own experiences of parenthood. Everything looks funny as long as it is happening to others, the day it is forced upon us,we defend ourselves with so much intensity as if it is happening for the first time to anybody on this earth.

Every new discovery, idea and breakthrough are projected from the higher source. One is just an instrument as the radio receives the waves or glass absorbers the heat and radiates it in its surrounding. One is compelled by its tendency to attract from the cosmos its like qualities and forced by its nature to absorb it and radiate it in the surrounding. That is why in spiritual terminology our body is considered a vessel, a flute, vehicle, boat, temple of spirit (spark of divinity) . Every physical phenomenon has its origin in the mysterious metaphysical world. The spiritual dimension is the source of everything we call creation, origin, growth or dissolution.

We are compelled by our Tendencies

When we are living in physical body, we are governed by our physical senses, (by the law of the land (earth). We can believe things easily comprehended by intelligent faculty of mind. Wisdom, (viveka) the higher faculty of our mind is buried under the weight of materially manifested world. Our spiritual connection appears to be an imaginary fanciful idea, as if an alien foreign land and we have no access and knowledge of its law (universal principles). Since intellect (lower faculty of mind) has limited capacity, yet it wants to prove influential and important. Ego is threatened by not being able to comprehend inner invisible, mysterious world, thus it criticizes, negates and rejects its existence altogether.

I can speak from my own experiences how tendencies are over imposed on us. I also used logical approach of mind to weigh the worth of my wonderful inner experiences which filled me with unexplained peace. After all which intelligent mind will settle for devoting time and paying high fee for some unheard, invisible knowledge?

I rejected this invaluable knowledge for lack of self-experiences with our guides, higher self ,a hierarchical order silently operational in the divine plan. Doubted its capability of erasing illusion and healing pain, criticized its claim of leading up the ladder of evolution .Internally bargained for its value in terms of money, material, time and devotion and planned to postpone it till I have finished never ending chores of this mundane physical world.

We are puppet on a string as quoted in Bhagvata Geeta in 18.60.61.Whenever we do not want to do a thing because of delusion ,we will do it even against our will, bound by our natural duty, karma. The Lord is present inside all beings moving them like puppets by his magical strings ..

When finally I took up healing as a means for further evolution, it was also my tendency forcing me to dedicate myself wholly to heal everybody of his sufferings . I wanted to be successful in every venture I take up and get recognition. Internally I knew all these things don't matter for me yet my ego needed boost and craved recognition by feeling doer of good deeds. Because most of the time we don't live by choice and with conscious awareness ,we live by the tendencies of the physical existed world which weighs heavier towards manifested visible realities. These tendencies get over imposed and mechanically take control on our conscious self . We are drawn farther and farther from our source of origin and delaying our backward return. So much so that even highly religious and knowledgeable people also say, " who knows how many births it will take to awaken and walk towards enlightenment "? They are only accumulating more and more knowledge , heavily burdening their mind and life, that they forget to smile at small wonders of life.

Ignorant people are filling with more and more illusions till it gets totally dark. Both stop expecting existence of any miracles and lose faith and hope in the higher plan of things.

The answer has to come from within

Though there is nothing new in the universe but for an individual who is awakening up, it is a new morning every day.

Transitory worldly knowledge to train our intellectual faculty is valued so much by us that howsoever learned the parents may be, still, they will enroll their child in the most suitable school and make him follow disciplined life. Though initially he is just mastering few alphabets and motor skills.

Things of necessity for containing our physical body like water, land, wood, food etc are God made or nature's creation, but they are also not freely available.

How can we then think such higher knowledge giving such deep experiences be bargained or grabbed for free?

Contrary to this if we can make our self-worthy, feel connected and can believe in it and accept it whole heartedly, it means we have already paid the fee. The mind is the only barrier -The fee is to break the barrier in the mind, clear the blockage from our system. Every process, path, prayer, and Sadhna is not to please anybody or God but to break this barrier in the mind, to make it accept, what is there. Whatever the mind can perceive and heart believes it, then there is nothing impossible to achieve. The journey of life is more inward than outward, the outer boundaries, barriers and victories are just the reflections of our inner world .Progress in the journey is indicated by the apparent change in surrounding, scenery and the circumstances. The change in our attitude, awareness, and understanding change the meaning of the journey. So, in the beginning, the meaning of my dream I had mentioned earlier but now I have found out the answer ' Ghar see chale the jab andhera tha'. It was taking me to the end of my journey when I would finally merge in that void that darkness from where each one has started. Erasing all the memory of all lives, all knowledge, and conditioning of mind and become devoid of the tendencies of swaying in one direction 'Then only one would be able to reach Home, merge in that origin of vast existence. Till the time there is knowledge, light , learning ,there is duality and we are forced by our tendency to become responsible , doing something and trying to become someone .But the ultimate goal is not to become someone but to become no one . Real home coming would be when Life comes full circle when it ends where it had begun.

3rd Case

Year 1992 is written on the calendar

Rohan February 2006

Rohan had only one session with me at his thirteen year of age, that too after much persuasion on my part as I wanted to know what relation we both shared in the past. There was nothing much revealed in terms of learning and there after he never willed to undergo any more session. But in terms of his present nature, circumstances, things can be co related.

Session– As I was guiding him back slowly, he reached a hill which looked similar to Dharamsala hills but was higher and vaster. There after he came down to one unknown street and felt sitting on a house as a bird. Then the bird flew away and became invisible.

He reached in a place where it looks as if some war had destroyed the civilization as everything is scattered and rotten in that area and insects are crawling on those destroyed and decayed objects .

Past life-"I am about thirty, thirty-two years old , sitting in one office. On the table, there are many files. I get out from the office, walk down the stairs and continue walking through the lanes. It is a foreign country, in front of the road, there are hills which are covered with snow. Some ladies wearing scarves, long skirts and coats are also going somewhere. At this point, I asked him, which year is this? He gave a very interesting reply, ' I don't know, but wait a bit , I am going back to the office, as there is a calendar in the office , it must be written in that' . He reached back to the office and read the year from the calendar and announced, " it is written 1927".

"I am going back through those lanes to my house. I am alone in my room, wall fire is burning. On the mantle of that fire place, a photo of a man and a woman is placed. I am taking out noodles from the fridge and eating it.

I am sitting in a bullock cart and going back to my home town.

I am very small lying in the baby cot. Man and woman whose photo was in my room, are my parents and sitting near my bed.

I am three/ four years old boy and am roaming alone". I wanted to know about his house, his parents, why is he alone? He said ,when I was two-three years old , my parents left me with one middle-aged neighbor lady and had gone away to earn some living . My parents never came back again. There was news that they have died or may have been being killed by someone .That lady feeds me, looks after me well.

I am fourteen- fifteen years old and am alone at the river side. My foot has got hurt. I am dipping the feet in the water, it's very cold. I feel lonely.

Now I am back to that same house where I live as a grown up man of thirty two. I am alone sitting inside the house. An old woman and man come to my house. I bring them in. They have a big gift in their hands for me". I asked him to identify who these two were? Whether they were his lost parents or the lady who looked after him or some other relative. He did not divulge any information on that, rather went ahead to narrate. He said, "I am taking them in a very funny looking car somewhere. I am driving through the curves of a hilly road. Road is not very good and at one point, car skids down and we three fall down the hill and die there itself".

After death"-I am being brought to one church; they both are taken somewhere else. Father of that church is saying something in a foreign language. It's not English or any language which I know in this life.'(That is why now he cannot understand what they are saying. There are few people around his coffin but none he knew personally there. He has been buried and some name with F is written on it.)

Heavenly experience – God is in the form of sunlight. I asked him, 'why has he come as my son? He said, 'I had helped you in one life, I had given you food, you were a sadhu (saint) and that is why we are here together. Studies don't interest me more; I have to do little of everything. I will help you later .God is already helping you.'

Concluding his session – Striking resemblance to his past life is that he was much attached to his mother, "were you a child of a dead mother in your past life'? His grandmother would retort by seeing him always clinging to his mother. He would not communicate much with others even in the family. He would not even eat or drink milk from any other person's hand. Once at his two years of age, I had to attend some important formal ladies club meet. I had fed him at twelve o' clock in the afternoon and till the time I was back at 9 pm, he had not even drank milk. He had skin allergy which started growing after six month of age (was this because where his body was laid, the place is manifested with insects and everything is decaying? Another peculiar habit he had was that he would not eat anything till one or two o' clock in the afternoon and had hardly slept peacefully till three years of age through the night. On a lighter note was his soul experiencing jet leg? As he had lived in anther far of country in his recent past life)

At the age of three year he was lost in crowded street of Kolkatta. For about an hour, till he was found, everybody in that place felt hopeless of finding him back. At that young age, he could not speak clearly and give his address. I had black out and was nervously praying, Oh God, will I never get him back now? It was at that age only in the past life that he had been separated from his parents.

As a teenager, he doesn't have many friends. He can pass his time on the computer and along with his pet dogs .He is fond of visiting places and photography.

In 2008, we had visited Leh Ladakh region and many time we went to rivers and mountains this year. He had injured his toe nail and suffered pain in it for few days. I was reminded of the memory of his past ,where he had seen that he had hurt his feet and is standing in a river alone, the water feels cold . The water is very cold like the Ladakh region but he was not alone in this life.

Nadi Astrology –Described his personal traits correctly and giving some guidance in his future course of life . One prediction which may look unbelievable to most is that this is his last birth, as he would start working towards this direction by the time he is in his forties .Though I am not here to convince skeptics or prove something, I am only here to describe many things already known to people and still there are many things existing between heaven and earth unknown to man. Yet I want to explain my reason for believing in it. If he would complete remaining work of conquering his inner boundaries, he may be liberated at the end of this life. Because we are continuing the journey of life since eternity. What all lesson we have learned, what need to be learned, we do not remember consciously. It is only enfolded in due time. I can even vouch for my first case (Kriti) that it is her last life because she had worked on other virtues in previous lives. And her God had said, 'you need to go back to earth one last time and fulfill your obligation and I give you the choice, where ever you want to be born.'

4rth Case

I Had to Come to You, so this accident happened.

Shivali 2005 Nov to 2008

Depression, Frightening dreams, Accident .

Shivali had three, four sessions with me but never had seen any past life so far. In her first session in November 2005,as I asked her to request her guide to be present there, she said, it is my late grandfather (her grandfather had died before she was born ,but she insisted that I can still recognize him) Her mother was sitting with her at the time of her session. She became very emotional and was in tears for some time and then she refused to go beyond that, so her session had to be discontinued midway.

Her second session was in October 2006, As she was away in hostel in Bangalore and she was staying with a girl who had very orthodox outlook towards life and was very frightened in the dark. Shivali was also getting affected by her behavior. Shivali also viewed her roommate's negative problems and we healed those things through her session

Third Session -October 2006. She willingly volunteered for Ayan's healing along with her, which is described earlier in this chapter.

There after also she had been having frightening dreams .She sees darkness and is filled with fear. She and her people are hounded by Gun fires, running away from some terrorists and trying to hide in some safe place .The whole process was making her feel scared, uncertain and exhausted, yet finally she could manage to reach the secure place.

October 2008- She asked me to do Reiki for selection in a job

And I felt so much pain being released from her

She requested me to do Reiki for seeking selection in topmost airlines as there was campus selection after finishing hotel management course . She was very hopeful and deserving candidate. When I was doing Reiki for her selection, I had gone into deep trance and felt that so much pain was coming out from her hands and feet, which was released through my hands and feet. I did tell about this to Ayan but warned him not to tell her , thinking that she will lose hope and become depressed .I had my own doubts in her selection as I felt something grave was coming her way and this healing has averted that. Within a week she met with an accident and broke her right little finger and damaged scooter in the process. Her finger had to be sutured and later wire had to be inserted to make it straight as her finger was getting disfigured.

She did not succeed in this selection and when she was to go for another such selection, her grandmother expired all of a sudden leaving her alone to appear for selection exam, making it unable to write and manage her documents with her injured hand. Now she wanted to heal for her finger because her injured hand became her first priority.

I am not going to be swayed by worldly things for ever

Her session in October 2008 was for healing her hand. She did not see anything, not even her fractured finger. She did feel the energy passing into it and rejuvenating it but beyond that it was dark. Subconsciously she said, 'I am rather happy that I haven't succeeded in this selection. I don't know why I am happy that my finger is broken'. I asked her to see the cause for her finger, originating somewhere from the past .She said, ' no, I haven't done anything in the past to deserve this pain and suffering'. I again persisted then why are you going through this pain, there has to be some reason? She said, ' I am also wondering how this is possible for my right little finger to break, when I had landed on to my left side hand and chest'. She kept quiet for some time and then continued, 'actually I had to be with you. I mean I could not be otherwise, so this happened '. I was surprised and confused and asked her to elaborate more. She said,' I am so fascinated by mind and its working, I want to know more and more about mysterious ways of its functioning. But there is no one to satisfy my queries. You are the one who can provide some answer to my quest. We both would be of immense help to each other. I know whatever I am doing now ,studying or trying for job and material things, doesn't matter at all to me. Same is with you. Rest of the people see everything in terms of gain and loss but you are not like them and you haven't yet got a single person ready like you, who will think these things secondary. She went on, 'I want to request you one thing 'I asked,'what? She said, 'I want to help you in editing your book'. I told her but you don't have time as you are pursuing some different course. She said, 'this is the tragedy that I want to pursue something closer to my heart but my commitment to creating a good future doesn't allow me time to work for that. But this compulsion will be only for four-five years. I am not going to be swayed by worldly things forever. I will definitely help you'. I told her that my book is ready and I cannot wait for this to be released after four-five years. She said, "but you haven't yet written it completely, the way it should have been, there is some more editing required" .

Till then I had not thought of penning her case at all other than her session which has already appeared in Ayan's case. When she said that you have to edit your book properly, you have not yet done so. I tried to convince her that to my knowledge, I have done the maximum and for eight months I have been waiting for somebody to come forward to edit it. But to no avail. So I have decided to go for printing it. She said, '"yes, by seeing it somebody is going to come forward to help you in editing it". After having some such conversation we ended her session.

Why I am writing her case?

There was nothing to write about her case as she had never seen any of her past lives. She had not seen anything in her healing session, so I had decided not to write her case. But I was reminded of the dream which I had in February 2007. That dream is still very fresh in my memory .I was to go to Bhuj for my outstation healing and teaching camp organized by her mother Mrs Ghotia . I had no help to take over family responsibility from me in my absence . So I had employed a boy through agency in February. At that time I had this dream.

My Dream in Feb 2007 -I hugged and recognized she is Shivali

In my dream ,I am far away from my home and some mishap has occurred in my house, in my absence. I can feel some Blood drops sprinkling on me, even though I am away somewhere from where I cannot reach back home in time .Something tragic has already happened. When I reach back home , I see Rohan ,my mother in law, one helping boy is lying bleeding, injured and crying in pain . Mother in law is saying, 'oh my God, my head is broken '. And there is injury and blood on her left side forehead. In the dream itself, I start healing her, she is healed and then others also are healed. One by one they start getting up from where they were lying on the floor, in different rooms. But there is someone lying on one bed .It seemed he is already dead, as his injuries are deep. I feel very sad and regret loosing somebody his life in my house. Yet I start healing that person. Slowly he gets up as if coming out of a deep sleep or coming out back from death. I hug that person in happiness. When I hug her and I recognize. She is Shivali).

After having this dream giving me warning of some untoward happening in my absence at my home, I started healing my house and all these people for safety and security.

The day I was on the train going to Bhuj , I got a phone call from my home , that my mother in law has hit her left side forehead and there are bruises and slight bleeding as she hurt herself against the corner of the bed. I was convinced that this is the feedback to me, just to show me how the healing of something more serious accident could have happened.)

When Shivali told me that I have not written elaborately my cases, the thought of that dream came to my mind. Her healing for selection in the job done by me and during that negative projection in the form of pain released from her through me also became alive. There was something definitely fatal coming her way which has got healed this way, not only by me but by her mother, who now and then does her healing for various reasons.

My Dream in Oct 2008

I cry in the dream saying that she is not our Deepa now, she is somebody else-The day Shivali was to come to me for healing for her finger, the previous night I had a very vivid dream. In which I see many events of our life and somebody is telling me many things about the course of events taking place.

1. Ayan is discharged from hospital but he still looks obese. It reminds me that I have to start healing him for obesity again.

2.Then my mother in law wanted to prove me wrong ,pretending to be quiet and still, but wakes up and says that she was listening to what all I was saying that she is not alive. Again she lies down in her bed without trouble and we all know that she is expecting her end and dies peacefully. I think within myself, a very peaceful way to depart.

3. My father is searching his shoes, but they are of different sizes. And he is running fast. I try to help him, so I run behind him to catch him. Somebody else is also running with him. He is my cousin Ajay. I fear the danger of them meeting with the accident because of their speed. By the time I reach them, they both fell on the ground. By the time I manage to catch my father, he looks just like sticks (skeleton) I pick him and hug him dearly.

4. Someone tells me that Deepa has come back (rebirth). I ask, "Where? The answer comes, 'as Anaya". I presume must be Neena's child born is the year. (In reality, someone had just opinioned this prophecy and I thought it can be true) I start crying saying, 'but she is not our Deepa now, she is somebody else. I try to recollect who Anaya is. She is Anuja's daughter.

I try to recollect who is telling me all this, and I presume, it is she(Shivali) who is coming to me for her healing session next day .

But next day Shivali had a session with me,she did not see any of these things. Thus I got convinced that I would be revealed in dreams all the things because I need verification thus somebody else will be telling me all of it just to verify things already known to me.

My state of mind I felt no urge to live

In November 2008 I was going through a very strange phase as I felt no urge to live. I thought my work is over, what I wanted to know, I know it for sure now, if people are not ready to accept the truth, which I know ,then I have no purpose left in this life. I think this life I had to live and work this much only. I know nothing goes waste and life never ends. Rest will continue in the next life. I did not feel enthusiasm and interest in healing others because I had realized that I cannot be life guard and saviour to others, if they don't want to take step forward. So many people have been healed in the past four five years by me but after wards no body truly believes and be ready to openly acknowledge the importance of healing. After they are healed and get busy in their usual affairs of life, they forget their pain and problems as if it was a distant dream happening to somebody else. If people cannot accept the truth I want them to know, while I am alive because of mental barrier, they will do so after my death. I felt as if this is the stage of accepting crucifixion for the good of humanity. I wasn't depressed in the usual sense, I only regretted not been able to share what I had already achieved in this life. I told about my feeling of no desire to live, to my close associates. Susnigdho, Ayan, Shikha, Anjana and others. I asked them to pray for me if they want me to be alive, otherwise I don't feel any urge to live more . Though I did not want my research work to go unnoticed and lost. Because again in my next life, it will take me time to grow up and retrieve this knowledge. Some made fun, some consoled me, and few openly said, 'no, you have to live for us'.

It was at this time that I got a call from Shivali to thank me. I asked her for what? She said, healing me for selection in the Air lines' .I told her, 'but you did not get through '. She said, 'that is why I want to thank you more because had I been selected in that interview, I would have relaxed and not tried for other places. Now due to recession and economic pressure on the airline industry, they have not taken any one even from last year's selected candidates' and who were already in training ,have also been terminated. So I am thanking you for doing Reiki to me for seeking job and always advising me that whatever will be for my good in the long run, I will succeed in achieving that'. I felt bit happy on accepting such bitter truth positively by a twenty years old girl. After few days she was selected for another very suitable job in a top most hotel. This time I expected and accepted her thanks with applause.

Note - In past two years after Deepa's death, I have cried twice in my dreams, regretting Deepa's loss. Loss of young and capable life is a great loss, not only in worldly but in a spiritual sense also. Because of initial twenty-five years, we will again have to go through the stages of growing up in learning motor skills and synthesizing emotional, intellectual and spiritual connection.

Deepa's case will appear in next chapter, (stumbling through obscurity). I have understood that no one is living only for himself alone . We live fifty percent for ourselves and rest fifty percent for others around us. When we don't have the courage to face the challenges to walk the actual path we are supposed to travel in this life or others are not accepting us for what we are and helping us to overcome our short comings, the journey is cut short. As Deepak Chopra says, 'there are no accidents, no failures; there are only some reasons which we have not yet understood.

Chapter 3

Stumbling Through Obscurity

✣ ❄ ✣

Case 1: I knew I will not be happy but I could not help

Deepa Nov 2005-

Abusive husband, No children, Deteriorating health

Logically Deepa is my failure case yet I am writing her case as it happened in the beginning of my career as a healer. I pay tribute to her soul for revealing mystic mysteries and teaching me valuable lessons through her sessions. Everybody wondered why she is not getting whatever she desires and rightfully deserves,even though she is good looking, intelligent, hard working and ambitious. Now making it clear that her mind was not freed from the past memories of helplessness, sadness, and unfulfilled desires. She did not want others to know about the ugliness going on in her life. Her husband had openly warned her to keep a distance from her relatives . To maintain peace in her life she was gradually learning to resign to his order as her fate.

(The beauty of intelligent faculty of our mind is that it tries to present to the world a happy and contented picture in spite of facing numerous upheavals and turmoil within us).

As I had opened a healing Center by then, I suggested her to learn Reiki and try to heal her relationship with her husband. She wasn't convinced, rather she had decided to put up with all the unpleasantness, he was creating in her life. She did not want others to know her plight to prove herself wrong by declaring her marriage failed. I was somehow guided to heal their relationship and continued distance healing.

My Vision –November 2005. It was on one such distance healing process in the morning that I suddenly saw her standing in front of me, showing her left shoulder and telling, 'Look now the situation has become this bad ,he is beating me here'. I was startled and disturbed. I messaged her to talk to me whenever convenient .When I told her about my experience ,she was also surprised at how is it possible for me to know what exactly transpired in their home at that same time. Now she elaborately told me the ugly fight taken place with her husband in the morning. Gradually she started opening up to me and I promised her all possible help.

By now I was also practicing Past Life Therapy I had even discussed her case with my teacher Shamta Sirohi and She said, 'she is allowing herself to be victimized by her husband because she is guilty of some past deeds, take her past life sessions and bring her out from this guilt, break away this cycle'. Whenever I got an opportunity, I took her session and she easily slipped back to her subconscious mind. Being a beginner and a novice as a past life therapist at that time and her casual approach to such healing ,made it bit confusing for me to comprehend, whether she is talking it consciously or is it the subconscious feedback.

First session– She immediately reached in one beautiful garden and felt very positive, cheerful, jumping and dancing. There is one hut, vision of Ram Sita and Hanuman. She was seeing a sea of clear water but as she was flowing in it, it was getting darker and turbulent and she started becoming uncertain and uncomfortable. I asked her to step on to the land. At this suggestion, she started seeing few houses and some people who she couldn't recognise.

Memorable day– Death scene. She started seeing her death scene and said, 'it looks as if I have suffered throughout my life and I have died now. People are dressed in white clothes around me , I am searching whether anybody known to me is amongst them. I don't find anybody known to me mourning my death. Even I don't feel any attachment to any one there. In fact, I am happy to be out from this miserable life, where I had no body to call my own. I am seeing my pyre is burning and slowly people have dispersed from there'.

(I thought she is seeing one of her past life, where she must have died of living unhappy and unwarranted life. But now I realize that this was symbolic of her this life's death. She had already created her end this way in her mind.)

Now she herself reached to the time when in this life, she is being forced by her husband to come out from her happy and peaceful life to lead this miserable one. She said,' I knew I will not be happy but I could not help, that is why I did not listen to any one giving me correct advice to stay away from this relationship'. Now the happiness and cheerfulness had vanished and she was feeling helpless and remorseful.

I wanted her to feel happy and peaceful thus I asked her to see any happy event in her life.

Future- She started narrating, 'I can see a newly constructed white colored house. I am in side it; kitchen has got granite on the floor and wall. I look the same age as I am now. There is one handsome man wearing track suit with me in this house . I don't know him but we share a very good relationship. May be he is my husband .We are on the first floor. People outside are walking on the lawn. It looks as if this is a house warming party. This house is in some plain region because climate is warm. I am wearing a beautiful night gown'. Thus by giving her positive suggestions, we discontinued the session.(Without my realizing at that time that she is seeing her future life (may be next life. Hut could be signifying her poor miserable shattered condition of her present life. Now the newly constructed house is signifying her safe, beautiful, contented life and harmonious relationship with her husband ,which had been missing so far. That is why, she was seeing herself almost same age in next life but living with a man whom ,she has very comfortable vibes.)

You assured me all possible help

Deepa December 2005-Second session- Her guide Sri Sri Ravishankar ji came alive in her mental screen. She said, 'I have been able to face so much adversity in life because of Guruji 's teachings and blessings'.

Past life- I asked her to go back to the origin of her relationship with her husband. She immediately started narrating, 'I am in a village in a hilly area leading a simple life. I have four sons and I am very short tempered,so is my fourth son. He is very domineering and he wants everything on his terms. I have no time to listen to his demands as I am busy with my domestic responsibilities. In one such heated argument, I lost my cool and beat him with a thick stick which was lying nearby. The boy has fainted,' then she corrected herself saying, 'no, he died on the spot.' At this she recognized this boy to be her present husband. She continued, 'I am shocked as I have killed my own son, I don't know what to do. I called my brother and sister from my parental home. Now she herself recognised those people present in this life. My elder brother in this life is also my elder brother and you are my elder sister in that life. My brother has refused any help, saying, "We have our own problems, what we can do now". But you assured me all possible help ,saying, 'I am always there for you'. Now you are helping me to hide my heinous deed and true incident from others around us. We declared that boy had died a natural death. I am regretting now. I live with this guilt and pain all through my life. But you were always there in my hours of need'.

Note- (and I wondered at the perfect divine plan, how she met her present husband, got attracted to him and he lured her to marry him. Her people had sensed and warned her of the trouble in her life, instinctively she also felt she will not be happy with him yet she felt trapped in this relationship that she did not have the guts to back out. She was resigned to her fate and went ahead; she wanted to work out her past karmas this way. It was not a mere coincident that I was the only one from her side to attend her marriage because others weren't willing. Being in the same city, I could not refuse her.

Nobody would have even dreamt at that time that I will be the one to bring her out from this unpleasant relationship. She had said in her session that I had promised her all possible help in her past life. But I had vowed now to bring her out from continuously following a mechanical cycle of living unhappy, miserable and unfulfilled lives. Her in-laws and some people detested my unnecessary interference in her affairs. But seeing fatal cause coming from the past, I overheard every body's warning and threats. I did not want some accidental death to happen this time so that they again get caught up in this cycle of revenge and guilt)

Past life – My husband is a Pujari in the temple and he is my present husband. She continued, 'there after again I am in a hilly place but slightly different one in another life time. I am wearing thick check printed clothes and have tied a head gear as worn in hills by married ladies. I am living in a big family; I have no happiness in life. I am only doing routine household chores day in and out. My husband is very short tempered. I have no children, no emotions, and no desires as if waiting for my life to end, I am dying in my middle age of some chest infection. Now, my husband is missing me and very angry at himself and God. I am also feeling bad seeing his miserable state now".

Past life – I am a Rajasthani lady, I don't have children – 'Now I am in a Rajasthan like place. I am married. I have had many miscarriages but no child is alive. I am very weak and unhappy in life' .There was nothing much revealed in this life except that she was again unhappy and living unsatisfied life.

Past life– I am a (Begam) Queen of a Mughal Emperor.

I jumped in the well and ended my life.

I asked her to see any other lifetime which has got some relevance to her present life. She reached back to the time of Mughal life. She said, 'I am dressed like the begums of Mughal Emperor, as we see in the movies. And it is just like a picture story that he is an elderly king and has many women kept in his harem. He doesn't give me any importance though I am of Royal origin. His promiscuous lifestyle had contracted some infection in the genital organs which have also infected me. I am very sick and frustrated. I ran out from the palace and jumped into the well and ended my life'.

At this, she herself started comparing her that life to present life. She said, 'I always craved for love, security, and caring but never got it. I had nowhere to go. So I ended that life. Same is in this life. And here she confided in me, her secret intention, ' in this life also I had decided to end my life this way some day when I will not be able to bear it anymore. Because I have nowhere to go back and my husband knows it very well. That is why he doesn't let me keep any relationship with you. So that you don't help me because he is afraid of you'.

(Thereafter I became more sympathetic towards her. I warned her, 'never ever think of doing such ghastly action again. There is no peace after death if you die in repentance and sufferings').

My Vision --Message for her

Whatever changes has to be brought while we are alive

(As I was healing her distantly,one fine morning I had another vision, rather it was a message for her. In my deep meditative state I felt my distant Aunt who had died few years back, as if she is scattered somewhere in an open area. I can hear some voice telling, 'who will make these people understand that whatever changes, it has to be made while we are alive. Afterwards nothing can be done.' I called Reiki symbols and healed that scattered energy , I saw it turning in to a womb and I wasted no time in directing it to Renu ,who was being healed by me for infertility at that time. I could realize the relevance of all these cases practically teaching me ,the mysterious working of life and significance of healing these simultaneously by me. Otherwise why would my distant aunt's healing be done this way, so many years after death? Who was least in my mind while she was alive or even after her death. But she had some relation with me and I could relate to her state of fear and confusion. This was a practical lesson for me in healing a dead person, who is stuck in the jungle of confusion avoiding higher ascension fearing harm due to ignorance. Though, I had no intension to heal her because she wasn't in mind at all. Here again I give the credit to the higher beings /guides ,who are like ministers in the God's assembly, assigning this cause to someone like me trying to tread the path to heal humanity. They try to help both the parties by bringing healer in contact with the beings who need such help and guiding us to do the needful. Otherwise, who would have shown me the womb and prompted me to direct it to Renu ?

I do not claim to have even the fraction of this much wisdom in me. And I had never seen a womb in ultrasound , the way I was shown this one. In fact, my strong logical mind was left wondering at this unexpected unusual experience. Had it been some unknown ignorant being appearing in my vision, I would not have been able to relate to it so aptly. Had it been someone closer to me while alive, I would have considered it my conscious mind's longing making him appear in my vision. This experience was to confirm my belief in the divine working of the universe and the proof of the part I am playing under the hierarchical order.

(My illiterate aunt (Taayi) while alive in her old age whiled away her time in useless and unpleasant abusive talks. People used to advise her to take God's name instead. She shuddered with fear and replied, 'no, no, I will not take God's name, by taking God's name I will die and I am so fearful of death'. So it was understood that such ignorant person would remain scattered and confused, hiding in the earthly realm, making difficult for her guides (higher beings) to collect and help her ascend to higher abode after her death.)

By now I clearly understood that Deepa had some relationship with me from the past. Consciously she did not want to confide in me for unnecessary burdening me with her worries She was pretending to be strong and wanted to take full responsibility for her action. She was handling things with poise but her soul was bruised. She was also facing the dilemma as she did not want to give a chance to anybody to prove her wrong in marrying him.. I tried to persuade her, ' do not let your ego come in between , if you have done one mistake , accept it and don't give your life for one small mistake. It is not easy to break away from the cultural, religious and social conditioning of right and wrong and accept ourselves failure and unsuccessful. This was a clear message for her because she wasn't daring to make some changes in her life while alive but was thinking of escaping from sufferings after death. Why else her soul would appear in my vision telling me the terrible state of her husband beating her? This also made me stronger and I assured her all possible help without any guilt. As initially I was also faced with a dilemma as people may blame me for breaking her marriage.

She just wanted to get rid of him.

Her personal life story is of much relevance alongside her healing sessions. After realizing difficulty ahead in living in such abusive relationship, with great resistance, she decided to separate from him. When she informed her people, they also agreed to her decision. She was living separately from her husband and planned to file a divorce. She was so accommodative and forgiving that she wanted the mutual divorce and did not expect anything in compensation and create more ugliness by mudslinging on each other. She just wanted to get rid of him. Even though the lawyer consulted by her had assured of all the laws were favoring her and she has entitled her dues legally. But her husband was so adamant that he wanted to delay proceedings of divorce. He still could not believe that she could dare to stay away from him. He had openly challenged her saying, 'I had cut all your wings and you cannot fly. 'Meaning he had forced her to break all the ties with her near and dear ones and she had nowhere to go'.

I had taken Deepa under my folds to bring her out of this mess and continuous cycle of revenge, remorse, and suffering. She was staying with me for some time now. She also understood some significance in her staying with me this way and was always willing for having healing sessions with me. I asked her, 'do you believe in what all you see in your sessions'. She said, 'I just keep seeing and saying anything coming up in my mind. I don't give it another thought, what and why it is coming to my mind'. Seeing all these things in her sessions, she never told anybody anything except she told her mother that she was a Mughal begum in her past life.

Her dream - February 2006

One dead body wearing a sari was being taken in a jeep trailer

Previous night she was sleeping in the adjacent room and saw a frightening dream. She said, 'I saw, a body of a lady wearing red sari was being carried in a jeep trailer type thing. Her body and face was covered and feet were visible. She was being taken away in the opposite direction (North) from my parental house. Then there are two people climbed on a tall pole feeling very uncomfortable there ,fearful of falling down. One of them fell down on the ground. Seeing them at a risk, I felt very scared at this moment. Then I saw my late uncle (father's brother) smiling and assuring me. (She was very fond of him in her childhood; he had died in 1987 after a long illness (Parkinsonism disease)

Conversation with her late uncle. 'First I want to teach Astrology to my first wife'

Session – In the session, I asked her to see what is the significance of this dream? She saw the same thing again and said, 'she is a lady who had died long back in our ancestral house. I cannot see her face, though; probably she was my uncle's first wife". I asked her, 'Why she has come in your dream? A- She seemed to have been hanging out in my parental house. She had died while giving birth to a male child. The child had also died after her death but she wasn't aware of it'. I projected healing Light on that body and she was seeing her being engulfed by this Light and merge in it. She said, 'now I see my old ancestral house, how it was a few years back. In one of the room, the cupboards and this room are completely empty'.

Note – (house, room, hut also symbolize our body. The lady was not released from that house but after getting released, her room and the cupboard are vacant now. Symbolizing that she has vacated the room of the house where she thought she is still living after death)

Now I asked her, 'Where is your uncle? A.He is here smiling at me.

Q- What is he doing here? A-He says 'I was waiting for my wife'. Ask him how is he feeling in all these years after passing over to the other side?

A-He says I am enjoying here.

Q-What he has been doing there in all those years ?

A-He says, 'I am learning Astrology'. I was amused to see her talk about him communicate with us so casually.' I cannot say how seriously I took this conversation at that time. I posed a question to him, 'wouldn't he teach me Astrology? A- He says, 'This knowledge will come to you on its own, first I want to teach my first wife. Q'Where is his first wife?'A-She was attached to this house and could not be released up. Q-Even though she had died much before him? A-She was left attached to this house due to her child. He says, 'I am happy that you have released my wife from that house.

Dream: I am petrified to see A red blanket on a stretcher in the middle of the ground.

We continued the session and I asked her, 'why did you feel so scared last night '? She said, 'I see as if I am in my school hostel as when I was studying there. There is one medical stretcher on the ground. I get suspicious, why it should be in the ground? I go near it and am petrified to see now that there is a red blanket spread on it, which wasn't there earlier. She concluded , ' I was so scared and that is why next day I had high fever for a week . I erased this fear from her mind. She was feeling lighter now.

Nadi Astrology forecast -

These two years are very difficult for her, thereafter she will turn spiritual and have a peaceful life.

I had also taken her to Nadi Astrology Thumb impression forecast and their predictions were matching her present life situation very aptly. It said, 'she is having a court case against her present husband. She will find these two forth coming years a very difficult phase in her life. It will be very difficult to win this case against her husband. Everybody will be against her, her name and even her parent's name will be spoiled because of her. But after two years she will turn spiritual and lead a happy and peaceful life. She is even destined to have another marriage and may have a child. Or she can even bring up her nephew or niece as her own child.'

She was already aware of the challenges in seeking separation from her stubborn and humiliating husband because he had already started spreading false rumors maligning her name , just to harass and threaten her At these revelations, she used to say, ' I don't know how will I turn spiritual ? (because she had many unfulfilled desires) Sensing her aversion for turning spiritual ,I suggested her to learn tarot card ,she seemed interested in it and I thought probably her late uncle might help her in making this knowledge of Divination available to her.

What is Destiny? I was wondering what does it mean that she is even destined to have another marriage and even a child? I asked Nadi Astrologer to clarify, 'what does destined to marry again means, will she marry again? They explained, 'destiny means it is coming to you but it is up to you to take that opportunity or not. Like you are destined to have food tonight but you might decide to go empty stomach The food was there for you but you availed free will of not utilizing this opportunity. When not destined you will not get food from anywhere and you will face pangs of hunger and starvation.

This explanation has been very helpful in understanding and accepting her death. I had been satisfied by their predictions and could verify revelations of my healing session. I was wondering about her future vision, where she had seen herself with a compatible looking husband in a new house. But I could not convince others. They completely rejected these predictions baseless and any significance of healing her in any way. If good life ahead was predicted for her and if healing had some benefit then why did she die? Thus, her death turned out to be a big blow to my healing capabilities as well as Nadi astrology forecast. While she was alive, she wanted to show these predictions to her people, her near and dear ones. Thinking that they might empathize with her by learning that she was destined this fate. Except her mother nobody was ready to accept that destiny was playing a strong influence on her. Most intriguing part of these predictions was that the day she died in November 2006, now her people wanted to know what was in those predictions but the prediction cassette tape wouldn't run, making them remain in the dark. They condemned, criticized, dissected superficial circumstantial evidence to find the answer from the drama of her life. True and deep Knowledge is available only once we are mature enough to accept the bitter truth and not keep blaming God or others.

Message for me

February 2006 "Lord Krishna" Came through Deepa's session

You are seeking very deep knowledge ,thus need patience--In the beginning, at times, I was a skeptic and confused, am I leading in the right direction or following illusions and wasting my time? But such messages were like the bells ringing in a monastery to bring back my wandering mind to the actual path I was supposed to travel. Lord Krishna came through Deepa's session and my feelings were so intense that I could only cry in wonder and joy, whereas she wasn't moved much by this experience. She described in detail, "Lord Krishna is in the sky in an extraordinary chariot, stepping one foot out and one crossing the other leg. Sudarshan Chakra is rotating in his hand and it is emitting light. I asked her, 'are you not filled with bliss at such a wonderful sight'? She replied, 'my condition is like a patient who has sweets spread in front of him but because of being unwell he is unable to taste it'. I told her, 'then I feel as if He has come for me'. She said, 'yes, He says, He has come for you only'. I asked questions about my work, my relation, my connection with Him. She replied everything as I had expected or imagined. He convinced rather reaffirmed my belief saying ,'Long lasting and valuable the tree, longer it will take to grow and start flourishing, so is in your case , you are seeking something rare and very deep Truth,give people time to digest this truth. It is very new phenomenon thus it is taking time, you are on the right path, have patience, your effort will bear the fruit."

We are dancing in a circle, ecstatic in devotion

Past life- I regressed her to see any other life, where we might have been together. She said, 'it is Meera's (Renowned Krishna Devotee) life. We are all Meera's Sakhis (friends). We are wearing a colorful long skirt and blouse (ghagra ,choli) dancing in a circle ecstatic in Krishna devotion. Q-'Is Krishna there?' A-He is present there in essence and in our feelings ,though not visible. At this, she corrected herself and said, 'but now I can see that He is present with each one of us in person there.

Q-How does Meera look like ?

A-"She is in the beginning of the row, I am somewhere towards at the far end. The circle is very long. I cannot clearly see and differentiate you or her. I don't know whether you are Meera or standing next to her".

Message for me- You have to reveal this hidden Truth. August 2006

Lord Vishnu came in her session.

She was having severe pain in her throat, making swallowing very painful. Her crystal locket had fallen. In the session, I asked her, 'what happened to that locket? She said, 'it had turned black and was transmitting black energy towards me, and I am feeling so much pain. Finally, it had broken loose as it had become very heavy for me to bear it '.Q- 'From where is this negative energy coming to you?' She replied, 'my husband, my mother in law and one black magician are sending me this negative energy, which is causing constant pain in my throat.

'Q-'Why are they doing this to you?

A-'They want me to go back to their house, they want me to be enslaved to them'.

In the session itself, I told her that I am giving you another crystal which will protect you from all these negative effects and I started charging the crystal locket.

She became clairvoyant (Seeing invisible things internally) – After observing for some time, she started narrating to me, 'light is falling from your hands on to the crystal and it is emitting bright light'. I asked her from where is the light coming to my hands? She replied, 'from higher up, very high in the universe, its Lord Vishnu with Sudershan chakra in his hand passing on that light to you'. I was pleasantly surprised and could not contain my curiosity of Lord Vishnu being present there. I told her that I feel like to talk to Him. She said 'He is saying, "then why don't you talk, that is why I have come'? I asked, 'What is the truth about all these things you have revealed to me, the negative projection towards you by this tantric and your husband? Is anybody else in your family also victim to this attack? She replied matter of factly, "He says many are suffering due to such things, but my brother Sanjay is affected the most'. I further enquired, 'then why don't people fully believe all these things?' A-'He says,' this is the Truth, but because it is so frightening and complicated to comprehend, so people prefer to keep quiet and ignore it'.

Comparing life with the coconut fruit-

Then she gave the example by comparing life with the coconut fruit. 'From outside it is so entangled that is why outer covering is hard to protect it from this confusion and mystery. But as one enters deeper, the softer, sweeter and more harmonious truth is hidden. People lack that patience and responsibility'. I asked her , ' if people don't want to face the Truth , even you and your family don't have any faith in my work, then why is this being revealed to me through you ? A-'Because you have the courage and you have to make people understand , You have to reveal this hidden Truth. If your intension is not to harm anyone, things will touch and go, teach you but not harm to destroy you. You need not fear any thing in life. People will accept your work when I will tell them after I am healed completely". I asked her, 'who is giving you this insight of comparing life with coconut? She said I see two Beings, one looks like Isaac Newton and another one is Rabindra Nath Tagore. They are explaining to me this philosophy of life. When I am accepting their view , it is penetrating deeper in my mind, there is some knotted and coiled rope type getting pulled out from my abdomen. I am feeling lighter and happier now.'

I asked her after the session, 'do you believe in whatever you see and say in your session? She very honestly replied, 'I feel, I just keep telling you whatever comes to my mind and it has no purpose for me, but I know you are doing some wonderful work and these are meaningful to you. I feel happy that I can be of some help to you. Though not taking all these revelations seriously, she confided to me her desire that she wished two people should undergo past life session, so that the cause of their life's problems can be deducted. One was her father, who is a gentle soul but very blocked and principled man..Another was her aunt, who had become a widow at a very young age and lost her only son at his twenty-two years of his age.

Note -On 17 the March 2006 I had my first encounter with such strong negative force, while healing distantly an elderly lady from Kolkata. She had become unconscious due to a heart condition. I had a very deep inner experience while healing her, which shook me from the root. She regained consciously and was released from the hospital after four days. I was shaken but felt confident that Reiki can protect me from any harm coming to me while healing self and others because my intention is just to clear and release the negative energy back to its source of origin, from where it will be transmuted and transformed and recycled again in pure form.

The year 2006 was the beginning when most clients started coming to me for clearing of such negative influences, irrespective of their belief or faith in any such things. Negative influences in the form of psychic attack, spirit possession and black magic(tantric work) done on them. Such influences affecting me and my family were already revealed to me by my son Ayan. Neither our family had ever discussed nor did we have any belief in such things. I cannot say that I was very brave but somehow I had the courage and confidence in Reiki. I felt I am being guided and guarded by Divinity. I was also given proofs of it end number of time. These difficult and risky cases were my assignments to learn practically about mysterious energy world and also help in clearing this darker side of the truth from the face of the earth.)

Past life

(Kaal)Destiny is doing his Duty - Karma is the effect not the cause- Cause for Throat pain – In this life she saw that her people were sending her negative projection. I asked her to see why they are doing this to her, what is the root cause for it , I meant what was the reason for her to fall in to these circumstances in this life? She said, 'I look like a king fighting a war in the battle field. I have cut throats and killed many soldiers . Now I feel as if with the same swords, I am slashing my own neck ,that is why there is so much pain in my throat and I am unable to swallow anything.

Past life -Relationship with husband –

She continued, 'I see myself in another life. I am a very rich and influential lady. I am very arrogant and full of vanity. My present husband is a poor person. He is asking me some help but I am very insulting towards him. Now I can see that he was much pained by my behaviour. He is cursing me heart in heart at that time".

Past life– In another life, her present husband is a sage looking person with a long beard and long uncombed hair, doing some very powerful Sadhana. She said, 'I happen to cross him on the way coming back from somewhere. He is wanting to possess me. He has so much power because of his Sadhana and he is full of ego. I am a simple lady, very fearful of him". (in this life also he is a great devotee of Saturn planet and Ravana. Every day he worships his deity for two-three hours yet there after he is very unstable, abusive and mean to her) She can see in her session that his Deity looks like a tantric and he is projecting very strong negative vibes towards her. When I was healing her of the powerful influence they have on her, I asked her to find out from Tantric looking person, ' Why is he tormenting you? She replied, 'he is saying, 'I had to do it ' (*mujhe to ye karma hi tha)* I understood he represents Kaal , Karma ,Destiny. Creating circumstances of this life by mirroring all her past actions. Thus, he is only doing his duty.

Suffering means paying back in the same coin. Being on the other side of the stick and experience how it feels. Note -(On the core level it's our own doing or coming face to face with this important dimension of existential reality. Negative forces are waste /by product of living a life of separation, ignorance and confusion. If not disposed cautiously it may spread more negativity in the process. Thus accepting its existence and device ways to eradicate it for the welfare of the society is the need of the hour. Not to live in fear, rejection and ostracism of these things.

Breaking away from fear to secure future-

I wanted her to break free from this fear and her inability to have a happy and secure life. I gave her suggestion to visualize living a happy and peace full life. She tried to feel the same thing for some time but then she expressed her inability by saying , ' but I cannot be away from their influence for long because I am again drawn back to them by some strong force'. I asked her to see further what happens if you go back to them,how is your life continuing further?(Because I did not want to pressurize her ,simply to do away her relationship. May be she could have a happy and fulfilling life with her husband later.) She said, 'we are all very unhappy with each other, there are a constant fight and unrest in our life, we are not able to bear each other. I am living in constant guilt and remorse for doing this to my life. I have nobody to fall back or even console me. I am suffering silently'.I gave her healing energy, positive suggestions to make her feel stronger and independent, and then somehow she could visualize herself in a new peaceful environment.

Visualizing Probable Future- To break free from continuously following mechanical cycle in her past and strong negative influences of the present life, I gave her suggestions to visualize some happy future events. Slowly she was able to see following probable futures.

1. She said, ' I am teaching in a very good reputed school in my home town and I live in a house with some close members of my family. I am feeling happy and secure.

2. I am in some Tibetan Market type place, standing in one shop. A man is standing next to me probably he is my partner or manager ,who helps me in my business. This looks to be a jewelley, stones and cosmetics shop. I feel happy and contented in life.

3. I feel as if you(I) are standing on the stage and (she) I am standing next to you taking down some notes. Probably I am working with you in future.

4. Once she saw herself wearing white dress and descending down in a Kaali Bari temple in her city. She said, "I feel this is after two years from now. Pundit of that temple is my guide". She wasn't aware what she is doing there thus I told her to find out from Pundit and ask him, 'why have you come here? She said, 'he says, 'you always come here'.

5. In her first session, she had seen herself living a happy and contented life with a compatible looking husband, (it was predicted in her Nadi Astrology)

6 In the same session she had seen herself dead and people were mourning her death. I thought it was her some past life because outwardly she was keeping a brave front, but subconsciously she had created this future for her (symbolic death in this life) That is why she could not recognize any body in that incident.

Note - Before reaching to any one of this happy probable future, she had to cross difficult hurdles in her life. She had to accept her weakness of taking a wrong decision. She had to regain strength to cut away from domineering family. For that she needed some courage and self-confidence, which would come by pulling together her inner resources, seeking some spiritual connection. Since outward circumstances were against her, her people were not forgiving her. She herself also could not forgive herself for her past deeds and was making herself pawn to her victim in the present. She could not muster the courage to face all these adversities, by preparing herself to transform her life and make a new beginning in this very life. Future can be transformed by modifying past in the present.Suffering not transformed begets suffering. She had no stamina to face the harsh realities of her life and subconsciously she had chosen the last probable future.

Describing Ramayana – In one session she reached back to the time of Ramayana. She was describing the period as if she was herself there. She could not elaborate, who and what she is doing there. But she was seeing everything clearly. She said, 'I am in a place, as we see in the movies, In fact, it is much vast and bigger area than any real place. Here on the first-floor balcony looking open place, there are Lord Shiva and Parvati sitting on the throne. They are blessing people sitting below in very big open hall looking place. On the first floor hall, there is one elderly king sitting on a huge gold throne. She announced, 'He is king Dashratha (Lord Rama's Father).Q – Are you sure he is king Dashratha? A-"yes, haven't we seen photos and movies, she retorted"? Q-"Is it looking exactly the scene from some such movie or serial? A- "No, it's not exactly matching any TV serial or Movie scene watched by me so far. But I can make out from his fatherly look. Three young princes are standing in front of him as if asking permission to go somewhere. Q –"Who are you and what you doing there"?A- I cannot make out who I am there but I feel I am watching all this from the side . Q- "If he is King Dashratha, then there should be four princes? She expressed her inability to verify this anomaly in her observation. But she was sure about the king Dashratha and his sons. Q – "What more is there to observe"? A- "Now they are going to some very, big majestic room. They are going out of the palace. Q-"Is Sita also there with them"? A- "Yes, there is a lady also with them". She narrated course of their journey, " they are going through difficult terrains, high hills, crossing rivers , entering jungles. They live in this uncertain and difficult land for a long time, facing many hardships. Now looks as if after a long time they are returning back through an equally difficult path to the same place. They are being welcomed. People are dancing and celebrating their home coming".

Ram Sita Durbar – In higher dimension –

I am standing in my present body in front of Ram

"Hereafter the scene is changed. Now it appears Lord Ram (Ram Sita Darwar) King's Court. The place is not on earth but very high in the sky. They are sitting on a throne and other brothers are standing in attendance. Hanuman is also there. There are many people in the Darwar. She said, 'now I can see myself clearly standing in my present body in front of Lord Rama higher up in the sky. I am bending down to touch His feet. He is picking me up. I am in tears. He is patting me, consoling me. He is assuring me. All your sufferings are over, now what is there to cry"? Seeing such a beautiful scene, I asked her to feel this presence filling in each and every cell of your body. Let this peace and serenity be your essence from now onwards in your life. She said, "Hanuman is hitting on my shoulder with his(Gadda) weapon". Q- 'Is it hurting you"? A- "No,He is trying to straighten the bone in my left shoulder which had fractured and disfigured slightly, causing me some discomfort. He is healing me". I let her be in this blissful state for some time.

After her session was over, I asked her for her feedback on this blissful experience. She said, 'I am Ram Bhakta /Devotee and I have been blessed with his (Darshan)Vision". Apparently, she did not feel much convinced with all this. Even I could not make out much relevance of this session. Was she reviving her conscious knowledge of Ramayana, a great Hindu Epic and she is Ram Bhakta? So consciously she must have imagined and created this vision. When we read any scripture we feed this knowledge to our system.

Had she seen her meeting with Lord Ram after death before hand in this session?

This struck me later. Regression or meditation takes us back and forward in our mind to our desired and deserved destination. There are many levels (Lokas) in higher dimension. Death is just a small break, after clearing or failing in one class. A time to rest, recoup and prepare for the next class.

It is a story of a soul departing from his heavenly father on this earthly journey

Note - As I was writing her case later,I seem to grasp entirely different meaning from her this vision. Isn't it the story of every soul departing from Heavenly Father on his earthly journey (Banvas) living in the jungle of ignorance same way? Here we are facing the darkness of delusion , uncertainty, rough roads, ups, and downs, crossing turbulent rivers, struggling to free our mind from ego (Ravana) who has captured our mind (Sita) by deluding it with the artificial shine of transient material possession (golden deer). We can only retrieve our mind by killing and winning over our ego. That is why she wasn't seeing herself clearly there as she is not aware that everybody in the soul is represented by Rama (The Super soul). When she is back in heaven after completing the journey of one life (one class) she is standing in her present body (school uniform). (We are all sparks of Divinity, Bindu in sindh)drop in ocean , the Individuated consciousness of that all-pervading Super conscious. Alas, when we are admitted into this earthly school, we forget our connection with Source,we feel lonely and lost. We experience pain, miseries , helplessness at this separation) That is why we are trying to find our connection back to our origin ,first by searching for the worldly pleasures due to illusion ,thinking these to be able to give us the experience of that blissful state ,experienced at our union with our Origin. Because we have that original experience of our union with our source, we differentiate and reject one after the other, these to be temporary and transient in nature. Slowly reaching at this realization that we are all one and same. Collectively we are all gods incarnated in different bodies for experiencing separation and multifaceted facet of that one Great Reality).

I have seen many people who observe certain rituals or follow a particular ideology or worship some Deity, are influenced because of their past connection with them. Some cases have described in their session, the life of Krishna as we hear in scriptures. They cannot make out who are they there.(Could be they are not in any human form that time , may be some animal or tree or even just as pure conscious as it is said, there is consciousness in each particle. Or are they being given this vision to prove to me the truth behind our scriptural description?.(As few years back I was also getting influenced by the verdict of many others relegating these epics described in our sacred books to be the imaginative fictitious stories just like some movies or novels are purely factious giving us some moral lessons. But aren't some true stories depicted through documentary movies and books?)These people have described in detail the scenes as if they are watching this real looking scene happening in that place in very ancient time.This is not their conscious observation of watching any movie or serial because it does not look exactly same . Some have said ,this is on the earth ,some say ,this is in the sky. This clarifies the truth that there are different lokas or levels or heavens. After worshipping a particular deity or following one ideology, one reaches that level after leaving this body. He remains there in close contact with his Deity/Guides , preparing for forthcoming life till the time comes for him to take birth again. Once born he has to search for that knowledge, that path again here on earth so that he can walk on the actual path, to evolve further from there to the next class. But some get mechanically stuck in their rituals and do not find any changes happening in their behaviour. They have knowledge but they are not applying this knowledge in their life. This brings spiritual alienation resulting in disconnection from the source and giving rise to spiritual disease .

(Consciously she was not aware of any importance of my healing on her other than feeling relaxed and gain some energy and watch these inner visions with detached manner)

Her Death - It was Anjana (A gifted clairvoyant client) who had informed me that she is not readily taking healing. Deepa accepted that she is convinced that nobody can cure her until she collects some inner strength and make herself ready to face the world. But her health was deteriorating. Self-guilt, the frustration of failure, an embarrassment of taking the wrong decision and burden of blames by others were destroying her inwardly. When she was sick in the hospital, two days before her death Anjana had informed me of her vision. She said, "I saw, Deepa is stuck in some web type thing and is struggling to throw it open. But she is unable to do so. As if she is in a mud pitcher needing some help". I started sending her intense distance healing and she was no more ,after two days. May be her sufferings of all these lives ended in this one year time. She had no strength to face the challenges required to change her attitude so soon; thus she needed some rest.

She would have been instrumental in creating negative karma in her people-

If she would remain alive, change herself and become spiritual ,she would have been instrumental in creating negative Karma in her people,who were constantly criticizing and condemning her action. Thus, she was as if living her life walking on a double edged sword.

Lesson learnt from her case

Substitute healing –

1- She also became a conduit for healing her nephew, who was undergoing treatment for malignant knee bone condition.

2 Her brother and his wife were under severe stress and depression as their son was suffering from such fatal diseases. We would heal them often through her at that time

3 Her brother Sanjay, who was highly intelligent as a child but could not complete his education and is depressed and wasting his life. When we tried to heal him, she said, "He says, 'I know my guide has sent you to heal me '. I told her to ask him, "Who is his guide, She replied, "My late uncle, whom we use to call Baba ji". Q-"But how can I heal him because your family doesn't believe in any importance of my work"? A-"They will believe when I will be healed completely and tell them all these things. It will take two years for them to accept your work". Q-"When will you be healed"? An"I will be healed in two months' time from now ".(but it was exactly after two months from then, (one year after she appeared in my vision showing me her bruised condition(she lived no more.)

4 Anjana's mother had suffered a severe cerebral attack and paralysis of right upper limb and face. Deepa saw in that trance state ,in her head, she has clots and injury leading to deficient energy supply

in her body because of blocked energy flow. She saw a healing light going to her from me and doing her healing.

5 Sensing higher Beings – In her healing sessions, she saw various Higher Beings or God Goddesses do her healing.

1. Pain in the throat - she saw Lord Shiva is chiseling her throat with his Trishul trident, when, I am directing healing energy towards her throat. She even saw same thing being done by Lord Shiva to heal my throat which was also not very healthy (I also had very sensitive throat)

2. Feed back on my experience- I requested her to see in one of her session, the meaning of uncontrolled tears coming in my eyes during Durga Puja celebration in Kolkata in 1999 without much devotion and faith in such rituals (puja). She said, ' in one life you had worshipped Goddess Durga and after death merged in her. This experience was to remind you of that life's association with Durga Though in this life you didn't believe much in such celebrations'.

(When Deepa's healing was happening, I had one of my short past life experience, where I had died as a young five years old boy. After death, I was coming back to the same house as a soul and by seeing the picture of some Monastery on the wall of that house, I was crying uncontrollably. I clearly remember the regretful words I was chanting, 'I had said that I will remember but I could not. (Haan maine kaha tha yaad rakhunga par nahi rakh paya.) I also remember the mantra I was chanting when I was in the womb, 'yes, I will remember' (haan main yaad rakhunga). As if my every breath and heart beat was chanting this mantra. This experience was for me to see it with my soul's eye that how we forget our past connection and when remembered due to God's Grace; consciously, we are just not able to accept any such possibility but our emotion that time expresses our inner connection by crying in frustration.

Wandering souls healed through her

1 As those days I was mostly healing cases with negative influences. I myself had one such experience one day while taking

afternoon siesta. I had a vision of one spirit entering in the form of street dog in my house in the afternoon. I am feeling a bit scared though I am not able to see anything in the house but I can sense there is something invisible. I am also aware that I am sleeping in my room and I felt being pressed by this invisible energy. I healed it in that sleep cum trance state but I still wanted some feedback.

In her session, she saw that one lady spirit is entering the house and trying to connect to me. I asked, 'why'? She replied, 'she wants some help. She says that you will understand'. I understood because these days I was releasing such wandering spirits coming up during my healing sessions and I was doing the needful.

2 Durga and Kaali(Goddess) both are coming through you-

I had met with an accident in 0ct 2003 in Dharamshala, H.P but was saved miraculously. I asked her to give me feedback on that accident. She said, 'you are seeing one dog, which is turning in to a lady, who is wandering there because her child was buried in the grave in that place. You are getting scared and nervously losing the control on your car. I asked, "then how am I saved"? She said, "Now as if Durga and Kali both are coming through you and applying the brake and turning the steering wheel to reverse direction, it turned up and toppled upside down but you were not hurt". I asked her, "but why don't I remember all that subtly transpired there as you are seeing it now. She said you were shocked and you were not in your senses, so you don't remember. I asked, "What happened to that lady spirit"? She replied, "You started praying to clear that place from all such negativity and she along with many others were released gradually".

(The fact was that I had really become so nervous realizing that my speed is much more than it should be in that turning point. I gave up as I felt helpless suddenly to bring down the speed so quickly. All I remember to my surprise was that my steering wheel moved in the opposite direction in that confusion on its own, making the car turn upward instead of going straight down in a deep gorge. Later who so ever heard about that accident, was surprised seeing no injury to me or my vehicle. Whereas, that place was very infamous for fatal accidents. Though, by then I had discontinued doing Reiki, as I was trying other meditations to seek my spiritual connection. But this accident really made me turn back to do Reiki to heal that place, after coming to know from people that children graveyard is across this road. And when I had learnt Reiki in 1999, I had done different techniques to heal myself from future accidents till fifty years of age as taught in one of Reiki book by Paula Huron).

Concluding her case

Death is not the greatest loss in life; the greatest loss is when a relationship dies while we are still alive.

Deepa could not survive or should I say that she did not want to live life which was battering her soul along with her bruised body. Her soul had asked my help one year back so that at least she is freed from her past lives' unpleasant and painful memories, which were mechanically creating alike situations and making her undergo sufferings life after life. Yet, I was questioned by people about the effectiveness of healing. I had no clarification to give them as they know life only in terms of years being added to life and not adding life to years. Her husband and mother in law wanted to capture the freedom of her spirit, making her slave to dance to their tune. They wanted her to forget herself as an individual and wanted her just be a dutiful wife whose duty and destiny is to worship her husband like a God and obey her In- Laws at the expense of her own desires. They didn't expect something unusual, isn't it the religious philosophy of old Indian culture? Except her mother, all other relatives were only there to pin point her faults, making her feel failure by proving her wrong and themselves right. There were voices saying, 'she had herself jumped in the well'. This meant she deserved this treatment as she did not listen to them, as if they are always right as far as their opinion about others are concerned and they have never taken wrong decision in their life and if there is some unpleasantness in their lives ,it is all because of others wrong decision and doings.

By criticizing others, we become partner in the crime committed

I want to warn people, who are so conditioned to become moral guardian and judge others for their actions and condemn them as sinners or criminals. By doing so they also become party to the deeds committed. It's very difficult to judge from the present scenario that so many good deeds go unrewarded and many sins go unnoticed.

This is an attempt to save both of us from the sin –

I might be questioned what authority I have for writing her case after she is no more. So I want to clear my stand, in my dreams, I have cried twice regretting her death. Contrary to my above statement that death is not the greatest loss, but yes, death is a great loss of a young and capable person both in physical as well as a spiritual term.

Oblivion to the fact that I must have been party to her crime in the past, why else I would do all this for her without her or anybody else even realizing any benefit coming to her from healing. Still, I was questioned the authenticity of the procedure I am dedicated to. On a subtle level, were these people questioning me the authenticity of my past action? Where I had tried to save her from ostracism and punishment from the society. Could I save her soul from the self-blame and guilt? Probably that time I knew no other ways to do catharsis of her guilt, through confession, counseling or healing.She had suffered all her past lives and subconsciously she was drawn to similar circumstances in this life. In this life either she would have accepted her fate by being murdered by her husband or may have killed him in desperation or committed suicide in frustration. Or probably she could have continued to live as a dead ghost living in the same body without any emotion left in her body just adding years to life and accumulating more negativity for her forthcoming life.

I was ignorant of my past deed, though my intension was to save her even then but I was not spared from the consequence. That is why ignorance is not a blessing as popularly believed but it is a curse. And not sharing your knowledge with others is a sin. (which I would do this time if I do not share her case with others)

Did her soul come to me one year before her death to ask for help so that this time I could help in healing and recuperating her battered and bruised soul? (How accurately are people's voices metaphorically pointing to us our past deeds? She had herself jumped in the well. Also when people were asking me the effectiveness of healing. These people were reminding me of my involvement in her past deed and my failures in giving her right advice in the past. There I tried to save her by hiding the truth to save her body and here I had no explanation to offer them because I could not save her soul. But this time I know that I have saved her soul though I may not have been able to save her body. Writing her case is an attempt to save both of us from the sin by confessing our deeds, we had committed in the past.

So what if she could not live in the same body, her healing has healed her past lives. Along with her are also healed some of my past deeds of which I was unaware and ignorant. In a worldly sense, she caused me pain by failing me in bringing her out from her miserable life, but in the longer run, she became instrumental in teaching me some valuable lessons and also healed my action which I had done to safeguard her as per my understanding and capability at that time.

Deepa was also instrumental in bringing Anjana and Shahnaz to me for healing. Both of their sessions had convinced me of the conspicuous divine plan working for me and making me stronger in my conviction of explaining my learning through Deepa's case.

Note –It is important to understand that life cannot be judged from worldly denominator like success, glory, riches and fame nor is it seen as a sacrifice, selfless service, and renunciation. I have observed it again and again that there are always exceptions to the rule. Though it is observed that in accidental and untimely death the individual may not readily accept the transition from physical to spiritual due to shock , unfulfilled responsibilities, and desires. Yet one may do so and be released immediately to his higher abode. Contrary to it, people dying off long illness and sufferings may remain attached to physical realities and miseries. In spite of seeing them free from their sufferings, they still want to cling back to the same situation, making them earthbound.

Death is a small halt, like declaration of result of one class. Death is feared because fear is the darker side of the thing without really knowing what it is. Fear is of self-judgment, regret and repentance that we have not done well.

It is pleasure and celebration for some and failure and disappointment for others. Though pain at the separation with whom we shared and learnt important lessons of this life is understandable and accepted, just like moving away from the family , leaving for higher studies. More fitting example is of a girl leaving for her in laws home after marriage. It is continuation of journey, a step forward to accept new responsibilities and unfold new opportunities It is painful yet pleasure for all because it signifies progress and growing up process.

One cannot simply pass the final exam but has to learn every virtue by practically applying theoretical knowledge by working through relationships.

Everybody cannot work for Nirvana.-Why should every one work for Nirvana ? When it is a great service to be born as physical beings to the Creation and to the God Himself. Provided we learn to live a life of purpose, trying to learn the real purpose of our existence ,our spiritual connection. People detest spiritual knowledge or seeking higher connection because hearing these words , first thing comes to mind is renunciation. Being Spiritual does not mean renounce the world, wear orange robes and live in jungles or monasteries. Though we cannot negate the importance of these things also. But people think turning spiritual means stop living life of happiness, pleasure and fulfilment. There are no great purposes but small ones like acceptance, forgiveness and love, starting from self

,home, community, country and extending to the whole cosmos. It is like going from subject to subject and grade to grade. Every smaller reality, every smaller purpose giving way to greater ones. Every such small purpose fulfilled helps in strengthening its greater branch in the universe.

2nd Case

Dilemma of our Logical mind

Everyone is hypnotized; direction decides the destination - ***Narayan - 80 years November 2004***

I had taken up healing as a tool to progress spiritually, Like an over the enthusiastic child, I thought of doing my best by serving needy people and the nearest suitable place seemed this senior citizen home in Delhi .I contacted their front office and somehow managed to collect few inmates to discuss the possibility of healing and power of positive thinking. But they all were filled with remorse and helplessness. After living a respectable life and doing best for their families and society, now changing values had created a frustrating period for them in the silver years of their life. Though they all were not so unfortunate and miserable as their poorer counterparts, who are forced to stay in so-called Old Age Homes. They all were living there by choice, but there was no better choice than this. Everybody did nurse a sense of failure and a pang of pain somewhere in the heart in heart .

I met Mr. Narayan for the first time in Nov 2004 on my first visit to this home. He had a very serious demeanour making himself unavailable for such frivolous talks by a much younger person than him and that too a lady. People called him a diehard Vedanta follower as he was busy reading Vedanta most of the time. At lunch time he came to call his friends for lunch, seeing me sitting there, as a courtesy he invited me to have lunch with them. Initially, I was reluctant but later I gave joined them for lunch . This was the time that we both got talking. Others also suggested that he would be interested in my work as he is a spiritual person. Others outrightly refused any interest in such serious and obscure topic.'We have no such aptitude or thirst for spiritual knowledge. We are happy in our unhappiness and enjoying life in our sorrows. How can we forget our glorious past and hope for happiness when it is lost with the bygone days.' Mr Narayan extended his invitation to discuss about his learning in Vedanta. Promising to be back soon at least to learn something from them, if not able to teach them because of barrier of my age and experiences, I parted.

On my next visit, it was only Mr Narayan, too keen to talk to me. He confided, 'seeing you the very first day, there was some reaction in me. I got the glimpse from my past life in which you were my daughter. Now onwards you are my daughter.' He started treating me so. He even clarified, if your father or husband has any objection to our relationship; I want to adopt you legally'. I assured him of no such problem from their side. He introduced me to his daughter living in the same city; she may be few years older to me. His daughter sounded bit upset about his behaviour as she started explaining to me his depressive attitude, his moody nature and not listening to any body's point of view. He brought his youngest and favourite son and grandson who lived abroad to my house to get to know his extended family. His son requested me to visit him more often to give him company. As on his part, he was doing so by visiting one such home in a nearby area in his inhabited country. I maintained my stand neither by being too familiar with him nor by totally severing ties. His concern for me seemed genuine. He even talked to me every week from abroad, when he went there for few months stay. He told his family that he wants to be back soon because Nirmal is there. This infuriated his daughter in law. 'He prefers to be with Nirmal more than me'. Taking his daughter in law's side, I cautioned him, 'this is not fair on your part; anybody would feel bad if you give more importance to me over your family members'. He replied, 'I don't get along well with her, she has so much ego. I have already told you and I also tell others that you are the perfect human being, I have ever known.' I warned him and asked to take feedback on this account from my family and my mother in law. You can get my real picture about me from them, because nobody is perfect. Simply because we don't live together, that is why you find me without any drawback and flaws'. I could not defeat him in his claim and he maintained, 'no, when I say this, it is not to earn some favour or please you. This is my soul's voice'. Though not very talkative but he was very assertive in his opinion.

Whenever we met ,he would say, 'You are very precious to me, please pray for me'. I am this much healthy and fit because of your prayers and my parents' blessings. My father used to tell me that others prayers really work wonders for us'. In return for his affection towards me, I taught him basic Reiki but he could not develop the habit of self-healing and insisted, 'You must continue praying for me. I know you have some special power'. 'I tried to convince him that he too can practice healing on self and feel that power within him. There is nothing special in healing; Reiki is only a special meditation to get what you desire and evolve further. This is the same energy, which is spoken as prevailing in the universe in every particle'. But he insisted, ' I meditate and read Geeta' that's all. I have read Geeta twenty times in past many years'. This was evident from the underlined verses and summery written on the pages of his books. I really revered him for his keen interest in reading scriptures so intently.

Respecting his old age and empathizing with the lonely soul, I also started reciprocating his feelings. He always commented, 'what is this body, nothing, I am not this body. Our relationship is not of this body but much deeper than that of soul. Nobody loves you more than I do ,neither your father nor your husband'. Often he visited our home but never empty handed. He said, 'a father can never go to his daughter's house empty handed'. I felt very awkward as I did not want any obligations of give and take. I requested him to keep our relationship spiritual in nature and not make it worldly by exchanging material things. He somehow convinced me in accepting small little gifts. He said, 'all this belongs to you, I will give it in writing'. I protested, 'no, I cannot even think of accepting any material favour from you. Your children have right on your material possession'. He argued, 'all are well settled, I don't owe anything to them nor do I take anything from them'. I persisted, 'I don't need anything because I am not interested in material possessions ,.I do not undervalue your things, but why not donate it to some needy person'? He refuted, 'no all this I have earned with my hard work and sincerity, I am free to give it to anybody and I want to keep it in the family'. On his invitation , rarely I along with my family visited him. Once a week he would talk to me on the phone inquiring my family's welfare. We always talked about spiritual aspects of our life.

He would not accept any of my words without logic. Once I told him about my observation regarding our being animals in the past. He rejected this claim on account of his learning. He emphasized,'animals cannot contain the complex human mind,Vedanta says that once we have evolved to become humans , we don't become animals'.I reasoned, 'then what happens to the people who are mentally retarded or have even less IQ than animals? Where is their complex human mind that time'? I also reminded him of the famous story from scripture, where highly spiritual King Bharata became deer in his next life due to his excessive attachment to motherless baby deer'. He could not accept my reasoning immediately.

Later he told me, 'I think it may be possible for a man to devolve to become the animal. I remember an incident from my childhood. My father used to feed milk to a snake, who had occupied one full floor of our seven storied ancestral house in Karachi. I use to tell my father not to feed this lecherous animal so that he will be forced to leave the place and we can utilize this floor. My father cautioned me, ' Narayan , don't talk like this , actually we are not the owner of this house ,he is the actual owner of this home. Alas, he had become snake as he was so attached to this house'. I did not understand it then, I think he was right, so you may be right too'.

Past life- Unconsciously he had acknowledged me as his daughter from the past. Consciously he wanted feedback from me on my reaction to his attachment. On his request, I regressed him to see our relationship in the past life and I had to rely on his revelations. He confirmed, 'in one life you were my daughter and died of typhoid at forty years of age. This life we lived on the bank of a river in Gujarat'.

Past life-'In another life you were my friend's daughter but I loved you more than my own daughter'. This was a foreign place. He even told his name as H.A.Hunn and the girl's (my) name is Merlyn. Alas in that life also you died of typhoid at sixteen years of age. In both the lives, I had been left heartbroken after your untimely death'. I could really feel the pain reflect in his emotion at that moment.

Past life- Seeing his keen interest in Vedanta, I regressed him to see any past life which has some relevance to his interest in Vedanta. He reached back to a very ancient life. He said,' I see the Baby Krishna (Baal Gopal) as He is in the posture hanging in my room. But now I see Him in reality in flesh and blood. I am one of the fellow friends (sakhas). I am playing with many such boys of my age. But I am very far from where Krishna is. My name in that life is also Narayan'. I asked him to be near Krishna, touch him and observe more intently. He said, 'no, no , how can I go near him? He is so bright and powerful. I feel I have no right to touch him'. I could not break his conscious barrier and he would not go near Krishna. He described his that life in detail and died in his very old age but still healthy (this life also he is healthy and lives an independent life at ninety years of age)

Past life -In another life he said, 'my Guru is Viveka Nanda. I was his follower, when I was an English gentleman. I always talk to him and he brings me out from any bad situation. You were also his disciple in that time. You were more sincere than me. My Guru says, 'your meeting has been organized in this life this way because of our past connection with each other and our Guru . Otherwise how can you think it is possible for you both being from such distant land and different culture and age to meet and recognize each other'? I asked him, 'why did we meet so late in this life? He said, 'that is my karma, I was destined to suffer so much. Now only the time has come for us to meet and help each other'.

He could not believe in his experience

He insisted, 'I want you should also see the same truth, then only I will believe in it, otherwise I think it may be my imagination'. I tried to convince him of my inability to see any relationship with him in the past. Not only him, I could not see any relationship with anybody so far. I confirmed his revelations may be true as diseases and accidents are repeated in many life times and I had suffered with typhoid exactly at the same age in this life too'. But he could not be convinced, why I cannot see any such relationship with him in the past. Thus he dismissed his experience as his wild imagination.

Once after coming back from a visit to Haridwar, he enthusiastically said, 'I met a great saint there and he said that he can tell me about my five past lives'. I told him that this is the irony of us human beings that we cannot trust our own inner voice, vision and feelings to be true ,where as we totally accept others opinions and observations about us to be true. That is why you can believe the saint but not what you saw yourself through regression and what you yourself felt by seeing me for the first time. He persisted, 'no, but my only hitch is, then why can't you see the same thing? If there is some reaction in me, then there has to some reaction in you too'. He would not listen to any of my explanations that meditation and healing is done to erase the memories from the past, which may be unnecessarily causing sufferings by excessive attachment to any person or situation. On the contrary he gave his philosophy that meditation is done to remember and bring back the past alive, which is also true .

Desires are the Seeds that bears the fruit

He could not believe that I do not have many worldly desires but I desire higher things. He clarified, 'Nobody can be without worldly desires. I am full of desires and I want to be born again and that too in the same family as my grandson's son. Even my guru has told me the same thing (in his vision) and in next life, you (I)would be born as my son. I am sure to get what I want. Because desires are the seeds and they bear the fruit once the time comes for them to be ripe'.Yet he wanted my feedback on his claim. I agreed, 'if you so strongly desire, it may come true, provided your deeds are in accordance with your desire'. He felt relieved by this confirmation and declared , 'I have never done any bad deed in my life '.When I tried to explain that same way my desires of seeking higher things and liberation can bear fruit when the time is right as I am also working in that direction . He felt I am being childish and quipped, 'Oh beta,(child)that's a very distant dream for all of us . God knows how many birth it will take to reach that stage'. I reasoned, 'at least we can try to desire higher things when we know that our desires can bear the fruit'.

What more proof I wanted that we create our own future, pleasant or not so pleasant? I could not but wonder about the veil of maya, illusion and self-righteous attitude of individual creating same cycle all over again. He does not get along with his family because of clash in their ego, attitude and changing values. He is living an independent, lonely life. Yet he wants to be born again in the same family as his grandson's son. Not only him, he has even fixed my place to be born as his son in his next life. 'Next life you will be born as my son of that I am sure, there after I cannot say whether you will seek nirvana or any such higher thing.' In this life he is attracted towards me unknowingly yet does not follow any of my philosophy, still he desires me to be born as his son in his next life. Without realizing what purpose it is going to serve, may be waste one life time again.

He reads Vedanta and has got enough knowledge which he wants to share with me but when we meet he is busy sharing his worldly aspirations, achievements, and desires. The time to share the true knowledge is always pushed farther. Once I told him about the Vedanta discourse by Shri Partha Sarthi going on in the city for three days. He felt very happy to attend it. Later he gave me feedback about it , thanking me for informing him about this lecture. He said, ' I attended his discourse for seven days, I also met Swamiji alone for two hours and asked him many questions and felt enlightened. He has changed my life. Swamiji was also impressed with my good health and asked me, 'it is nice to see you so healthy and independent in advanced old age. What is the secret of your healthy body? He continued, 'I told him, 'I drink two pegs of whiskey every night to keep myself healthy and remain free from depression. Swamiji was very impressed and said, 'keep it up'. Now Mr. Narayan prophesied his opinion about Swamiji, 'he is also very energetic at this advanced age, he also must be drinking whiskey to keep him cheerful and healthy'. I was bit put off by this allegation to carry on his habit on the pretext of the green signal from a saintly person.

I was comparing the truth about the fact that the people and world outside us are just the reflections of our inner self. Was this to test the philosophy of non-judgment which I was trying to practice in my life? Yet, I could not remain without analysing which part of my inner being is reflected through him. Pretension, telling lies, spiritual complex, egos, I am confessing these hidden traits in me ,which may be reflecting through him. Why otherwise he should be attracted to me? Or was he craving for reflection of some desired higher virtues through me? Though I fully believe what Veda preaches, healing is just the practical application for elevating life from a miserable thinking body to feeling highest spiritual manifestation of our Divinity. Again I am judging whether it is my inadequacy not to be able to make him realize importance of healing and make him tempted to use meditation in his daily life, so that he doesn't have to deepen on whisky for dispelling depression but try to drink the nectar of bliss by attuning inward and get a kick stronger and pleasant one by realizing deep spiritual connection.

Slowly he was realizing my sincerity and dedication towards my goal, he felt sorry and lamented , ' you really have a jest for higher things , you should not have got married ,because of family responsibility ties you down and you cannot renounce and succeed in this direction '. I told him that family life is the greatest way to progress spiritually while performing all the social responsibilities without attachment. I am not attached to anybody that I would like to be born again in another lifetime. Off course, if I do not finish working out, my karma with someone or something, I may have to be born again. But from my side at least, I don't desire any such thing. Sympathizing with me, he opinioned, 'at least you should have been born abroad because in India people will not realize your worth. With your talent and sincerity, you would be admired abroad'. He could not digest when I said, 'I don't desire any name or fame. I want to reward and recognition from my higher self and from there I am getting feedback on my inner growth. Because I am becoming aware of the purpose of each and every situation and learning lesson from circumstances of my life'. He pities my immaturity and fanciful ideas and tried to dissuade, 'you should visit places, enjoy life because life is to gain experiences.' I replied, 'I am inclined towards inner experiences and it is my choice, not by any external force'. I think he felt hopeless about me. Yet we kept in touch and talked such stuff, not agreeing to each other's point of views for almost five years.

He Trusts me

I also usde to talk to his friends in his Senior citizen home whenever I visited him. Once he lost a great sum of money from the cupboard of his room. He had caught a fellow mate red handed and informed the authority immediately. His friends even warned him saying , 'since Nirmal also comes to your room ,there is a possibility of such occurrence in the future '. He said, 'I told them that even if the God comes down and tell that this can be true (Nirmal stealing), I will not even believe Him. Distrusting Nirmal is like distrusting myself'. Later he confided to me, 'they are surprised and suspicious of our relationship. I had told them that I will give everything from my room to Nirmal. They warn me that I have been hypnotized by you. They advise me to visit you less frequently'. I just kept quiet. He enquired, 'do you think I have been hypnotized by you'? I tried to explain to him what exactly is hypnosis? As I practice hypnosis and past life regression therapy along with Reiki and many other healing techniques. He could not follow much. I asked him, 'if you think you are hypnotized by me, is it harming you anyway? He said, 'no, I feel very peaceful and uplifted in your company. My thoughts are always directed towards higher realities and I feel free from mundane worldly worries.' I tried to convince him, 'then how does it matter to you, whether I have hypnotized you or not? He replied, 'no, it does not matter but because people say so, then why do people say so? I said, 'they are correct because as they are hypnotized by the material world, in that sense you also get hypnotized in my company towards your inner spiritual world'. The word hypnotize was not palatable to him, because others believe that I must have done something to control him. He said, 'then you please dehypnotize me. Hypnotism is not good'. I said, 'for that you have to go to somebody else who can dehypnotize you from me. He replied, 'but I don't know anybody else who can help me. I explained, 'Because I have not done anything knowingly to hypnotize you. You yourself formed ties with me saying that I am your daughter and made it stronger by meeting and talking to me. Then you stepped ahead by thinking and saying that I am the perfect person and God incarnated for you. You stop all this and slowly you will be dehypnotized'.

Hypnosis is nothing but guided meditative state

He always wanted that I should call him, visit him and reciprocate his affection. I did not want to tie down to somebody's praises and affection. From my side I did not want to impose myself on him. I was also wondering at the dilemma of a logical mind. How a person is swayed by outwardly influences and leaves inner call unattended? How one resists change and new knowledge „even if it gives him peace and progress? How one sticks to old habits and thinking, even though it makes his life sad, stagnant and monotonous? How one is so conditioned to judge and accept his philosophy to be the most honoured verdict from the Lord? God is testing our faith, our sincerity and our yearning. He is not impressed by shallow scriptural knowledge. Applying this knowledge in day today's life is more important than reciting verses and anecdotes. All the scriptures say, 'man is a spark of divinity; God has made man in his own reflection. God is omnipresent,but how much are we ready to accept it in our life? Leave aside considering everything innate and evil things originating from God, we can't even acknowledge God's presence in our loved ones or God speaking to us through people we admire. God is present in everything, every situation and being. We are seeking confirmation by mugging and memorizing scriptural verses. Alas, we stick to known and familiar zone, though it may be more stifling and painful..We are scared of the meditative or trance state which can take us closer to seeking bliss and divine grace..Hypnosis is nothing but guided meditative state, where as meditation is self-hypnosis, which is not easy to reach. Everybody is hypnotized and everybody is insane anyways. Difference is only of direction and degree. Wiser ones towards the inner world, the absolute reality. Intellectuals towards the material world ,the transient reality. Who is to judge, who is right, who is wrong? Who is losing by such arguments and judgments?

Note – I learnt from him that Ego is half God. This made me reflect on the contrariness in the statement that ego is the principle barrier in our path to seek union with that big whole, source of our origin. Yet ego is necessary element till we reach a certain point. If we do not feel ourselves separated from whole and from each others by creating individuality and personal traits then we have no grounding, no foundation on which we can stand to work towards realizing this union. The person denying any importance of ego is like saying; purpose of birth is dyeah only, so why do anything at all when we have to die one day. It requires an individual to stand out alone and create certain personality traits to strengthen his character. One makes his foundation strong by gaining any desired qualities like physical power, strength of character, material possession; intellect etc. That is why some trait is always dominant in every individual. As he interacts with World, his experiences make him reflect on his weakness and power. His wisdom compels him to learn to transform negative traits in to life supporting opportunities. Gradually he becomes the Alchemist to manifest the jewels of evolutions.

Ego – I want to elaborate my understanding of the much talked Ego in the spiritual journey. Like desires, it is very difficult to kill the ego. And it is next to impossible to become aware of our own ego and accept it in self. We may immediately pinpoint its reflection in another person. The more we kill the known and apparent ego and declare our self free from ego, the more subtle form it attains and becomes difficult to pinpoint. It becomes impossible to kill it since now we can't even recognize its presence in us. It becomes more dangerous like a revengeful enemy is more dangerous when hidden from us. We cannot measure or judge his power. We can notice ego in another person in the form of arrogance, proud, shrewd, pompous etc. and immediately decline traces of it in self. But do we know that pretending innocent, ignorant, poor , weak , generous; sympathetic or sacrificing is also a subtle and most dangerous form of ego. I also wish to verify Shivali's pronouncement in her last session, where she said that you haven't written your cases as it should have been. You have to edit by giving more clarification and comments from your side. I did not agree with her there and argued that I have done my best. My ego was stopping me from accepting criticism from a younger and inexperienced person. When I was reflecting on it later, I realized that I had decided to write only success cases. Thinking who would like to know about my failure ? It meant I was also measuring success and failure in terms of achievements and recognition. I was not writing the memoir of my inner experiences honestly . I just wanted to produce successful cases and feel champion in healing . I wanted to avoid writing my failures that would cause embarrassment and threaten my ego.

2. I had really not written much comments in other cases except Ayan. Why? Because I did not want to sound as if I am preaching people, I wanted people to read cases as it happened in its simplicity. If I explain more I will sound claiming myself wise and knowledgeable. But little did I realize the subtle form of ego where I wanted people to accept my work just as simply revealed and innocently gathered truth reflected in different life stories through sessions.

Now I understood,ego is really half God. That is why it is difficult to separate it from life. In the physical world, we are always confronted with the duality and confusion, living life on the edge. More so with the spiritual journey, which is like walking on a double edged sword. If I explain , what I know ,I may sound egoist , thus I wanted to kill my ego. I now recognize my apparent ego and am trying to win and embrace it in the form of my pretension to be most humble , modest, ignorant and innocent. Wasn't it subtle ego wanting approval of my work from people even though it may cost me suppressing my wisdom and authenticity ?

There is a reason for everything. The knowledge about self is within everyone. Only thing is we have to retrieve it. From outside, we just seek approval of our inner knowledge. I also had this knowledge from the beginning and would speak it out but people would not accept my knowledge because it did not match my experiences and my level of being at that time. So I decided to suppress it for the sake of seeking approval from them for fitting in the conventional norm of the society. And I started becoming modest, humble, suppressing this knowledge farther and farther. That this became my tendency, a compulsion, and my habit. Now I have recognized it as my subtle ego, as this is separating me from the higher world by making me think the doer of this work. Thus I am using safety measure to stop my ego from becoming visible on the surface. Now I have recognized my ego both ways, it's my duty to explain what I know. How does it matter whether others accept it or not?

3 rd Case

Kartikeya 17 years

December 2006 Restlessness Lack of concentration.

History –Eighteen years old Kartikeya is a very sensible, and obedient boy. From his young age he started taking house hold responsibilities to help his working mother and supervise his younger sister. Unlike his peer group he is religious and visits nearby temple regularly with offerings of flowers and water. He promises his parents to do well in studies but finds it difficult to sit and concentrate. Visits to doctors and psychiatrists have not proved much helpful.

Session – He easily slipped deep in his subconscious mind and started describing. First he started viewing his probable future.

I have observed that teenagers easily go to their future in the beginning itself. Because they are at a threshold where their energy is focused more towards future. That is why forth coming fatal accident or opportunities can be seen as whatever is coming up in near future is displayed first ,provided we are ready to accept and work in that direction or have courage to face it.

Future - He started describing, 'I am twenty years old, sitting in a class room. It is a different country probably, because all the students looks from different race. I asked him to observe keenly as to what class is this and is any known person sitting in the class, as I wanted confirmation in regard to time and place. He said, 'it is a fashion designing class and one of my friends Varun is also sitting with me. Q-Where is Varun at present? A- He is studying with me in eleventh class. Q- How do you both look? We both look same as we are now, only thing I feel we are now about twenty years old. We are wearing slightly more fashionable clothes'. There after he elaborately described the modern gadget and setting of the class room, thus I concluded he is been given glimpse of his probable future. To be more sure, I asked him to see further what is he doing after three, four years. He said, 'now I am working in some office, I look twenty five years old. But it is a different foreign country, not where I did my course. My parents live in country of my origin and I am in contact with them, I send them money'..All this will happen in the future but before that he had to get over his present problem, So I asked him to go back to the origin of his this problem.

Past life – He regressed to about ten years old boy in his past life. He said, 'I am standing outside a small house in a village. I am wearing kurta payajama.. My mother is tending to the fields in nearby area. I don't have a father. I help my mother in the field. I do not go to school.' I asked him to see what he does for a living ,when he has grow up to become an adult. He said, ' I am about twenty years old , I sit in the market in a tailoring shop and am stitching clothes. This is the same village ,where we have little land. I am not married, my mother has grown old. After some time she is no more. I feel very sad and lonely.

I am about forty years old and I have moved out to a nearby city and have opened a small tailoring shop there. I am very efficient in my work, people appreciate me and I am doing well for myself. I have not got married and I am living alone in one house. I feel some void and loneliness. I am growing old in age.

I have reached in my sixties, my health is deteriorating. I cannot do any work, I keep laying alone in my house.

Q "What disease you are suffering from, Where do you feel discomfort, Don't you take any treatment?

A-"I am suffering with cancer. I have cough, congestion and pain in the chest. I don't take any treatment. Probably there is no treatment for this disease or I cannot afford any treatment".

Q-'How do you sustain, is anybody helping you there '?

A –'Sometimes somebody out of compassion gives me food, but most of the time I go hungry. Gradually my disease is increasing and I am in unbearable pain and discomfort'.

Death –'Languishing alone,one day , I die alone in that small room. .

Q- 'What happened to your body after you are dead, did anybody find out and cremate your body'?

A- 'My neighbour comes to see me after a long time; He opened the door and found my body lying dead. He went to collect few people. Some people out of compassion carry my body to crematorium. There is also one pundit chanting some mantra.

My body is Placed on the pyre to burn'. Q-'What is pundit chanting? Isn't there any change in you by hearing this mantra'? A –'I do not understand its meaning. I only feel relieved to be released from that pain and loneliness'. Q '-Is this the reason that you feel restless because you had faced so much pain in your body in your past life'? A- Yes, whenever I try to concentrate my mind in studies ,the same suffering is experienced and I become restless '. I healed him by touching his body and also gave suggestion to his mind to feel released from the memory of that life. He burnt the painful memory from this body along with his past body. Which he felt going back like bags full of some thing in it. Gradually he was feeling lighter. When I asked him to see some happy future event, he said, 'I am about forty years old, I am in London. I am going to some place by one very brand new car. Q ' What are you doing there , since how long are you living there ?But he said, ' I am on my way to some meeting. I think but on the way I have severe pain in my heart '. I asked him to see further what happens to him. I also wanted to confirm whether it is happening in this life or has happened in some other time? By this time he was tired and unable to see anything further. I healed him silently and brought him out from trance by giving positive suggestions. His mother was also sitting near him and amazingly listening to whatever he narrated. I suggested them to have few more sessions, so that his future discomfort can be erased from his mind. I also told him to learn Reiki or practice yoga, Pranayama which will definitely calm him gradually as the memory will slowly be released from his mind.. He did not have another session with me, so I had to be content by knowing this much from him.

Lesson – Time is not the greatest healer , mind is.Grave diseases, accidents, unpleasant circumstances are the outcome of unresolved issues from the past being repeated in the present and leading to more pain and miseries in the future, if not cured from the root. Healing is the only ways back HOME after successful completion of the worldly class. If we are failing the test ,we are again repeating same grade in subsequent lives. In such cases death is like changing a school in the hope that the new school and surrounding may provide some fresh breath, some new insight to understand the subject fully and be able to pass the test finally. Skills are also refined over the time. Talent is nothing but hard work of many past lives.

4th Case

There is a hole in the center of my head.

Pawan 13 years Feb 2006.

Dyslexic, Unable to study, Excessive hunger

This thirteen years old boy was brought to me after much persuasion and convincing by his moher of no harm to him from healing . He has dyslexia and is finding it difficult to cope up with the study in higher classes now. He is a good basketball player. He also has problem in controlling his hunger. He over eats and finally lands up emptying his bowel, making him feel hungry in no time. This is quite embarrassing and causing inconvenience to him and his parents. He looked a healthy boy except his problem of restlessness and lack of concentration in study. He was giving his exam with the help of a hired writer.

He rushed to see his successive past lives and reasons for his present condition were contributing to his present problems in life.

Session – He easily started describing his inner world. His guide came as Lord Ram.(Though at present he is following different religion). I asked him, how does Ram look?, He said, ‘ he is wearing Dhoti and crown on his head. There is Trishulin his hand. I ask him to see the origin of his problem. He reached to one of his past life.

Past life - He said, ‘I am living in a some small town in hills of Himachal Pradesh. My mother is my present mother and her name is Rekha. I have same sister as my sister that time. I am studying in the some city in the plain region . Then I went abroad and I did MBA. Now I have opened a Garage in my city. I am married. I meet with an accident. I suffer a head injury and I die. This is year 1720.

Past life – Now again I am in a village in hilly place. He describes his guru is Vijay. He is my neighbour. How and for what he is his Guru he could not say anything about it. I have parents but I do not go to school. Probably there is no school or it is not considered important in the village to go to school. I play and roam around with my friends. I do not know any of them now. There is some fight taking place and I am also involved in it. Now, we are hiding in some place. I am caught and people hit on my head and it is bleeding heavily. I lose conscious. My mother is crying inconsolably. And I have died now.

Past life -Now I am born as a poor fisher man. There is very little to eat. I am very thin though I am a grown up young man. I am not married because I cannot support a family. My mother wants to see me married. I do not recognize her in this life. She dies as she had grown old. When I am in my thirties, I slip from a big rock while fishing and hurt my head; it is injured at the same place where it had hurt in my last life. But I regain conscious and soon I am able to walk and continue my routine work of fishing. But my body is very weak. Slowly my health is deteriorating and I am losing any interest in life as I cannot earn anything. I die in my forties, feeling freed from that wretched life of poverty and hunger.

Past life -Now I am born in South India. My father is my present father and his name is Subramanian. My mother's name in that life is Lakshmi. I do not know her in this life. I study engineering and come to Delhi to pursue higher education. I complete my education and am working in Delhi. I start having a headache. I am going for a treatment. Nothing is detected by the doctors. My trouble is increasing and affecting my life. I am unable to continue working further. My father had come down to look after me and get me treated. But I die in my thirties. My father is inconsolable. I was the only child of my parents. This life was from 1930 to 1960.

Preparing for this birth- I asked him, 'which life you had after this'?. He said, 'there after I was born in 1990'. Q –'Where were you for all those years (1960 to 1990'? A- 'I was in the sky. I wasn't born on earth'. Q-'what were you doing in the heaven'? A-' I was preparing for my next life'. Q- What sort of preparations you did for next life'? A-' I don't remember now. I had to be born to my previous father'. Q -Why? A-'because he so desired.'Q-' What was the reason for your coming this way to them (adoption)' A-' There is no reason. I was born to people who did not need me'. I tried to help him by explaining my understanding on adopted children rather I wanted feedback on my understanding and asked him saying , ' because you could not have been able to come to them as a natural born'?. A – 'Yes'.

He remembered his past lives year wise

Surprisingly he rushed to count year wise all his past lives from year 1600 onwards. I had recorded his case but his voice is so low that it cannot be made out clearly.

Healing-Now I asked him to see his head , how it looked when he died of that undiagnosed headache. He said, 'there is a big hole in the center of my head. That was causing this pain'. I asked him to see that hole getting healed with the healing light..He was seeing different colours of light entering the area and now that hole was sealed. His head looked healthy in that life time. Now I asked him to see each life one by one to heal his head from injury and he did it so. He was seeing the effect of head injury in his body getting healed. He himself said,'yes, now I can see alphabets clearly and read properly. In that trance state he started reading a passage as if it is written on the board. I asked him,' from where are you reading this passage'? He said,'it is on my mental screen, a passage which is in my English book'. This passage must have been revised in the class but that time he wasn't able to read because letters were not stable. But the sound was stored in his mind as now without any questioning from my side he started reading it on his own. Now he sounded confident.

Hunger-After all the past lives' memories of head injuries were healed from his mind , I asked him, 'why does he over eat'? He said, 'because I had starved in one life. So my mind fears that I may not get food, thus I cannot think of leaving any food..I feel the urge to eat everything then and there. But my mind was injured and it could not digest and absorb everything. I am forced to evacuate my bowel immediately and my stomach is hungry again'. After healing this memory from his mind and also giving some positive suggestion to his subconscious to break free from that life's scarcity memory. 'Eat as much you can easily digest and utilize'. There is plenty to eat now because now the circumstances of your life are very different. You have surplus to eat at any given time.

Guides -I told him to ask his Guide , is your healing complete or you need some more session with me. He said , "my guide is Ram ". I asked, ' Lord Ram?'. A –'No, Lord Ram was my guide in my fisherman's life". He says, now my problem from root is healed but it will take some time to get completely cured. I don't need any further session. I will be cured gradually'. I still wanted to know the reason behind his head injury in all his past lives claiming his life. In this session he could not say anything in this regard.

Lesson–Being novice , lacking in experiential knowledge and not getting any conclusive answers in my sessions, is the reason for giving heading for this chapter 'stumbling through obscurity.'

His mother also was sitting by his side during his sessions and she also exclaimed, 'no wonder his brain has deficient functioning, he has been having his head hit every life'.

1. I was left wondering whether in this life also he would have met same fate and died of head injury. But by erasing this memory from his mind, this cause has been healed as he said, 'I am healed now.' He wasn't ready for further healing at present. He needed some time to gain some strength after coming out from so many lives' fatal memory.

2. Hole in the center was for atoning some deeds of his previous life where he must have been perpetrator of such action on others? That in many lives he is meeting fatal end via head injury. It has become a mechanical cycle for him.

3 He was sent to me to learn that how some of us are caught in this never ending cycle of meeting the same fate. Healing would break free him from it. Even, if his brain function does not improve in this life at least he is out from meeting same fate i.e. dying of head injury and carrying same memory forward. I am sure more healing

would definitely improve his condition provided people understand the importance and efficiency of healing and learn to have patience.

4. He verified my belief that adopted children have strong ties with their foster parents. They cannot come through normal channel that is why this adoption opens up the opportunity for their union.

5. At times he had some guide appeared in his mental screen. Proving presence of higher beings always guiding us subconsciously without us being aware of their presence. He is now in different religion but he had seen some guides with whom he had relationships in his past lives, now he does not believe or recognize them in the present.

6. His case may raise some doubts as he was describing few things which may look odd like,doing MBA or Engineering and all in that distant past. Actually our mind has got this faculty of transferring the information in to equivalent quantity of present time. He may be doing equivalent study in those days known with this name today.

(This is my own experience that our conscious mind goes back to past lives and analyse, deduct, criticize and evaluate as per our conscious understanding of the subject. Because there is no past or future for mind. It is only present. That is why if someone does not follow my instructions consciously, he may not be able to explain any inner experiences.

I have been given proof of this phenomenon in one of my past life experience. I had felt myself in the auto rickshaw type thing moving down a steep hill. I am also on the top of it as if hovering over it. Then I am myself analysing how is it possible to drive auto rickshaw in such steep road. Actually that may not be an auto riksha but four people carrying my body (dead body ,that is why my consciousness is hovering on top of my body) making it equivalent to having a four wheeler ride,.

In another life I had seen myself releasing spirit who had possessed a lady. I am also healing that lady by releasing that spirit and also wondering, did I have this healing knowledge at that time also? But this experience happened to me now, when I have this knowledge. I am going back to that remote life now with all this knowledge , so it is possible to utilize our present understanding there and heal that event which was not healed in that life. This is what is meant by the statement one becomes the director, the actor and the critic of his life .

5th case

Vasudev- Worries for his daughter Nitu - Abnormal hair growth on her back 24 Dec 2005

Nitu was a ten years old girl with abnormal hair growth at about two inches roundel at lumbar region in the spinal column. She had undergone permanent hair removal operation last year but the hair in that area grew back again with coarser texture. Now her father had brought her to show her in Army Hospital R&R. As she was still young and not herself disturbed by her problem ,so she was advised to wait for two, three years.. Since, he was known to me, he somehow got convinced that I can provide him and her some relief. I myself wasn't sure whether healing can really do some miracle in her case and I was very clear in explaining to him my stand. But he still insisted and I suggested him few healing sessions and also promised to continue distance healing. He agreed to come to me whenever convenient for him.

It is worth mentioning here that he is the only person who without understanding any procedure or seeing any visible positive outcome , kept bringing her to me from far off places like Jodhpur and Ranikhet once a year for four years and also assuring me that something positive would come in due time.

First I took Nitu's healing session. She was very reluctant to speak for not only was she less communicative by nature but was also finding it difficult to describe as she wasn't able to understand and put in words her inner experiences. I also realized that he is more concerned about her, where as she is innocent and really do not understand the longer consequences of her problem.

I suggested him to take session for healing her problem, which he willingly agreed.

Session– Past life - He is seeing a rough patch of land in the garden, where there is nothing grown. There is also a well, a temple and a school in that garden. He said, 'I cannot see myself but I see a cart going on that rough road'. I asked him to follow where that cart is going'? He reached in one village.

An old man is taking bath there outside under a tree. He has put a tilak (red vermilion) on his forehead. Now he is going to temple. He declared, 'this is a jain temple. I can make out from the pictures on the wall and decoration in the temple. Though I cannot recognize the pictures on the walls. Some ladies are entering the temple'. He wouldn't move from that temple to any other scene in that life. Thus I asked to see at least death scene in that life.

He said, 'there is a dead body under the tree, whose limbs are dried but face looks fresh with tilak on his forehead'. Though he did not recognize or relate this person as him. He kept looking at this scene for long. He said, much later a man in white clothes come and put this body in the cart, which is pulled by two buffalos. One man is sitting and driving the cart but since I am following this dead body so I cannot look at the driver. There is also one camel coming in my vision as if it is walking with us. Some villagers also have gathered to look this procession move ahead on the road. After some time they disappeared.. The cart is moving very slowly and as we are crossing another village, the people from that village also come forward to look this procession and start walking with us. As we near a far end of the road at a dead end, they have pushed this body down in the (nala) deep gorge). He is sincerely following the fate of this dead body. He said, 'I have come down along with this body. The crowd from top has dispersed but I remain there itself with this body for a long time.

Healing- Not wanting him to leave the body and move away from there, I asked him to see the last rites of this body by burning in the pyre, also, throw back all your present tensions, worries and bondages carried forward from that life in to this life. He did as advised and I asked him to roll the unwanted hair from Nitu's back and burn these along with his body as these are also apparently causing him excessive worries. I asked him to move ahead in life from there as that chapter is closed. He moved out from that gorge but he said, I am again back to the same village and same scene is following. The man under tree is taking bath, then I follow him to the temple and I see the same scene, people coming and going in the temple.

Guide-I strictly told him to move out from there and move up in the sky to meet his guide. He said, 'yes, Mata Vaishno Devi (Goddess) is my guide. I had visited Vaishno Devi abode few years back. I am in the same mandir now and She is blessing me. Though in this session I could not find any relevance of his daughter's problem yet I felt he was very stuck and stagnated in his past . I wanted him to break free from this mechanical cycle of going back to same place where he was standing till now. One session wasn't sufficient, so I advised another session with him.

Session -In his second session he reached to a place where a man is standing out in the field. He has got Rajasthani attire and surrounded by his sheep. I asked him to look at his face, whether he can recognize him. He expressed his inability to look at his face. He kept glued to this vision for a long time. I asked him to move away from there but he retorted, ' how can I move until this man moves from there?'. Then I impressed that this man is moving away from there. He said, 'no he cannot move because he is fixed there. He is statue (putla.)' So I dissolved that vision from his mind by burning it in the universal fire. It took much coaxing and convincing from me to move him back to any important scene in his that life time, when he is watching this statue of a man and feel unable to move away from there.

Moving back in time, he said, ' I see a women milking a buffalo on the ground floor of a small double story house. She is coming up to the house and empty the milk in the pan. She is boiling the milk. There is one child in the house. She gives milk to this child to drink.

Now one man comes from outside. This seems the family of these three people'. He couldn't recognize, which one of them is he there..

Another scene – The man brings the grass from outside and gives it to buffalo. The child looks grown up now. Here he just presumed may be she is his daughter Nitu. There was nothing more happening in their life.

Death- I asked him to see his death. He said, 'the same man has grown old now, the woman also has grown older.. He is dead. People are around his dead body. They are burning his body and he is watching all this from far.

Healing– I asked him to throw back all his worrie, attachments or ignorance from that life affecting him in this life in to the pyre.. He saw it going back in the form of balls of wool getting collected and burning in the fire there. I told him to pull out the hair from his daughter's back from the root and burn them in the fire. After this asked him to move up in the heaven to meet his Guide. He said, again Vaishno Devi is there to receive me. She is blessing me.

I asked him to see some happy future vision, he saw his sister's wedding ,which filled him with pleasant memories.

Summary– I feel he was ignorantly stuck in his past life. Where he is not even aware about his own body. Though he is seeing some body but he cannot feel that he could be that man. May be it is his religious teaching that he feels detached to that body that he doesn't relate him to anybody there. Yet he is bound to his past life which is seeking reflection in the form of excessive worries for unusual problem in his daughter.

He has been some pundit in that life but he did not have awareness. May be he just followed rituals and others teachings blindly. He never desired or intended for self experiences. This session may have been organized to show him that he has been in to different religion in different region. Which might enlighten him towards the diversities of life and make him open to start experiencing himself these multifaceted aspects to life one by one?

Summary of Nitu's session – She would see an area full of long thick grass. One squirrel like animal and many unexplained things.

When I asked her to see the cause of abnormal hair growth, she only saw her ethereal body, where hair have roots in the form of some black pipes (vein like) connected to hair under the skin. These pipes are feeding hair roots deep within the flesh. Slowly she saw these pipes are being pulled up and dissolved by burning. Gradually the under skin area was becoming clearer from these pipes till it had become clear. Finally she said, there is no hair or their roots visible to me '. On the physical level her coarse and dark hair were becoming softer and lighter and easily pulled up as compared to deep rooted hair which were painful to pull up.

It is my presumption that her mind had the memory when she was in the form of grass grown in a place. Or does it remember being a squirrel ,camel or such tailed animal reminding it of its tail, still nourishing the hair in that region. By clearing her mind of the supply to hair roots in this area now the place can be free from hair growth.

This is the reason for giving his /her case under this title obscurity because she is the only case where I could not clearly ascertain any connection in the past life. I could have done without writing this case but later I have enough evidence to prove the problem to be reminding her of her connection to some vegetative or animal species. May be I would not have accepted his /her revelation of her connection in those species as that time I wasn't open to this truth.

Note:

1. It really doesn't matter whether our body gets buried in the soil or burnt in the fire until one becomes aware and use his body as a vehicle for his soul. Till we complete this earthly journey ,we have to keep account of each and every pain endured by this vehicle (body), safeguard it for the comfortable travel to the distant Home land and also upgrade it with changing needs of the time. Our body in this evolutionary journey is represented in various form like cart, car, bus, train, boat, ship etc.

2. I have observed that where ever we abandon our body in the past, with whatever damage , the same injury or pain would be reflected in our present body on various levels (physical ,ethereal, emotional, mental ,astral ,spiritual) depending which level have caused it damage. We have to go back and retrieve it, heal it, rejuvenate it, make it strong enough to capable of moving ahead.

3. His case also signifies the blocked attitude of many people stuck with considering their religious philosophy to be the last verdict from the lord. They are like that man living in a cart era, when life was so simple and slowly moving. In that life he may be perfecting only one virtue like mechanically following rituals without actualizing its meaning in his life. Like new admission in the nursery class is made to mug up the syllabus before they can really understand its abstract teachings. The child so enrolled in the school doesn't know ,why he is in the school. He may repeat the answer by copying his elders the purpose of his schooling.

4. Same way it may be the beginning of his schooling in seeking his spiritual connection. Because he cannot understand much complicated intricacies of life. He is not even aware who is he? Who is driving the cart? Who is putting the dead body on the cart? It's not in his hand finally what they are doing to his body. He doesn't know who the dead body is yet he is hovering around it ignorantly because he doesn't know where to go from there. Because consciously he must have followed body is immaterial, not important. But after death he was not free from the debt from this body, thus he was left behind observing it helplessly and ignorantly.

5. Statue also signifies a body without soul (consciousness). Do we go to another life after death without freeing from our past and live like a statue ,a living ghost of our own past ,a body without conscious ,not knowing who I am, where and why I am here. and who is the poltergeist that keeps troubling me because I do not remember what I owe him?

⋙ ⋘

Chapter 4

A Step Forward

✣ ❉ ✣

Void -a blank space -I have observed ***few people reach a void or a blank space .*** A stage where one reaches when one has finished working out his negative past karma. Void is a place where one is resting for the moment, before he can step forward to take up new assignment. Though nobody is free from action and its consequences but after getting freedom from negative karma, there is freedom of deciding the direction to be taken according to ones desires and interest. It is a stop gap stage ,like a student after finishing his school exam is taking a short break till he again resumes further course or take up a job suiting his calibre. Till the time one is under negative karma, he will have to deal with that phase first,, mechanical cycle (Kaal chakra). Negative karma can be compared to a student failing in some subject in his previous class. As a student failed in a subject has to pass his failed subjects first, even though he is attending his next higher class. That is why he feels trapped,,always getting what he detests. It is important to pass all the basic subjects from the ***school syllabus***, and then only one can avail the freedom of selecting subjects of his choice in the college. Like a debtor has to first pay back his debt, then he can think of spending or investing his money as per his desire. A ***state of liberation but not released from bondage of body and life***. This is the time when one starts becoming aware of him being part of the Divine plan. He feels responsible for himself and does not blames others or God for his circumstances. That may be the reason that many do not go to their past life immediately and see them in some blank or void space. Because before starting up some action to serve the higher purpose through his body, he is living in limbo. That is why ,one may be content and peace loving yet feel confused and pained by seeing diversities and miseries around him.

This I realize now that in my first PLR session ,I was in the same stage at that time. As from past many years I have been healing my life through Reiki. My past was healed and my energy was being channelized. I was awakening and searching the path leading towards the higher purpose of my life. I was absorbing right knowledge coming to me through various means. Finally when I decided to take up healing as a means for further spiritual evolution. I was being given clues and guidance in the form of some visions, dreams and intuitive thoughts. In my visions I did not see any God form or Deity but I saw people from this life and some dreams giving me messages.

It was not easy to understand the deep meaning behind the **dream** in which I saw my Reiki Guruma is telling me, ' if you think you will earn money from your healing center ,then better close it'. When I tried to explain to her the purpose of opening a healing center that earning money is not the main aim ,though it is not considered wrong as is widely accepted in Reiki practice , give and take for maintaining balance to ensure fair exchange of energy. Seeing my strong logic , she gave up arguing further saying ,' I tell the same thing to everybody '.I was confused ,why my Reiki guru is giving me contradictory advise as I am trying to bring the knowledge of healing taught by them into practical use by opening a healing center. Then why is she asking me to close it and thinking that I intend to earn only money from it? She could well understand my intension that my main aim in opening up a healing centre is to devote my life for healing by making it my profession for the purpose of seeking inner connection and spiritual progress and also service to humanity. Had she spoken these words outwardly (it was a dream) or had I not accepted them whole heartedly my Gurus, I would have taken this advice adversely thinking that she is not my well-wisher as she does not wish for my progress. I knew there was some **obscure** guidance for me through this dream. Because if without no conscious conflict in my mind with her or her teaching on this subject and without my expectation, I had this vivid dream of her , then their cannot be any confusion and adverse message in this. Though I had accepted them my Guru's for Reiki teaching but I cannot claim to be that devoted to them that I could expect such close interaction with them internally (appearing them in my dreams amd visions). In fact, outwardly I always had some hesitation thinking them to be highly knowledgeable and thorough professional. As per popular belief, I too would have imagined and expected some God, Guides or spiritual beings appear in my visions and dreams, giving me messages.

This I am explaining to awaken few people who have reached this place/stage and do not know how to progress further. They have got stuck in this void. They have not fully surrendered and their logical mind has become very strong. People do not want to step ahead as it is comfortable living in a familiar zone. We do not want to learn new things because learning new things means unlearning old knowledge,wipe the slate clean. This is very difficult because our knowledge is the foundation of our life. Unlearning it means shaking this very foundation. This is called a *trishanku* state. People become devotee and want only to worship, remember stories of God, learn the verses from the scripture but they do not follow it. They do not want liberation for fear of stepping in to some unfamiliar zone, a next step in the evolutionary ladder ,where each one has to learn and become their own master.

1 st case I Am My Own Uncle Kuldeep January 2006

(Pricking pain in lumber region)

History – Kuldeep is an eighteen year old sincere and hardworking boy. He had a healthy body and tall figure but he had nagging pricking pain in his abdomen from past two years when cycle had hit his abdomen.. He had consulted many doctors and took medication but everybody declared, there is nothing serious. For few days the pain was very severe which subsided slowly but nagging pain still persisted which was causing him discomfort all the time. He feels though he takes good care of his body in terms of good diet and exercise but he is not gaining weight and doesn't feel very healthy. He had no understanding of healing or past life therapy but conventional medicine had not helped. So he wanted to give it a try.

Session – As soon as he was able to slide back in his mind, he reached two years back to his present life Guru's Ashram from whom he had taken initiation at that time. Many other people are also standing around that place.

He reached back what seems to be a jungle in his native village in Rajasthan, 'I have never been to this place earlier but I can make out that this is the jungle outside my ancestral village in Rajasthan My parents had left this place much before I was born in Delhi. I am feeling bit scared as it is evening time and its getting dark '.

Pain Abdomen – To know the cause of his present pain, he reached to his ancestral village in Rajasthan and is inside his ancestral house. He is seeing his father who is much younger at that time, he can recognize his grandfather, who resembles his father. (Though he has never seen him in this life) He is pleasantly surprised and announced, 'I feel ***I am my own uncle (main hi khud apna taaya hoon***).Yes, I am my father's elder brother. My wife (taayee) is also there. My younger brother (my father) is not married yet. We all are sitting and talking something. My wife is instigating me to take share from my father's property and start living separately. But I love my father and brother. I don't want to part with them so I disagree with her. She gets up from there and goes inside the house. After some time I come to my room. My wife is coming with a glass of milk in her hand and gives it to me to drink. I drink the milk and sleep in my bed. I never woke up again. (For the world he had died in his sleep but his subconscious remembers what all he went through when he died.

Death - He said, 'I am having severe pain in my whole abdomen, much like how I keep having now, but more severe and excruciating like glass is cutting my stomach. I am feeling very helpless and in agony as I cannot shout or call anybody. I think my wife had dissolved the poison in the milk, she wanted to kill me.

He continued, in the morning I am found dead in my bed. People have collected around my body. They are crying, my wife is also crying but I feel she is just pretending. She is not crying in fact she is happy internally. Pundit is also there, people are carrying my body to ghat (crematorium). My body is kept on funeral pyre (chita) My father (present grandfather) is carrying a mud pot filled with water (ghadha) on his head and taking seven rounds around the pyre and then dropped the pot down from his head. My brother (present father) is lighting the funeral pyre. I am feeling very sad , bit scared and helpless at this moment.

Healing -I asked him to feel and mentally throw back the poison from this body. The memory of that life pain was still imprinted and causing similar symptoms in his present body. He felt severe pain at this moment, much like he experienced at the time of his death. I had to stop and heal him for some time. I also gave suggestion to his subconscious mind that the body which experienced so much pain due to poisoning had been burnt. So all the pain and suffering from that life is burnt with that body. This is different body, entirely new life; it has nothing to do with that life's pain full experience now. It took some time for him to feel relieved of that pain.

I continued further when he felt relieved of that pain, 'my father and brother are talking about the date for immersing my ashes (Hindu ritual of picking up the bones and ashes from burnt pyre and immersing in the Ganga river mostly at Haridwar or Gaya with prayers conducted by pundit.. So that the dead is totally released of his present body and immersed in the vast universe through fire , water and prayers) (***but did he feel released from that life's pain and helplessness?)***

Heavenly experience-I asked him to go up in the sky from there. Now he is higher up in the sky , one person with crown in his head is sitting on the golden throne. Few girls are standing in a long queue. I am also in the long queue. One person with some long paper roll type thing in his hand is writing something. I asked him to find out from those people ,why did this happen to him ? He got the reply and conveyed to me, ' because in one life, I had hit my wife , so she had felt intense pain and was full of revenge for me. She either wanted to cut me off from my family so that I will keep craving for their love and feel pained by separating them from myself or else I had to die and leave life mid-way. Now the justice is done. I intuitively told him, then this must be ***Dharam Raj,*** and the person with paper roll is ***Chitragupta.(***According to Hindu mythology, Chitragupta writes all our deeds in his book and we have to meet the same fate once the time comes for our karma to be ripe).

I asked him to find out from his Higher self, is he healed from past karma and what will be his future? He answered, ' my life ahead is good; whatever I will do, I will get back. I am released from my past'. He was working in my office as an office boy so I casually asked him what about our work ,where you are working now? He said, ' Dharam Raj will not comment anything about it'. So I brought him back.

Post session -He was very surprised by what all he saw and felt. He narrated to me about his family. His parents had left their ancestral house after his grandfather's death , leaving all the property back in the village never to return back. They were suspicious and scared of their sister in law's behaviour. Kuldeep is the youngest of three brothers in the family and his parents had never discussed anything about his uncle's death. I cautioned him not to discuss anything with his parents. But he did just the opposite and asked them point blank, 'did my aunt give poison to my uncle? They were startled and wanted to know, why is he asking this question all off a sudden ? He told them about his session and much like I had expected, they told him to be cautious of me as I might be doing some black magic or some such thing, otherwise how could I let their son know their hidden truth. He was relieved of his pain thereafter.

One day he had a dream in which he saw, there are many people sitting on the benches and we are disturbing healing water to them. I am telling him to give it only to people sitting on the front row.

Concluding session – I had seen only two three people reach that place (Dharam Raj). Rest of the people had reported different levels in the higher dimension. Could be those who had to give back their life in return of their past deeds of taking some body's life had to get clearance from the Dharam Raj's court.

Rituals are of no use if the parting soul is filled with excessive revenge, remorse or attachment. Could be by performing different meaning full rituals, the one performing it is reminding himself to understand the meaning of such rituals later when he is dead that this is what each ritual performed for him means)

Was he revengeful towards his wife and wanting to be born nearby her and pain was a reminder and at the right moment he would do something to take revenge or was he sympathetic and felt attachment for his younger brother(present father) and wanting to be nearby them ?

2nd Case My guide says, You have to heal me! Ayushi January 2006

(Healing the future) Backache and leg cramps

Ayushi is a seventeen year old girl studying in plus one and she is having backache since past one year. All the investigations and medication have not been able to relieve her of the pain.

I tried to heal her through Reiki and regression session. In each session she would see all the black spot in her energy body being cleared through healing and she felt relieved. But within a week, would have pain back again. It was bit confusing for me. She did not go back to her past life in initial two sessions. If the cause is not in the past, then why does the pain reoccur again after being cleared in the healing session? If the cause is in the past, then why doesn't she go to her past life, to the origin of her present pain? I also felt very unusual for a young girl of her age to have such backache.

Now I know that she was sent to me to teach me rather practically show me yet another dimension of healing that is ***healing the future***. (Though the future is nothing separate from present , its continuation of the past modified in the present. If that modification is not done, certain incidents can give rise to fixed outcome in the future.) What we call fatal end or accidents, outcome of negative experiences or coincidences and fortune from positive experiences. I got the clue, when I asked her to find out from her guide, ' why are you not getting healed ?what should I do to heal you ? Her reply was , ' I my self seems to hold on to the pain , that is why it comes back again and again. ***My guide says , you have to heal me.*** (Her guide was **white Light**)

Session I– She is sitting in the garden and is very lonely. When requested for the guide to come, some people and light descended in that place. When I guided her to go back to the origin of her present problem (backache, fear, depression) she reached back to this life's situations which were trigger points.

I am in my class room in tenth standard and all are made to sit and study on the ground in the school campus. We have to write test and have to bend forward to hold the note book and this stretch causes pain in the same place in my back (L1,2).

At home I am sitting in the bed in a bending position covered in a quilt. This is my normal study position but it stresses my back.

Once I am trying to get up from cushy low sofa at home , I felt shooting pain at the same place in my back. I have to sit down there itself as I am unable to bear this pain.

While filling water in the cooler a heavy bucket caused pain in my back.

In all these moments there was no injury to her back but were trigger points. Hence there was no question that the pain would have originated in all those situations.

When again I guided her to go back to ***the origin of the pain*** , she started viewing herself in her house in R.K Puram, when she is five years old wearing a frock. She is feeling very scared and knocking the door from outside but nobody opens the door for a long time. Q- From where are you coming alone to this house ? She reached a temple near her house. ' I have come to the cemented parachute slide in the lawn of the temple. I am climbing up the steps to reach the top of the parachute slide but I trip and fall down, I am crying now.

Hearing me cry one sadhu is coming towards me and picks me up. He is taking me inside one hut but it's not his own hut. I can see one of my cousins who is one year older to me , is also there tied to the ropes . I am so scared now. Sadhu went inside one more room'.

How she escaped from there ,she doesn't remember but now she sees herself knocking the door of her house and her mother and grand-mother opens the door. She is still shaking with fear. She somehow tells them about her cousin whom she saw tied in that hut. They reassure her and go to rescue her cousin.

Thus the fear of that time was hid in the back bone. Maybe she was hurt when she had a fall , as she felt some pain in her body at that time but where exactly the pain was ,she could not pin point. But at present she can see pain in the form of black ball in her lower back, which is being pulled out and sent for burning through healing. Pain is also in her knees , in her head, at the back and same way it is being cleared from her system. She can see the healing light filing l up that vacant area. And now she can see her body as a pink colored healthy skeleton. There is no black energy anywhere in her skeleton.

In her second session again she saw the same negative energy which is collected as within the week she followed the same routine and the pain resurfaced again.

Future My Boss hits me and I am lying dead on the floor !

Session- II Within a week she back again with backache. I asked her to view the origin of the pain as last time she had seen her body clear and freed from pain. I was expecting her to go to her past life incident , where she must have physically hurt in that place. Instead she progressed to future with some significance.

Future - She said, 'I see a small wooden window, it is opening up and I am entering in to it. I find myself standing on the ground floor of one modern looking multi-storeyed building..The place looks as if it is Kolkata. (Though she hasn't been to Kolkata so far in this life.) I am standing in front of one flat. I seem to have come here by mistake. A young man opens the door. He is my boss. He is very angry, as I seem to know some of his secret, which is in the file, I am carrying in my hand. We both are having a heated argument in the room. Suddenly ***my boss hits me at my back and I am lying dead on the floor.*** ' I asked her to find out with what did he hit her. She said, 'I cannot see that, it could be a knife or a pistol. I felt something hit at my back, where there is pain and I fell dead on the ground . I am twenty five years of age'.

(She had externalized her fear in to the future and created this fatal accident for herself.)I had to ascertain from her the definite time, whether it happened in her past or is this happening in the future.

Healing – I guided her to rewind the scene. Go back and come as if rewinding through the door. You don't know any secret of your boss ,you don't know anything which can harm him. Try to make amends with him, inculcate your faith in him , pacify him that even if I come to know some secret about you , I will never divulge it to anyone. I tried to erase all that fear and negative thoughts from her mind, which she had projected in to the future. She tried following my instructions but felt failed and replied,' He is not listening to any of my requests, he doesn't trusts anyone. He is going to kill me at any cost. I cannot escape from there'. When nothing worked to convince her or she failed to convince her boss about her being harmless to him in her subconscious mind ,then I asked her to hand over the resignation letter to that man and come out from that room and never to go back there. She did the same and came back to her home. She said, this is not my home in Delhi , where we live now. My parents look more matured than what they are now, so is my younger brother looking grown up in age. I am twenty five years old at that time (because she sees herself in this life in future ,at present she is seventeen years.) By now I was convinced that this is happening in her future.. Now I told her to write a nice application for a decent job and send it to one very good office. She did the same thing and she sees herself in one comforting environment where one middle aged gentleman is her boss. He addresses her as 'beta' and she really feels fatherly affection in him. She elaborated, 'yes, I am feeling very secure now and we both are wearing white color dresses. In my previous office I always felt fearful and was in black dress. Thus by giving her subconscious mind positive suggestions, we ended this session.

Session III.- This week the pain was more severe and I asked her to see if her future is healed ? She again reached to the same place where she is going to be murdered..Seeing her boss she feels very scared. Because now she already knows that he is going to kill her. They both are wearing black dreses. I healed her by sending healing light and also asked her to resign from that office again. After that she herself reached back to that comforting environment ,where her boss is a fatherly figure. 'This is some tool company in Kolkata. At home, my younger brother and parents are there. I tell them that I have resigned from that office, as I was not feeling safe there. They are happy with my decision'. Now she feels much relieved and said , 'now the pain has gone as I have avoided that accident from happening to me in the future'. I also gave her suggestion that she will never go to such an office again where there will be some threat to her life. In case if she is faced by such situation, she will have pain in her back and she will be reminded that this place is not safe for her. Her subconscious had accepted this suggestion as she nodded in affirmation.

Past life I -Now I asked her to go to the root cause , why all this is happening to her in the future? She sees a road where only big trucks and few buses ply. It's not very crowded like present time. She concluded this is the road in Najafgarh, where she is attending school now. So I thought she is again seeing her present life time. Not seeing her going to any of her past life, I gave her blind instructions just one last time to go back to her previous life times. She again sees the same road and said, 'I am five years old wearing a frock and standing on the road. A truck comes from the back side ***and hits me at my back*** and I am knocked on the ground, my back is broken and ***I am lying dead on the road***. Few people collect near my body, one lady is crying uncontrollably, may be she is my mother. My body is being carried to a place near my house and buried there'. Healing the memory of that injury and pain from her past by dissolving her body with the dust. She saw, now beautiful flowers have grown there.

Past life II- *I am sold to the tea planter.*

Next week she was much relaxed and free from backache but she said ,' from past one year,,I have cramps in the legs and arm and pain as we get when we do so much physical work.'. To see the cause for her pain and cramps in her body, she reached to a place which looked hills and there was so much greenery around. There were some small green bushes and a typical smell in that atmosphere. She recognized that smell and said, ' these are tea plants, I am in the field along with many other people plucking the tea. I am sixteen years old , wearing a head gear and some funny looking dress which I have never seen in this life. I am bending down wards and plucking the tea leaves. My hands and legs are tired of doing the same work every day'. When I asked her, why is she working so hard, she replied, ' because ***I am being sold to these people*** and I have no escape but to listen to them even though I am so tired. But one day I manage to slide down the hill, hiding myself from their eyes, thinking to reach my parents. I reach at a river bank; I am sitting in a boat and rowing it to reach at the other end. But I am weak and in the middle of the river there is so much force in the water that ***my boat is turning round and round. I don't know what to do now?*** She sounded alarmed as if she is sinking. ' I am going in to this whirlpool as my boat has turned and sank in the water flow'. I assured her let her that body drown which was so tired and exhausted. I held her hand and made her feel alive, assured her that she is safe and nothing is going to drown her. She was convinced. She felt lighter as her body was feeling lighter after releasing from those cramps.

Concluding her session –

Did she become unconscious and went to her subconscious mind, where sadhu is taking her inside the hut? Her cousin is also already there tied up with ropes. Could sadhu and rope be signifying our tying down to fate because in her past life also she had died at that age. Why otherwise cousin should be somewhere near their house though she lived much farther from their house at that time. As she could manage ***to escape from that sadhu, did she defy her death this time?*** That is why initially she felt, at home they are not opening the door for her but now when she comes home towards the end of the session, her mother opens the door for her and reassures her.

When I asked her after the session, she said, "I do remember the fall in my child hood but do not remember going to any sadhu or my cousin being there". Was this memory of that unconscious state after the fall which she could recollect now in this regression but not otherwise?

Same way as she was destined to live a short life at five years but could win over her death . At sixteen year also she had died drowning in the river. By creating same symptoms of past life pain in this body ,was her subconscious giving her warning that something fatal is coming up? She has been searching ways and means for releasing this pain ,as she clearly saw that at twenty five years of age in this life she is being killed by her boss.

Destiny means whatever good or bad we have created will be relayed and relased through us. If the fear of accidental death of past life is not released from her mind, it will create circumstances leading to similar fatal end in the future. Now she herself has seen it being cleared from her system and she is seeing herself healed from that destined future.

The capability of younger and flexible person makes it easier to release mechanically repeating past experiences which can then be erased by replacing with healthy outcome. Less flexible mind of much grown up person is not ready to believe in any miracle and would not consider healing a viable option. Whereas ***nothing is miracle, everything has to fit in the scheme of things by creating sufficient energy.***

3rd Case ***Proof of healing the future***

***He is calling me - Renu April* 2008 –**

Lack of sleep, worries , depression , Vision of burn accident

Though this case happened much later in **April 2008** but since she gave me direct evidence of how fatal future is created when certain issues are not resolved in the past and how healing done in the present heals our past ,bringing considerable liberation from meeting the unpleasant destined outcome in the future. Coincidently I was also guided to keep recording of her session.

Note – The words are insufficient to describe correctly sequence of events of the healing session. Life is not a word or a picture but a full flowing three dimensional drama. As in a session one may experience issues of many life span needing attention in a fraction enfolding in his mind. It is just an attempt, a trailer of the drama, trying to write sessions in sequence.

In March 2007 after coming back from Bhuj , I had this dream.

Dream – (*I dreamt that I have gone to Bhuj and there they have sent me to their beauty parlour. They are doing my facial, applying gel to my hair. I am seeing myself in the mirror, my face is looking so fresh and my cheeks are shinning. But I feel I have wasted half a day in the parlour and how am I going to finish my teaching and healing in another half a day? They are asking me to postpone my return by a day* *and inform my home by phone.*

I am also falling short of Reiki course books and I am contemplating to talk to Reiki Healing Foundation to send me the books by courier. But will these reach in time? This thought is also bothering me. Some men are asking me, ' is it true that we can meet our guides through regression session'? As some of their colleagues have described to them their experiences and I am explaining to them how this is possible')

In April 2008 it was my third trip to Bhuj . On my arrival at Bhuj, Mrs Ghotia insisted that I must get myself relaxed and refreshed before I venture in to hectic schedule of teaching Reiki and take healing sessions. I was reminded of this dream which I had one year back about going to parlour and I agree to go there . In the parlour I met this beautician who was very creative, intelligent and hard-working but off late she felt nothing is going to last long. She lacked that enthusiasm which was noticeable even to other people around her. She was already enrolled to learn Reiki along with her husband during my visit this time.

As we got talking while she was working on me in her parlour, I told her I smell as if something is burning. She convinced me that it is the dead skin in your face which is burning as the electric roller is working. And this set the motion of our talk further. She said, 'I am very petrified of getting burnt. If I see some other person with burn injury ,I feel the pain as if my body is burnt'. I asked, 'have you ever sustained burn in any part of your body in this life ? She said, 'no, even though I have never had any burn in this life ,but I feel as if I exactly know how painful it is to be burnt?

Her vision -Then she went on to narrate her present state of mind to me. She said, ' these days as soon as I close my eyes for meditation or just to take rest , I always have a vision , in which one pan 'kadhai ' full of boiling oil spills before me and I turn my face away from it as if to protect my face from being burnt. I also see the hospital and burn ward. I haven't slept in real sense from past one year since this started happening. As soon as I close my eyes, the movie of this vision starts rolling and night passes watching it. In the morning I feel very lethargic and burdened as if everything I am doing is temporary, there is no long lasting attraction to my work as it used to be earlier'.

I sensed something serious coming up in her life in very near future and advised her to have a personal healing session, so that exact cause could be ascertained and healing done accordingly. She agreed and arrived next day early morning.

She said, after talking to you yesterday, I felt bit relieved and also had a slight nap for a short time for the first time in past many months and am feeling bit relaxed. So I prepared her for the session by explaining to have confidence in my ability to heal something unexpected coming up in her session. Anything can be healed provided you are ready and listen to me, and I mean your good at any cost, you have to have this much faith in me. We proceeded with the session –

Renu He is calling me

First Session – Immediately she slipped back in her mind and started having clear picture in her mental screen. She reached in a garden in her home town in Chandigarh. When I asked her to request universe to send her guide there, no body appeared only the thought of Shirdi Sai Baba came to her mind. She started viewing a house in a village and she is in *lehnga* and *choli* standing in front of it. She felt she had been to this house in her present life about a year back to condole the death of a young man of this house, who had died in a motorcycle accident. Since then the vision and restlessness in her mind had been apparent. Soon she was narrating whatever she was seeing.

Past life -I am inside this house in *lehnga choli*, where two ladies, one older and other almost of my age are pouring some watery liquid thing on me. I am resisting but I am weaker in front of them. I am totally wet. One of them has a match stick in her hand and lighted the stick. She has thrown the burning stick towards me. My dress has caught fire and soon it is touching my body. I am burning and I am running out of the house. In that air, fire is increasing more and flames are very high. Those two ladies are also running behind me and when I reach near a river they pushed me down. I am flowing in the river. The fire has slowly extinguished but the flow of water is very strong and my body is flooding along with it. Now I am out of my body but the body is still flowing far away.

One young man wearing *Dhoti Kurta* has come home to these ladies and is asking them , what happened? They are saying, ' she jumped in to the river'. He is very sad, he is crying, ' no. She can't do this' . He is not believing them. Slowly other people are gathering. Now he is arranging some people to fetch that body from the water. They put a big net and retrieve the body. The body is burnt badly. But the face is clear and I look very pretty and young. This man is crying and I feel so much pain for him. He is very nice. They have put the body on pyre and lighted the fire. This man is inconsolable. ***He is calling me;*** 'please don't do this to me. You can't go away like that.' And she herself was in so much pain , not because of burn but the cry of this man was as if making her restless.. I told her to pacify this man, maybe he is your husband in that life ,when these two ladies had burnt you alive. He could not bear your separation but tell him now to release you, you can't go back, your that body is burnt badly .. She started making request to him, 'please forgive me, please don't call me, I can't come back. Forget me'. She expressed her incompetence in pacifying him, 'but he is inconsolable, he can't be convinced. He is calling me back'.

Future- Here she herself reached to her future in this life.' I am in my house alone here in Bhuj. I am standing in front of the Goddess idol in my house, lighting a candle 'Diya'. As I turn to other side , my *duppatta* caught fire. I run out of the house and scream for help. Some people come from neighbourhood and pour sand and water on me. They pulled me to the ground, covered me with the blanket, trying to extinguish the fire. Now white color ambulance is coming. I am put in the ambulance. I am in so much pain. In the hospital my body is fully covered on the burn bed. It is this Air Force hospital and known people and doctors are attending to me. But my face is not burnt. Now my husband has been informed and he is inconsolable seeing my condition. My parents and my son have also come. Oh, I know now in that vision ,it was I ,who was burnt and put in the burn ward which I was not able to see earlier'.

I started healing her mind and asked her to actively participate in releasing this future projection of memory from past. She was mentally exhausted and emotionally shattered by seeing her future as she had recognized the event happening in her present place. I simply asked her to receive energy while I was healing her silently and feel relaxed not to think of any of the pain full things which she had seen just now. After a while I brought her back to her present. She described everything with certainity what all she saw about the course of event her life was going to take. I also guided her from my side and advised her to have faith in higher plan of things and have confidence in my ability to deal with such case. I convinced her of the possibility of transforming this fatal future. There may be some higher purpose in your coming to know this event in advance and you had already willed to learn Reiki. I asked her to keep chanting mantra, I am healed of my past. She could not be convinced fully as she has been already having such visions. Knowing her mental state, I started giving her distance Reiki on emergency basis and asked Mrs Nirmala Ghotia also to do so after discussing the session with her. She also agreed whole heartedly as she admired Renu's qualities. She felt pained to know, what all was in store for Renu in future. In the mean time Renu had also learnt Reiki and had severe heaviness in the head after the initiation and was not at all relaxed. This thought was constantly hammering her mind, how can such things change when she is seeing this from past one year. How is it possible to change the future? She was feeling nervous and lacked confidence.

Session – Her second session was scheduled after three days and I had recorded it simply for I might not be able to recollect her case clearly later as I will be attending many cases there. I had no time to write down the details of sessions, in case something significant comes up. Before starting her session she described to me her mental state and inability to experience anything during Reiki class as she was constantly fixed to her previous session's outcome. She said, I did have sleep for quite some time in past three days and remember some dreams.

Dream – I am standing on the balcony of my parental house in Chandigarh and I look down. I am calling out to my sister. But she does not come forward. I see my mother has fallen there and lying flat on the ground of our house. Now I realize that must be the reason that I was calling my sister to show my mother fell on the ground. I woke up with a fear that she might be dead. I am quite upset as some such thing should not happen to my mother. We proceeded with the session to heal her past memory and also ascertain what message this dream had for her.

Session – She reached her home town Chandigarh. She is roaming here and there. There is one man with her whom she could not recognize any one from this life. Now she is walking on one footpath, ***there is one white dog walking behind her***. On the way there is big hole on the road and the dog fell in that. She continued walking further. Now she is seeing one cute little girl behind her. She looks exactly like her but she is little girl of four five years. Now she has reached the big crossing road and her younger brother is with her. They both are happily chatting away sitting on the green grass on that crossing. From this scene her mind went back to her past life where she had seen she was burnt by two ladies.

Past memory was ***healed***

Past life- She started seeing the same house and she is inside it. These two ladies come forward and are trying to do what they had done to her in her last session. She boldly announced, 'but this time I have stopped them from that. Q -How did you stop them? A- I held one lady by one hand and pushed another away throwing the match stick from her hand. Now I am not burnt. I have not fallen in the river this time. I am watching all this from the side. I am feeling safe and happy now as I have been able to stop the fatal accident happening to me. (*With so much of distance healing, her own effort by chanting positive affirmation ,her Reiki learning had given her strength and she was seeing how she herself is able to avert the accident or rather her own murder in the past . Because this fearful and revengeful memory was creating burn accident in the future of which she had no doubt because she was seeing vision since she had visited this known place from her past life in this life to condole one young man's accidental death. Could this man had something to do with her past life (was he her husband in the past life and calling her back or the visit to this place triggered the fatal memory of her past life ,reminding her to fall victim to same accident, though in a different place, body and situation. I had to grasp heuristic insight regarding all these things, not going in to much detail because there were more important and interesting story enfolding in her vision.)*

Her subconscious was relaying to her healing of the past fatal event

Session cont.. Now she started describing the incident where her past body was cremated. She said, 'same young man wearing earings in his ears and turban on his head, is there. He is calling me. But now he is going and laying down on the same pyre ,where he had placed me that time. Now both of them are lying on the pyre and burning together. (There was confusion in her explaining and my understanding. When she said both of them,I asked, who are both of them? She said,' he and the one who was I, that time. That me also went there and lied down by his side and they both have been burned in that pyre. They both are waving me saying good bye. That time I had felt attached to that body and felt pained at the separation from this man. But I didn't burn this time. I am watching and waving them standing at the side. Those two ladies, who had burnt me last time are crying. Seeing me they have gone inside their house. I am happy now as ***I have averted the fatal accident*** happening to me.

Symbolic inner journey

'Now I see a photograph of my husband and I ,which was taken at the time of our wedding but I see there is my son also in it now.

Now we sit in a car and drive it on a long road. One side of the road is a high wall ,other side is open and blank space. Our car skids down this blank space and we reached the ground with yellow mud. There are two roads ,one goes to the right, other to the left. We are confused which road to take, husband says right but I insist on left road. Finally we take the right road and reach station house (station commander house in Bhuj where I was taking her session). This was symbolic journey where she would get one road leading towards guidance and upward journey in her life.

Healing the future accident

She continued, 'We have come home now. We go inside the house, my son is watching TV. We both go inside our room, we are very happy now as if some burden has been lifted from us. We make love to each other and feel very satisfied. Now that fire from the lamp is not burning me, instead I can feel some attraction towards it. As it is holding and leading me to the temple and making me sit there. I am sitting there in meditation. There is one yellow colour light shining on my forehead. It's coming from Shiva's hands. I am feeling very relaxed, released and satisfied. The light is telling me to dance and I start dancing. I have come out in the open, going round and round.

I am standing outside my house where earlier I was burning, but now I am dancing there. My husband is feeling awkward as what people might say. He is asking me to stop dancing but I continue dancing and have reached in a very big ground. We both are very happy there and all three of us are dancing in celebration. Now we are back home with our son. We are eating food. They both are feeding me. I am feeding them. We are lying on the bed. We feel completely satisfied and loving towards each other. We have everything. My husband is very proud of me'. (Dance was symbolic celebration of life. Fatal memories of the past released and she had been freed from meeting fatal end in the future. Thus she is feeling relaxed and light in mind. Now she can progress further)

We have everything in life

Future – She continued, 'he is giving me a gift. It is paper of a flat which he has purchased. I tell him I am pregnant.. Initially he doesn't like it as he is taken by a surprise (as he himself is suffering from deteriorating health due to chronic ulcer and both of them must have decided not to have another child) then he says, but you use to say earlier that you don't want another child. But now he also happy at this news. I can see my big tummy. Now I am in the same labour room, same doctors and staff is attending to me. I asked her to clarify, 'what do you by mean by same, you mean where you were admitted after the burn ? She corrected ,'no ,not here ,in my home town in Chandigarh where my son was born. I have delivered a beautiful daughter'.

Now she wanted to convey to me her surprise and said, you know who is my daughter? I already had something ticking in my mind before she announced, 'the same little girl who was with me in the beginning. But now she is very small, just a new born but I know it is she. She is very fair'. I nodded in approval and said , 'that is why she resembled you so much there' '. My husband is happy to see her. My son is loving her. My parents have also come to see me.'

Now we are not living here (Bhuj) ,we are in another house in some other place. My husband is not in uniform.. He looks very healthy and smart. My daughter is growing fast but my son looks the same. I am not working; I look after kids at home.

Now I am going somewhere. I know the roads are like Nasik because my cousin stays there and I have been to this city. There is one empty shop, I have entered it. There is work going on inside. Two people are asking me what to do and where to fit things. I am giving them directions to put doors wardrobes and shelves. Now it has become my beauty parlour. Its running very busy,I am not working there. There are two to three people working and I am sitting in the counter and watching them work. People are coming and going and looks satisfied with our service. I am very happy. I thank God, close the shutter; put the lock on the door. Now I have come to pick up my kids. I think I have left them at some one's place. I go home with kids. But our house looks as if it is in Gandhidham. (Could be first she will work in Nasik and then purchase a house in Gandhidham or place is not important but her state of inner peace ,sense of achievement is.

My husband also has arrived home. My daughter goes and sits with papa. I go to kitchen and bring juice for all of us. Girl spills the juice on papa but he doesn't says anything to her. My son is saying, ' look what she has done, you don't say anything to her ,had it been I ,you would have scolded me severely'. To this my husband is saying , 'she is my daughter'!. So the son is asking, 'am I not your son ? Husband says, ' you use to do so much mischief'. She confided here , ' now we really get very angry at our son'. I consoled her that could be because there are many things troubling you both, so you could not tolerate little bit naughtiness in your son. She continued,' now my son is looking towards me as if getting reassured that at least my mother is always there for me.

Avoiding to see the fatal future for her father –Continuing session forward ,I asked her to see ahead ,what else is happening in her life? . After seeing this happy go lucky family tale in the future,she moved on to see something and appeared sad. I asked her what are you seeing ? She said, I don't know why I am seeing something but I don't want to see it ? I asked her, ' are you not able to follow what you are seeing? She said, 'it is about my papa but I don't want to see'. I asked,' is it something negative which you don't want to know'? (I understood her higher self is trying to acquaint her of the forthcoming event but she is not strong enough. One side she would take time to integrate her life as she was destined such fate and in another side she would be faced with something unpleasant in her papa's life. So I asked her to relax and healed her for some time.

In the meantime, seeing the readiness of her mind accept ,delete painful past and relay pleasant probable future so easily, I realized the importance of teaching her through this guidance being given to her. She knos how she had changed her fatal future. Now she is convinced about it. She is even learning Reiki. It is a good way to show her the importance of healing or rather acquainting her of the value of this higher knowledge.)

Significant of coming to Station house (symbolic)

Intrigued at all the sequence of events leading to her session, right from my dream to our meeting her in the beauty parlour and her telling me about her phobia and mental state. I wondered what is the significance of her healing this way. I asked her , ‘ earlier you said that you have come to station house. What does it mean to you because it, is leading to some significant changes in your life ’? She kept quiet for some time as if trying to recollect or retrieve something from her mental screen.. She reached back to the same event when they had come to the station house.

She said, ‘ we have come inside, where we are greeted by sir, madam and their elder daughter (station commander, his wife and elder daughter). My husband and son touch their feet and I hug mam (madam) dearly and we are leaving that place’. Q- Why are you meeting them or rather touching their feet and all that ? Are you indebted to them for something or just like that? A- I am thanking them for changing our life. Q- How have they changed your life? A -Till now we use to come on a scooter to this house but now we have to come in a gypsy jeep. My husband is not in uniform though he is wearing a cap. I also look more grown up now as if we have come from a far of place. (She was seeing symbolic vision showing progress in their life.) Q- How have you progressed in life, I mean what made you so happy, contented and successful for that you are showing gratefulness to these people? This is important to know because you know that so much fatal has been healed from your life. Yet you also are aware that there is something fatal coming up in your papa’s way, which is making you pained and scared that you don’t even want to see it. But you know what is there, burying it from your sight will not make it disappear until some remedy is done, but if you know something with which you can erase or heal such things in your and others life ,you will feel at peace and in control of life.

Now she described that scene further and she said, ‘we have come outside their house on the gate to leave that place. Ma'am is saying bye to me. I don't feel like to leave her. I am feeling very sad. I feel much attached to her. I want to be with her always. Sensing my emotion, ma'am is saying, don't worry, go now, I will call you. I am crying and saying, 'I don't want to go. Sir and ma'am are saying , 'don't say like this, you better go now'. Their daughter Shivali is laughing at this. We leave that place'.

Q Why you do not want to leave them. A- I want to live with her. Q- Why do you feel so? A-Because she ---(pause) because she cares for me. I feel protected with her. I work for her out of love. I don't want anything in return for it. I feel ,how should I pay her back. She doesn't understand it, no, she understands but she sort of doesn't care for it. Q -Why do you feel protected and this gratitude for her , I know they have done so much for you but is there some deeper reason for this ? She kept quiet for some time as if searching this answer from her subconscious.

Past connection– After some time she was surprised to see her ma'm in some different shape and place. She continued, 'she looks very slim and younger ,she is in a sari. She is bringing me milk to drink. I am small but ***I am a boy***. She is annoyed with me. She doesn't like me, she has pushed me out from the house. (I thought maybe she is talking of this life when Mrs. Ghotia was younger but when she sounded pained by her behaviour and said that she is a boy . I realized she is talking about some past life).

Past life- Now she was totally in to her past life that she was showing her resentment for her Ma'am and addressing herself as a boy. She sounded chocking with emotion and helpless. 'I am an eight years old boy though my hair is long. I am wearing white shirt, gray half paint and I am attending school, sitting in my class. Q -What is your relationship with this lady (Mrs. Ghotia)? A-I don't know. Q- Is she feeding you and looking after you ,is she your mother, does she love you ? What is your feeling about her ? A-She doesn't love me ,she is not my mother. She is troubling me, hitting me; all she is doing for me is as a burden. Q-Does she looks exactly how she looks now?

A-'No, she doesn't look exactly how she is now; she is slim and very short tempered and busy in her household work. I am very helpless, I am alone with her. I feel like running away from this house but I don't have any place to go'. Q-Who is she to you, who is her husband, why are you forced to live with her? A- 'Her husband is not her present husband, he is somebody else but he is my father in that time. She is my *chachi*(Aunt) no, she is not my *chachi*,(she was bit confused about her identity and I concluded that she was her/his step mother) I am complaining to my papa about her ill-treatment , 'papa, she hits me'. She is showing him with her action that he is very naughty. Papa is not listening to me but taking her side. He pushes me away saying, 'you go away from here'. He is not my present papa. They throw me out from the room and lock the kitchen. I am angry. I drink the milk and throw away the glass. Seeing this again she comes and hits me. They have thrown me out from the house and locked the door.

Here she moved on to the relevance of this scene in her present life. She said, 'now again I am seeing my present husband, sir, ma'am and Shivali (their daughter). Now I am greeting them but this time she is loving and caring towards me. That time she wasn't. Now I am saying , 'I will not go'. She is telling me, 'now you go, I will call you. You will stay with me'. (Showing how the healing of that past memory had happened, in this life she loves and cares for her)

I asked her to see, ' why were you thrown out from the house , what had happened to your mother , why were you forced to stay with your step mother , what did you do after you left the house. What were your feelings at that time? Gradually she started narrating her past life as the vision was enfolding in her mind's screen. She said,' I am very young, seven eight years old. I am wearing school uniform and I don't know from where the tie and school bag has appeared and I am going to school.

I am in the school sitting in the middle of the class room. I am happy as if I have forgotten that painful incident of my home. The school closes and I come out from the gate. I am looking here and there as if waiting for someone. I see one lady walking briskly towards me. May be she is my aunt. She holds my hand and takes me away from school. We are sitting under a tree. She is feeding me. She loves me. She is wearing sari and looks slim and has got spectacles on. She puts me to sleep on her bed.. In the night also she gets up and looks at me lovingly. I am growing up living with her'.

(She went on narrating this new lady's appearance and her behaviour towards her (that boy). I asked her to find out how she is related to her (him) in that life ,giving her some clues ,whether she is your mother or mother's friend or some other relative ,she could not clarify) Instead she opinioned that she looks like my present *Taayi* (paternal uncles wife).

She continued, 'now we have moved to another place. Tall multi-storeyed buildings, broad roads, it's a foreign country. I am grown up now. I am working in a big office. This lady comes to receive me here also from the office as she use to come to receive me from my school. I am finishing my work and going with her. This building doesn't have boundary wall, so it is open from all sides. As we come out, ***there is a breeze***, pushing us and we have a free fall from very high story and land on the ground. I can see she has head injury, my spine is broken, neck ,head ,back is paining at that time. I do not feel much pain for myself but feel so much for her. I am much worried about her. She is also looking towards me.

She is dead **,**but I don't die. People have gathered, they take me to hospital for treatment. It is a foreign place. My treatment is going on and I remember that lady so much ,I miss her . Now this lady in that life time (Mrs Ghotia) comes to the hospital. She is grown up more in age by now. Now she is caring for me but I do not pay any attention to her. I am angry. She is loving and feeding me. She is feeling sad that the other lady has died. She knew her. She is telling me now that ***she was my mother.*** But I did not know till now, neither she told me. I am all the more angry now.

I enquired her, if she was his (her) mother ,why were you not staying with her from the beginning and why your father was staying with some other lady? She opinioned that I was born out of wed lock; I was not a legitimate child. She could not give me her name. So she had given me to my father. And she herself was living all alone. She had no body to fall back. She was working, she took me back, after I left my father's place.

Now she started describing his step mother's changed behaviour towards her /him. . 'She is regretting her previous behaviour with me. But I am turning away from her. I tell her, I don't need your love, I don't need both of you. Go away from here'. Doctor is advising me, 'don't behave like this , they are your parents after all'. She (Mrs. Ghotia) is saying, ' I will take you with us'. One boy also comes with them , he is young. She tells him , 'he is your brother, he will live with us from now.' The boy loves me. He asks me, 'what has happened to you, why are you here? He feels lonely ,he needs brother to love him . So he is happy to get me. I am also not angry with the boy. He sits, talks nicely to me. He tells me, 'my mother told me that she threw you out from home. Papa cried a lot there after. But he could not say anything to mom. He was scared of her. So you come home at least for me. I am refusing, 'I will not stay with her. You can come and stay with me'.

He/she could not forgive them

They are still in India. Once I went to their house afterwards. Now they made me sit on the same chair, where they had beaten me. Papa also is sitting next to me. She is feeding me milk with love in the same glass. I do not like that milk; I don't like the milk she has touched. I have still not forgiven her from the heart. I did not eat on the same chair. I got up and sat next to that and ate there. Now I am leaving their house on my free will. Earlier they had thrown me out but now I am going happily with my free will. I am telling them I will keep coming to meet them.

Mixed Scene – Now I see the same scene when I am leaving madam's house. I am not sad now. I am happy; their son is watching. She is Shivali, their daughter. (I think that is why she saw only Shivali with them initially when she was leaving their house) it was a mixed scene. As if she is recognizing people from past life in the present. She said, 'She (Shivali) is their son there. He (son) is waving me bye ,Ma'am is also saying bye. But sir (Mr. Ghotia)is not same as my papa there. He is somebody else. She was getting entangled in this memory, so to take her further I asked her few more questions.

Regret and revenge leading to creating bitterness

Q-How did you live your life ahead. Did you get married? How long you lived and how did you die?

"I live alone. I am filled with bitterness. I am not married. Now I look aged. I live in the same house in one multi-storey building. It's a foreign country. My ***mother's photo is hanging on the wall.*** I keep the plate down and eat my food and sleep alone. I live alone but some time those people come to meet me. They are in India. Now they have come to call me for my brother's wedding. Now I am attending his marriage. I am quite elder to him. I look in my forties and he is a lot younger. His bride is my sister in this life. Both are getting married. They are taking my blessing. I give them a gift. I am not watching towards that lady (step mother). They ask me to stay with them but I do not stay back.

Holding on to dead person's memory resulting in fatal end

Death -I have come back to my home. That day I am very restless. Seeing his marriage, I repent and ask myself, why am I all alone? I feel very restless. I am taking medicine,some tablets. I am feeling scared also. Q -Did you take more medicine? A- First I took two three tablets and drank water. I am feeling scared. Then I took more medicine. Now I lie down. I am sweating, I remove the blanket, I am lying down. But I am seeing that marriage scene and I am cursing my self , ' you deserve this destiny only. You cannot love anybody else'. Now I call my mother saying, 'mother, please call me to you now. I do not want to live here anymore. I don't have anybody as my own here. Only you are mine'. She also says, 'ok then you come to me now. Q – How did your mother tell you this? A- She is speaking from her photo, she says,' don't think, come to me now'. I took many tablets, drank water and I lay down. Now I have stomach ache, pain in the heart,, vomiting. My head is jammed, legs are aching and a severe pain below naval. And I passed toilet in the bed itself. I fell down, banged my head on the wall. (I did not want her to see her suffering much thus I asked her to finish watching soon as if she is viewing some movie and not feeling the emotions of that person in herself). She started describing herself there as a third person now) ' he is suffering so much , he is roaming here and there in the room. Now he jumped out from the room and fell at the same place, where he had fell with his mother'.

Her attitude had attracted strong Negative force in her

She continued , 'there was something in that house which forced him out from the room.' Q – What was that, which forced him out from his house and threw down from the building.? Is there some being, or it's your feeling that there is something that forced him out ? A – No ,there is not any being but it's a feeling that there is some force. ***The strong wind***. First it rotated him around in the house. I think earlier also same force had forced both of them down from the building.. Again today same wind is blowing. Q -Can you see this wind ,how it is forcing him out from the place, because wind does not make one fall from the building ? A – 'In the wind ,I can see a ***women figure***. Who is dancing like this and this (she was rotating her hands to show the movements of this figure in the wind) She is dancing forcefully and with the intension that who so ever is here, should move away. She is not doing anything to him , not touching him. He is standing at the window. In her hand there is some instrument something like this (showed with her gesture) sometimes she plays that instrument with the hand. I feel she wants that I should vacate that place for her. I should get out from there, so I jump down. I fall there only where I had fell earlier with my mother and I can again see my mother is still lying fallen there. *(She was repeating this scene because I had asked her to see what forced him to jump* *from there, earlier also this powerful force had forced them to fall*) She said, 'It feels my mother is still lying there from the time of our first fall but I am falling for the second time at that same place(*this could also be as he did not let his mother be released from his memory. He kept his attachment for her only and finally he called her, he was responsible for holding her in that place.* So in his mind she was still laying in that place.)

She continued, 'earlier she was watching with sadness at me, but now she is laughing at me. She is laughing at me sarcastically. Now people have gathered there. From the top of the building, ***she (invisible force is looking like a lady)*** is watching down. ***She*** is also laughing. Then ***she*** looks around the house, she looks at my mother's photo and ***she*** throws it down and closes doors and windows forcefully so that I do not go back there. ***She*** lives there itself. But nobody can see ***her***.

(She (Renu) clearly saw that keeping dead person's memory alive by hanging photos and showing excessive attachment is not only harming us but the dead person also from progressing further. We are not allowing them freedom to move ahead in life as we keep them trapped in their past and forcing them to become ghost.)

Positive attitude, praying changes the negative in to positive

Q Did ***she*** throw down somebody else also like ***she*** did to you?. Renu observed internally trying to find out the answer, she moved ahead to see what happened there afterwards. She gave her observation, 'the house is on a very high building. Now somebody is walking up the stairs. One old man, old woman and a young man with their luggage are climbing up and have reached this house. Young man is their son. He places his parents in that house. They are foreigners, because this place is in some foreign country. He is very fair and one thing peculiar about him is that his head is balled in the center. His parents are holding his hands as if they don't want him to leave. He is trying to pacify them, he says, 'I will keep coming frequently, you understand my problem.' 'Son is feeling bad for them. But he leaves the place. Old couple stays on.'

She (the invisible women of wind)is sitting on the stool next to their bed. ***She*** is watching and listening to them while they talk. But they both cannot see ***her***. They sit on the bed. They work and go around in the house. Now I can see only this room, I am not aware what is happening in the whole house. It is the same room in my house, same curtains, same bed. But that place is vacant, where my mother's photo was hanged. Now they have placed some other photo on that place. But I don't know what photo it is. It is not some person's photo. It is some scenery. Below it ***they light candle and incense sticks'***.. I prompted her , ' may be this photo is some church or Monastery ?'. She confirmed, ' yes , it is a photo of a church. Old man is praying , old lady is lying down and saying , ' today I am feeling so much pain. I do not like this bed ,I will lie down'. The old man says, 'you lie down on the sofa'. Old man lies down on the bed. ***She (invisible woman***) goes and watches the old man and ***she*** feels pity for him. And thinks , ***'no I won't kill him'.*** Old man also feels pain.. Now the old lady is out from my view. I cannot see her. Now ***she (invisible***) is serving him, pressing his legs. ***She*** dusts, swabs, cleanse the room. Make their bed, spreading sheets on their bed'. With great surprise she informed ,' The ***same lady*** who had thrown me out from this house ***,she does all this for them.*** Whenever they feel tired or have pain ***,she*** presses their body, does the work for them. Now they both are happy there. When their son comes, she makes him feel unanted as he does not like to stay there. He goes away soon. Now old couple is happy. ***She*** is also happy with them. ***Earlier she was feeling lonely and dancing forcefully that if someone comes in my way I will destroy him***. But now ***she is happy with them as if she has merged in them***. When they both talk, ***she*** sits down and talk with them. ***She*** lives happily with them.

I wanted to know how her past memory is healed ,so I asked her Q -What happened to your life thereafter ? A-' I again see that village where I was burned as a young lady . I am standing in the same house. This is not my parental house, I have been married in this house. I have come from another village, my parents are sardars in that village. Again same thing is happening. Q- 'But you had seen that same thing had changed.) A –Yes, now I have protected myself , I am not burnt.

Forgiveness is the key to healing

I asked her to go back to her parents in that life, where he/she was abandoned and he/she could not forgive them and her /his life ends in suicide. I explained, 'Because you could not forgive your parents ,that is why you met this fatal end in the next life and also projected fatal accident for this life. Ask them to forgive you, they had already asked forgiveness from you, but you did not forgive them. That life is over now'. She said, 'yes, I am happy now, now that fire is not burning me. It is like a candle flame spreading light in my mind. I am asking her forgiveness, I am again back to my childhood. I am asking forgiveness from her but she is touching my feet . She is not getting up. She is turning to side and crying. She is saying how can I undo what I had done?.It will not go from my mind. I am telling her, ' I have forgiven you ,but she is not ready to believe me. How many time to tell her , 'please forgive me, I have forgiven you '. I encouraged her , 'go forcibly embrace her and ask forgiveness'. She replied, 'she is saying, I will repent, she is not able to forgive. She wants to do something for me. There is so much feeling for me in her. She is asking herself, what should I do for her.? I have forgiven her'.

At this I asked her, ' how you felt when you had not forgiven her? She said, 'she is very old ,she is alone ,her son and daughter in law are not living with her. They are living abroad, where I used to live. My papa is not alive. An old man helps her in her work. She keeps lying on her bed. She is repenting now'.

She is dead now , they have placed her down. There is wheat grains placed near her head(a custom in some place) Many people are sitting around her body. But today also she has that guilt. She is not remembering anybody else, her son, daughter in law, she is only remembering me. She is folding her hands, asking me orgiveness forcibly. (Renu sounded very emotional and chocked). 'How many time do I need to tell you,I have forgiven you'. But she is asking me to say that I am your son. I am saying, 'yes, you are my mother. I touch your feet, I forgive you'. Now she is happy. She is folding her hands and saying ,'I will do something for you'

Q What is the deeper significance of your meeting in the station house? Because none of you were aware of this. Was she to show you a way out breaking free from your fatal destiny? Now see how she has been instrumental in transforming your life. Now she was describing this life's situation, 'Ma'am called me and told me to learn Reiki. I agreed and I did it because I could believe that it will definitely do something good for me. I feel she is feeling so much for me that what should I do for her that she is cured. Then same thing is coming up --- earlier I wasn't happy, I lacked the will to do anything. Now I feel positive and go to my work happily. Now we have gone away from this place'.

She had been already shown her future both fatal and after healing her progress. By this time we both were tired thus giving her suggestions to keep practicing Reiki and heal her life , we ended the session.

After the session, though she was slightly embarrassed but was quite firm in her observations. She felt confident this time that her fatal accident had been averted. She gratefully said, 'I know I have got new lease of life, I will definitely benefit from it.' She gave me permission to write her case with her original name.

Lesson – Her case makes an interesting and enlightening story verifying truth depicted in certain movies and fictions.

1. We are in tune with our future through our mental state ,dreams and fears. We cannot handle it that is why we try to brush it aside thinking it our mere imagination or fanciful idea.

2. Dramatic effect of healing fatal event in to harmonious life are evident in her case. It was healing, which gave her subconscious mind the guidance to stand up and strength to emerge as a winner.

3. Rejecting our fear will not vanish it, if there is something, it will only disappear from our life if we apply some concrete effort and change our attitude.

Suffering /accidents/fatality is not a punishment, a final verdict from lord. That is why this life is only a preparation, not real at all. Changing our attitude, the life will automatically change for better.

4. Revenge, grudge, blaming others or delving in guilt or self-pity is the source of suffering. Forgiveness, taking responsibility for one's own life, loving self and others unconditionally is the key to heal ,progress and evolve. It is through change in mental attitude of the victim, not the other person whom he holds responsible and thinks that he is not forgiving.

5 If we have strong intension to come out from our suffering then nobody can stop us, even the dreaded enemy will be ready to forgive us, because everything is in the mind of the victim. It was Renu who had all these hidden memories and grudges in her mind and she is suffering. Mrs. Ghotia is not suffering because she may have repented and asked forgiveness. As Mrs. Ghotia had also turned healer by now and doing many healings herself. So along with others, her hidden causes were also being healed. If she was holding Mrs. Ghotia responsible for her miseries in one life, it was Mrs. Ghotia in this life instrumental in bringing her out from her fatal causes.. Making it evident that ***culprit and victim have to work together to help victim come out from hidden past trauma***.

6. Physically we may be living in the present time but if some strong memories from the past are not resolved,we are hypnotized in that event, re-living same experience in the present scenario. Our own ghost is scaring us, creating vigorous poltergeist activity turning into accidents, murder or any other crime. That is why others cannot even feel the intensity of one's inside turmoil and pain. But for the one who is experiencing, it is as real and more painful than the pierce of a knife or touch of any physical object.

7. Opportunity knocks at every body's door, whatever the circumstances may be. Nobody can force us to change direction in life. That is why we always feel standing at the edge and wondering which path to choose. We have free will ,provided we feel this deeper connection to our higher self and pray to guide us to lead in the right direction enabling us to enter the right door.

8. Revenge and grudge creates negative environment attracting more powerful negative force from surrounding, forcing one to commit crimes ,in this case suicide. At the same ***time same negative force can be transformed in to positive by praying and positive attitude***. This highlights the importance of doing prayers, meditation, and rituals with heartfelt feelings. By bringing change in the environment ,one is not only reaping the harvest of health ,happiness and peace for self but is also helping the negative aspect which is the outcome of faulty thinking from the face of the earth to transform into positive and help in leading a progressive life.

9 We can recognize people from the past if they are present in the present life irrespective of change in their looks, age, race and even sex.

Case 4 **I had told lies and also stolen things'**

Kritika, Snake fear. 1st June 2006

Eight years old Kritika was very keen to have a session with me. Her father was fearful and reluctant as children might project their wild imaginations which may affect them adversely. As he could not experience anything himself in his session thus rejected relevance of any truth in others' revelations. He declared whatever these people describe with closed eyes is nothing but their wild imagination and fantasies. Her mother had experienced some relevance in her healing session and was encouraging her children to have sessions so that something will be healed at least. I did not have to waste much effort in regressing her to any of her past life, which in any way was related to this life.

Past life- She is living in a hilly village as now also she lives in hills of Shimla. She said , 'I have same name and I have parents whom I don't recognize now. I have one elder sister ,she is my younger aunt (bua) in this life. I go to a school in a nearby village but my sister doesn't attend school. She helps our mother in household chores and in the field. (Striking resemblance to this observation is that her younger aunt hasn't completed her school education in this life also). I see my elder sister is getting married. When I asked her, did you get married later in your life? She said, 'no I do not see my marriage instead I am in the jungle cutting stems of the tree (pine tree).I am about twenty three years old. I have climbed high on the tree and suddenly I slip down and fell on the ground. I am unconscious. Now I am being taken to hospital. My uncle (chacha) is carrying me on his back and he is my present grandfather. He is very fond of me (who loves her very much even in this life also). I remained unconscious for a long time. In between I became conscious for some time and then after some time I died.

After death –I asked her to go in the sky after her body had died. She felt bit uncomfortable. I asked her, what happened? She shuddered and said, '***black horned yam doot with big sword*** in his hand is standing in front of me. (Yam is considered minister of death and yam doot is his agent according to Hindu mythology. At the time of death he causes unbearable pain and torture depending upon the deeds of the individual). She continued,' it's so frightening to see him. I assured her, ' he will not do anything to harm you. Just ask him why you had to meet the fatal end in that life? She replied, 'because in one life I had killed someone. In fact here after she herself said few things on her own. She said, my parents don't have any relationship with my grandfather but they have relationship with my grandma from past life. My mother was my cousin's wife in the past life'. Giving her positive suggestions and asking her to visualize pleasant, safe future we ended the session.

Past life – 2nd sitting – I asked her to pray for her guide to be present there ,so that she can feel secure and protected . Her guide came a gentle man with pant and shirt. I could not ascertain what connection she had with him in any of her past lives. When I asked her to find out how he is her guide? She said, 'he is your guide, that is why he has come to safe guard me.' Not going in to much detail of this guide ,we continued further.

She said, ' I again see I am in a hilly village but a different location. I am the only daughter of my parents and my name is Leela. I am studying in the school in plus two. It is a typical village school where we don't wear any uniform. Now I find myself married and living with my in laws and husband in another house . My husband is an alcoholic. He doesn't do any work.. I have started working to earn some money. He keeps asking me for money and waste it in drinking alcohol. Like a typical story, she said, ' I am fed up with him , if I don't give him money then he beats me up. Even my in laws cannot do anything to stop him from his addiction.

This time he is asking me for more money. I am also adamant now. I am not giving him. He is beating me ,thrashing me. Still I don't let him snatch money from me. Frustratingly he flanked a rolling pin (*belan*) at me. It hit on my fore head. I am hurt very badly. I am bleeding profusely and falling unconscious. Seeing my condition, my husband ran away in fear of getting caught.

Death- I die after some time. People have collected, my parents are crying uncontrollably. I was their only child. She was getting connected emotionally, I tried to detach her from there by seeing her body burnt and dissolving all her painful memory of that life with that body. As a young child she could readily do as advised and moved up in the sky.

Meeting in the sky – This time she did not feel scared. She herself went up and met her guide. She herself sounded the verdict on her accidental death, 'because ***I had told lies and also stolen things'*** that is why I had to live a violent life and die young. I asked her, it means you could meet the same fate in this life also ? She said, yes. I was reminded of the fear of her father that she might see something frightening and it was true. Sensing the higher purpose and some deeper meaning to her healing session. I asked her , ' you don't understand the deeper meaning of my session. Why I am healing you this way ? She replied, ' ***because I had taught you to believe in God in one life***. I asked her in amazement , 'what , I did not believe in God and you were my Guru? 'Yes, long time back, I was a sadhu and you had no belief in the existence of God'.

Past life- 3rd sitting- This life she is in the plain area living in a city. She felt intrigued and wanted to express her observation and she said, 'my mother in that life resembles someone I know now . Q- 'Whom? A, - 'you'. After sharing her surprise with me and also getting reassurance from me, she said, ' I go to school in the city. Again one more surprise waited for her and she announced , 'my present grandmother is the headmistress of my school. She is very strict'. She continued, this life I was married and had children. I lived a very good and happy life. I asked her, why are you seeing this life ?(I think after watching fatal and short life it was to reassure her that she had lived all good and bad lives in the past). She said, because past two lives had been full of very unpleasant and painful memories but before that I had also had good lives'. There was nothing more significant in this life other than knowing these two people and getting reassurance of having lived a happier life. She moved on to another life.

Past life – She said, ' now I am an English looking girl ,my name is Nitu. My parents are Britishers but we live in India. She seemed quizzical and said, 'you are my elder sister here. You are six years elder to me and your name is Anna. We lived a very short life because we were killed in the riot'. I asked her,' why were we killed in the riot?'. She said,' it was our father's karma because he had made many people suffer and this was his dues to suffer heartache this way. Later he too died of heart attack'.

Snake fear – I asked why you are so scared of snakes? She said,' in one life, I am going to school and I see a snake on the way. I kill the snake with stones and stick. I have come home now. In the night one snake comes from somewhere and bite me. I am dead. From that time I fear snakes that suddenly it will appear from somewhere and bite me. I healed her mind and asked her to feel her fear being erased. I was also reminded of my own snake phobia. So I asked her, 'can you tell me the reason why I have fear of snakes? She dramatically said '***oh my God, you are also very cruel.***' I was taken back and asked her to clarify. She said, 'you are dressed as a hunter and in the jungle doing hunting. Now you are killing a snake with the gun. That is why you also died of snake bite in one life. From that time this fear is always there in your mind'.

Note – Her mother had confided that Kritika and her father does not get along well. This is even predicted in her horoscope. When she was born, her father had to be away due to his business and that too was going in great loss. I asked her in the trance state ,'why don't you get along well with your father? She said, 'actually we have to heal him also because there is some danger for him. His heart is very blocked'. She admired my work and felt pained when he and others would criticize me. Though he is a good human being and very religious. He chants some mantra yet he is very sceptic and non-believer in anything modern spirituality is all about. He believes in scriptural teachings which rejects everything that is modern. Guru and God were only incarnated in those eras and now all are frauds and cheats. He wasn't willing to accept any truth through healing and regression. Once he offered to undergo a session ,which wasn't successful. There after he became stronger critic.

Channelled healing of her father- I regressed her to heal their relationship and asked her to see why he has so much fear and heart blocked to accept few things which might be helpful. She said ,' he is being possessed by one spirit ,whom he had killed in his past life. It is clinging to his heart. It makes him irritable, restless and closed for accepting anything useful'. When I asked her to see his heart healed and freed from the possession, she said, no, he is holding it back, because if he throws it away ,his heart starts bleeding ,same way as he had bled this person's heart'. Thus I could not heal him in this session. So I asked her to see the reason why they both don't get along well? Though normal father daughter relationship was evident but the difference of opinion was unbearable.

Past life-She said, 'actually we were both brothers in the past. We had a property dispute and we killed each other. That is why we have to pay back in this way. He would suffer heartache while I would have lived painful unhappy or may be fatal life ahead. I healed them of that memory and asked them both to wish for forgiveness, love,peace and progress for each other.

Lesson - She verified the presence of Yam and his doot. She reasoned her short past life without any hesitation to be her paying back for her deeds in the same coin . Her relation with her father also had the story like element that they had to pay back to each, by being closest relatives and not get along well with each other and feel so much pain at each other's suffering. Because they were revengeful to each other and here they both were suffering unknowingly.

2 She described my deeds of being cruel as a hunter ,it is the reason for excessive snake fear in me in this life. She made me humble by apprising me that she had been my teacher as I was also an atheist once upon a time.

Next year onwards she started having bleeding from her nose frequently. As I started healing her and she was seeing ,there is one patch in her right nose which is causing weakness in the blood vessels in the right nose. Vein is getting ruptured and blood oozing out dripping through the nose. Healing is clearing away the blood , making light fall on the weak vein ,making it look healthier

Conduit for channelled healing for her uncle -She had been my first successful channel to heal her uncle of renal stone. She clearly saw, there is hard crystal type thing pressing in his kidney causing pain swelling and inflammation. As through her I was projecting healing light on his kidney, gradually the stones were getting crushed, area oozing out blood, pus and smoke to finally clearing away any debris in five six such channelled healing.

Future- She even visualized that at about twenty years of her age she would be getting attuned by me for Reiki. There were many other people working with me at that time..

Case 5

He wants to take revenge Nakul June 2006-

Collar bone protruding outwards ,back pain ,knee pain and epistaxis

Thirteen years old Nakul had right collar bone protruded upward from his child hood. As he was growing tall, the curve was becoming more prominent making right collar bone and chest protrude out and left side looked pressed inward. On exertion he also had pain in his lower back and on the knees. His parents were worried about his aches and pains and this disfigured collar bone.

Session – Disfigured bone could be congenital defect and its causes could be quite deep. First we healed his knees and then back. There is black smoke on his knees as healing light is falling on it, gradually it is becoming clearer. At the lower back there was a black patch which was getting cleared by healing light .

Past life -I asked him to see why is this dark patch and black energy there? He said, ' I am seeing myself in a different time and body. I asked him what relevance this pain and that injury have in his life. He said, 'I am a small boy of ten years of age in a hilly region. My mother is wearing sari and I don't have a father. (I concluded he must be in the hills of Uttaranchal Garhwal region as ladies in that area in the hills wear sari.) We have small land in the village but that is not sufficient for maintaining our life.'

I am attending a village school. We are playing Kabbadi game. One boy is throwing me down and hitting me at my back. My knees and back are injured. I am in terrible pain. I cannot walk. Since then these areas have got this pain hidden in the form of black spots there.

I do not study much as in search for some living I am leaving my village and going to small town. I take a train from there and have travelled far from my place. I have reached a very big city. There is so much hustle bustle there. I feel lost in that place. This is Bombay. Q- Have you ever been to Bombay in this life, how can you say it is Bombay? He said, ' I haven't been to Bombay or even to Delhi but I know it is Bombay. Q-Any way, what are you doing there? He said, ' I am in search of some job. Q Where are you living ? A-There are many people like me in that city from different places, living like one lives in hostel or Dharamshala. I did some odd jobs for few days and returned back to my village. I get married and have four children. My wife wears sari. I am doing farming in my land. As I am growing old my back problem is becoming more prominent. Q I asked him , 'does your collar bone also has same defect in that life. A –Yes it is curved and looking protruded outward. I die in my eighties. In two sessions he was free from knee and back pain.

Past life-. In the next session I asked him to see how his collar bone looks in this body as I started healing it. He said, it looks curved and broken from the side. As it is taking healing light gradually it is getting joined together. Q Why is it broken and curved? A- I am an Indian soldier in the Army. One English man is brutally crushing my collar bone with his hard shoes. It is getting broken and detached and I die there itself. Q-Why did he crush you with his boots ? To find this answer to the origin of this problem in him in past many lives ,he went back to the life where he is the perpetrator of the action.

Past life -He said, 'now I am an English looking man living in India. I am very arrogant and hateful towards Indians. There is some procession and I am very angry at them. I want to stop it and I fire at them. Crowd has dispersed. I catch hold of one poor Indian and crush him under my feet ,same way as I had seen some English man crushing my collar bone. This person sustains so much injury in his back and knees. His chest bone is completely broken and detached from the joint hanging loose. He died there itself'.

Healing - I asked him to see this man and ask forgiveness from him. He refused saying, he does not want to forgive me as I had caused him too much suffering. As he was tired by now or not able to forgive himself for the pain he had caused to another fellow being and thus not ready for healing ,so I could not convince him to make amend with his victim. To make him feel detached from that memory I asked him to see his injured neck bone getting healed and joined together, which he readily agreed. After this I asked him to meet his guide, he said, 'my guide is Shiva sitting on Mount Kailash. 'I asked him to take blessing from him to get healed and cured from this deformity. He said, ' he is already blessing me '. At this I asked him why am I healing you?. He replied because I had also healed you in one life. He said, 'I can only see that you are injured and I am applying you some herb lotion on your injury. That is why you are healing me now. Q Why is Shiva your guide? A. I see myself as a sadhu sitting in Shiva Sadhna. He is giving me darshan and blessing me. Because of that only you are healing me now. Q Ask Shiva what does he say about my work. A- He says, she is going to become great in few years. Q- But why are you not ready for healing , why have you refused to ask for forgiveness from your victim. A- What can I do, he is not ready to forgive me. He is right because I had really caused him grave injury and death. At this we ended the session.

He and Kritika are my nephew and niece. Twice I made him conduit for healing his uncle of kidney stone and he also saw same thing as had his sister Kritika seen. But he wasn't interested, rather convinced of his complete healing.

Next year, when I met him he had a problem of bleeding nose frequently. I healed him by touching his forehead and nasal area. He saw his nasal blood vessels are fragile and burst open due to smallest extra pressure on them. Healing is making these stronger and healthier.

In 2009 he had turned seventeen and his bone was looking more prominent. I suggested healing and this time he agreed

Session – He started seeing his collar bone is hollow at one end and curved upward. The hollow end is taking healing light and closing slowly. Slowly the curve is also getting straightened. I asked him to see the cause for this defect. He said, it is same thing where I am hurting somebody on his collar bone. I asked him to ask forgiveness from this person. He said, no he is refusing and saying, ***I want to take revenge***. Q. How will he take revenge? Will he again hit you at that place and break it and kill you like you had done. A -Maybe, but he says I want to take revenge'. It was really hard to convince him to ask forgiveness from this person. I forced him now to see how this man is suffering because he has not forgiven you. He replied, yes I can see his right arm is paralyzed. He cannot work with it. Now I told him to convince this man to accept your heart felt forgiveness because by forgiving you , he will not only help in your healing but he will also be free from his problem. But he refused. Not agreeing to my suggestion, I told him to see this man being healed..He said ,yes his right arm is getting light and slowly as if coming back to life. After his arm was healed he said, now he is ready to forgive me. I am feeling free from guilt and feeling confident of complete cure for my problem. Now.

Concluding his session-

1. We are victims of same circumstances ,which we were perpetrator of some action once. Causing pain to other person is causing pain to self. We hold our self,guilty and pay back in the same coin that is why he was not willing for healing. He felt the other person is not ready to forgive him. Other person is just the extension of our own self. Where there is a question of asking or forgiving the other person involved in the problem, it is always your readiness and conviction which matters.

2. The other person holding you guilty may himself be suffering some untreatable disease and not knowing why this is happening to him. Your readiness and forgiveness not only heals your problem but of the other person too.

3. We all were Good and bad, cruel and kind, saint and arrogant some time or the other. We cannot judge things from what appears in the present ,which is just the tip of the iceberg. It is easier for younger and ignorant person to accept all tiger and lamb in us ,but a rigid mind will laugh it all as weird imagination. How casually he told me that he was sadhu and healed me once when I was in need. That is why I was healing him without his or his parents' understanding any relevance or any importance of healing

4. He had this problem in many lives. With this much healing continuity of cycle has been broken and further damage arrested..

5. Complete cure in chronic diseases takes time and many sessions. Which helps in increasing his awareness, acceptance and understanding of the mechanics of healing. Thus learning and practicing yoga, Pranayama mediation and healing techniques in everyday life is necessary component for complete cure, further progress and evolution in life. ***Disease means some blockage at the spiritual part***, severing our connection from the source of origin. Healing erases that block, connects back to the abundant source. It is only our mind which rejects possibility of miraculous healing. Whereas nothing is a miracle, everything is science. If stem cell implant, mutation of genes is possible, why not healing?

6th Case

Dark Cloud in the sky is threatening me

Why healing is painful and varies in time to cure ?

Pushpa 36 years May 2006 to 2009

Giddiness, nausea vomiting, lack of Appetite causing progressive weakness.

Pushpa is having above symptoms from past two three years at a regular interval once in a month . She is slim, active, talkative and positive in nature. She feels she is otherwise healthy other than when she is incapacitated by this attack for two three days. Her health has deteriorated considerably. She became very fearful of my touch as her problem would get more aggravated after the session. She would encourage others to have healing sessions with me including her two teenaged children. It is her positive outlook and eagerness to become healthy that she still dared to have this session with me. Even though there was no positive outcome in these past three years in her condition yet she gave me the opportunity to take her session once in a year. Because deep inside in her vision she had herself seen the grave cause beyond physical or modern medicine's approach. And no wonder she had started stating lately that she fears soon her condition is going to turn into a tumour in her head. Her worries were genuine as she had become less positive ,lost lots of weight with no appetite at all. She would retort, I am a living corpse till all my body parts are dissolved and finished.

Session -I am not going to write much detail of her past life story because in each session she had seen her head getting hit in the same place where she experiences pain now making her head spin and throwing her in a quandary.

Past life –2006 June. In first session to see the cause for her headache and giddiness ,she is seeing herself in her past life at about eight years of age playing in front of her hut in a hilly place. Suddenly she slipped and hit her right side head on a sharp edge of a stone. There is profuse bleeding and she is lying unconscious there. After some time she is out from her body ,seeing her dead body lying injured and unattended there. At this sight she started having same symptoms again. I healed her silently asking her to relax and keep saying positive affirmations. After some time I asked her to see the wounded area healed. She reported that wound is getting congealed and stitched up to make the area look clear.

Heavenly experience –to make her feel detached from her previous body, I advised her to go up in the sky and meet her guide. She said, 'I am in a very beautiful garden in the sky . I see somebody is sitting on the bench there. He looks to be some character from Mahabharata time and here she declared, ' ***he is Bhishma pita maha***'. I enquired from her, 'is he your guide? She said, 'no ,I just met him on the way to go to meet my guide. My guide is ***Lord Shiva*** sitting on Mount Kailash. ***He*** is blessing me. There wasn't any communication between them so I advised her to come back to the present and feel happy, healthy and progressing. After the session she surprisingly asked me, why did I meet *Bhishma Pitamah* in the garden? I had no concrete answer to this query. I suggested her she needs few more such sessions to have complete cure. To this she agreed at that time but as after the session she continued having those symptoms of giddiness for whole day. This frightened and made her doubtful whether healing has triggered her existing problem more. She could not dare to have another session same year. Next year when we met again , she was fearful yet she gave in and we had healing session.

Past Life- 2007 -She is seeing herself again in the hilly region village but in a slightly different setting. This time she is bit grown up teenager and going to jungle near her house. In the jungle its dark and she slipped down on a rock and hit her head again in the same place. There is injury and bleeding at the same spot and she is lying unconscious for a long time there. I healed her and she saw her wound being healed and felt bit relaxed.

Conduit for healing - Here after I even asked her to see her husband's problem because he is very blocked and does not think positively about healing . He has firm belief in Ramayana,which says that Kaliyuga will be full of fraud people claiming to be gurus. His firm opinion is that modern people have devised such things to cheat or misguide people. I asked her in that trance state what is causing such orthodox attitude in him ? She saw there is black energy band around his heart chakra. On seeing deeper ,his heart is clogged with blood and blocked. Why? He is stabbing somebody in the heart in his past life and now the same wound is inflicted on his heart, making him feel suffocated and restless. We directed healing on his heart and he was feeling bit relived now.

I also made her a channel to view her brother in laws' kidney problem whom I had healed last year. I had made her children channel for healing him when he had suffered severe renal colic. She saw exactly the same thing and some light going to him and healing his kidney. She said, 'I can see some child is carrying this light from you to him and his kidney is getting cleared and healed'. I asked her to see the child properly and here she recognized them to be her children. After the session her symptoms appeared again and here after she developed phobia of undergoing healing again.

It was not a mere coincident that I made her conduit for seeing and healing her husband for his blocked heart. It was to make her open to accept the effectiveness of healing irrespective of her not getting any direct benefit so far. I could sense her willingness for healing but could not force her due to her past unpleasant experiences after healing. It was genuine to resist further healing as she had felt more troubled afterwards. It was like getting my teeth extracted at the time when there is an acute infection and pain in the teeth. Her wound in her mind was very raw causing this problem more severe in her upon touching that part. Which meant her time was not right for seeing and healing such raw wound.

March 2008,She had severe watering in her right eye as a piece of grass had rushed in it. Which was taken out by one God gifted local specialist, who was clearing away such objects accidentally falling in people's eyes and ears. Seeing her discomfort and irritation in her eyes I suggested gentle healing.

Healing-She started feeling some heat and light entering her irritating eye. Soon she was able to see there is some hole deep inside her eye which is filled with pus. Healing light is clearing it by draining it out through her feet. Gradually the hole was being healed by the **Light** energy passing on to her.

Dreams giving me guidance - I had few dreams regarding her, which prompted me in healing her now and then whenever I heard about her being unwell.

1.Once I saw there was some argument going on in their family with me. Nobody is agreeing to my point of view but she is accepting it openly.2. Once I saw there is flood everywhere in their village. I am standing in knee deep water and I notice somebody has put my clothes for drying on a tree. I know Pushpa has done it for me. 3. Once we both were sitting in a jeep going on a familiar road. I am naked and I am asking her to borrow clothes from two known ladies living in the nearby area. She said that none of them are at home so that we might not get anything.

April 2008, I had a dream that though her son is bringing me recognition on his birthday but she is giving me something very unpleasant to eat. I did not understand its meaning then..Her condition was deteriorating in past few months as frequency of such attacks also increased to two or three in a month as compared to one in a month. I understood the message it was giving me. Her past few healing had healed her past life memory. Frequency of attacks were clearing away process. Her body has deteriorated much while clearing all her past painful memory ,she might not be able to cope up clearing away her pain in this body which she had projected for her future. She was right when she said that this way I am going to get brain tumour soon. In spite of my sincere effort , her belief and willingness in healing , she was so fearful because her body was too weak and could not withstand the clearing away of so much pain.

Her sister in law Nilam mentioned to me in one of her dream which I felt was giving me some guidance.

Nilam's dream – She said, 'you ((I), Nirmal) , I (Nilam), Pushpa have gone to one fate reader to know our future. You both enter inside his house but I am bit hesitant and keep standing outside for some time. I have ten rupees note in my hand and fifty rupees note in my pocket. I am thinking to bargain with him first by giving him ten rupees, if he doesn't agrees then only I will give him fifty rupees. I enter in one room where he is sitting. I see, my cousin's wife who had died in a fatal accident three months back was already lying or sleeping there. I wonder as you both also go and lie down by her side. Confused and bit scared I gather some courage and somehow try to show my hands to him. I am showing my hands to him some time I am crossing right hand over left hand and sometime other way as if I don't know which is the correct way to show my hands. There after I don't remember anything what he had predicted.

2009 - I gave her distance healing for some time when I heard about much deterioration in her health. I could see her turn negative, her tolerance level dip too low and she had become anaemic.

In March, I got the opportunity to heal her son ,sensing her problem and inability to take healing from me ,I did channelled healing for her. He saw there is one orange spot on her mind. May be this was the area where she had seen her head injured. We healed that and gave her subconscious mind suggestion to be happy healthy and progressing. The result was that she boldly said, ' no matter what happens I am going to have healing session with you'. I gave her suggestion to keep chanting that she is happy, healthy and progressing in life. To which earlier she would argue with me saying ,how can I think positive when I know my suffering is beyond measure.

I also convince her that though there is no concrete diagnosis and treatment in allopathic medicine about your problem. The exact cause is in your mind and you and I know it for sure, why these symptoms are there.

Session –This time I was very gentle on her. As I knew her weak body is unable to take required healing energy. That is why she was even scared of my touch so I asked her to touch her body herself instead of my touch ,which ever part was being healed at that time.

First I decided to ***heal and balance her chakras.***

Third eye was totally dark, by giving it some light and making it turn clockwise. We proceeded to her heart, it was deficient in energy. It was draining red colour from her root chakra to compensate functioning. As a result her root chakra was also deficient in functioning making her physical body weak. Supply of blood to her whole body was low, making her feel weak and giddy.

Now I asked her to touch her head where it pains and gently healed her. She felt a stream of pus oozing out from the wound in her head which started draining down through her right side body as if a pipe is attached to the wound, which was emptying it out from the right feet. As it completely emptied the pus from the wound , she felt much comfortable.

Energy connection -I asked her to see her energy connection with her husband as he is very temperamental. His behaviour and remarks really affects her deeply lately as she feels her tolerance level has also dipped to all time low now. She saw, she is sending black colour from her solar chakra to him and he is sending fiery red to her heart. This was definitely because of some past unresolved issues. We cut the energy cord which was exchanging this faulty flow affecting each other negatively. We healed the raw area with pure healing ***light*** drawn from the universal source and wished each other forgiveness, love, healing and progress. Now we moved to head part where earlier she had seen wound twice.

Past life- She was seeing again that wounded area in her right head as her body laid unconscious on the ground there. We healed the wound ,she got up from the ground but felt very weak to move from there. She is still standing there. I made her relax for some time and healed her quietly till she felt energetic enough to walk away from that place. Now she focused on the third eye chakra ,which was stationary. Intending and directing healing light ,it started spinning slowly clock wise. She also saw this chakra moving and turning from brownish colour to deep blue in colour.

Now we moved on to focus any other area responsible for causing so much deterioration in her health.

Throat – There was a dark patch on the throat center causing obstruction in the passage of energy or prana going to her heart and stomach. As this was healed by intending healing light on it, she felt as if a pipe is opening up from her throat and blowing down fresh cool watery breeze to her stomach. It felt cool and comfortable in the stomach. Now she is feeling this cool comfortable energy spreading in her entire body. I asked her, 'is there some leakage in your throat center? She said, yes, 'there was some trickle of water drops oozed from throat spread around neck and chest. But when this light is falling on it ,these have dried and area is clean now.

Pranayama- Here I advised her about the importance of Pranayama, in spite of being so popular and easily available , many had advised her to give it a try but she wasn't able to bring herself to practice it. I apprised her, how her body is blocked and deficient in prana. Her stomach and heart are not receiving prana at all. She does not feel hungry and body does not get energy from the food which she forcibly eats as it does not gets metabolized in to energy in her body. Now she agreed as she herself had seen how the blocked channel had opened and pushed up some gentle breeze giving her cooling and energizing effect.

Higher dimension – I asked her to see her healing happening in higher dimension as I know that when we heal physical body on earth ,energy bodies are healed simultaneously in the higher dimension. She said, I can see, I am in the sky sitting on the bench. There is someone's hand on my head transmitting energy on to my head and whole body.

Significance of her healing She does not really know much importance of healing and even if it is freely available to her she cannot take it as she starts having pain..Her problem aggravates more making her sceptical and fear full of healing. I wanted to know from her subconscious what is the significance of her healing for me? Does she have any past life connection, does she has some revenge or hold me guilty for something , so that I have to heal her on my own interest ? She replied, 'no, I don't see any such reasons, I only see you are very high up and far away wishing and saying to me , ' wake up and progress in life. It seem something is just out of compassion on seeing my deplorable condition'. I further asked her, 'then why were you not healed in past three years even though you trusted me and had keen desire to get cured? In spite of my sincere effort you were fearful of my touch? She said '***there is one thick cloud*** which has moved farther now. It is still waving to me not to take it. ***It's sort of threatening me***. I asked her to see that cloud dissolve completely. She said, 'now it's clear sky and I feel quite optimistic and out of danger now.

I asked her to see what food or medicine is helpful for her to regain her health back. She said, ' I can see pulses, rice, chapatti, vegetable and fruits. Q- don't you need milk or any other thing. A- I can see banana and oranges and I already take curd and milk. Giving her positive suggestion to take frequent nutritive meals, practice Pranayama for faster recovery back to health and keep chanting positive affirmation like a mantra, we ended the session.

Post session- She told me about her ***dream*** next day. She said, ' in my dream, I am telling you , see how I am eating food four times a day now a days . I can even eat more than this'. I told her this is a positive sign as now your subconscious has started responding to positive affirmation and healing. Earlier you were scared that is why you could not bring yourself to practice anything positive. Now she started doing Pranayama also. But next day she again had same attack. I just touched her lightly and told her to be positive and optimistic. Don't fear it as recurrence, it is a clearing away process. The amount of painful memory she had projected for future had to be released this way. She was troubled at that time but felt confident. I kept giving her distance healing for few days till I felt guided to do so.

Note–How accurately our fear turns out to be true? She had projected this fear and pain for future and she had rightly prophesied ,it will turn in to tumour. She saw how the wound was filled with pus which was gushed down through a channel in right side of her body and draining out of her sole. That is why she was not cured even though her wounds were healed in the past because this was acute phase and she felt intense pain while trying to heal it, just as a raw wound would be untouchable to dress and stitch.

Importance of her case -

1. I was getting opportunity to take her session once in every year and I also had few dreams about her. Logically this can be explained because she is my relative but I don't dream about all my relatives and comprehend what it means as I understood in her case.

2. More importance is due to healing of my own problem along with her which had gradually surfaced in past four five years. I had occasional blood pressure and I noticed that in past few years when ever I visited my native place where Pushpa also lived I had severe tension headache and high BP for two three days. This also troubled me while traveling in high altitude area of Leh and Ladakh.

3. There were few other signs which pronounced some hidden cause was being healed from my system of which I wasn't aware. In 2007 Punam (Numerologist friend) informed me that in her meditation she had seen my right side head wounded as if sharp bamboo stem is pierced in it. Though I didn't take it seriously as I felt I am doing many things to heal my life but at times I had severe tension headache making me unable to move my neck, shake my head and sharp rise in BP. That time I would think I might have some stroke or die due to this.

4. 2008 had been very challenging year for my whole family and for me on the whole. So many of our past issues were being cleared. When something gets cleared completely ,a stage comes when we are left vacant , no hopes , desires or will power. Though I was very dedicated to my work but for few months I was bogged down by the lack of physical stamina and troubled by emotional issues that I wished nobody should come to me for healing. Gradually I lost interest in everything from eating, entertaining to socializing ,though I wasn't depressed in the usual sense. Self-dialogue and evaluation was continuously going on in my mind. A time came when I felt I would not be able to live further. Yet I had this hidden desire and knowledge that if I die leaving my work half way, it would be waste of higher guidance given to me to serve the real purpose of my life. I

had been given guidance about this difficult phase in my life through my intuitive faculty. I knew this phase can either make me or break me. So I just wanted to live to complete my work.

I have also mentioned this state of mind in first chapter page no 5. People are free to call this my imagination or whatever but I very well know that imagination also has some source somewhere. My imagination had valid source and I was fully aware of the direction my life was taking. I do not want to sound mysterious or arrogant by not mentioning simple reasons for my premonition.

A. Nilam's dream that Pushpa and I are lying down at fortune tellers place where her dead sister in law was already lying, signifies we both also have same fate coming for us.

B. Anjana's vision about my mental state. C. My own dreams and vision giving me direction about this difficult phase in my life. D.I felt lifeless and no energy to peruse my work for few months. I even informed few people about this and asked them to give me healing and pray for me as I felt my karmas are over now, there is nothing more I can do in this life. E. There were also few unexpected sudden deaths of people giving clue that life is very unpredictable.

6. I also knew that there is difference in dying with awareness at any age and dying at a ripe old age without being aware of your end and any purpose of this life. So I would be living with this awareness that if I live till my eighties, I will not be living for myself , I will be living to fulfill some higher purpose through me.

If I die in my fiftieth year, I will die with this awareness that I have worked upon my personal karma. I have healed and erased karma of my close people and few others who came to me for their healing. I have healed them to bring them up to certain level, beyond that it's not in my hand to change their destiny. It is in their hand to bring transformation in them. Though we have to do all the efforts to make things not in our control to make in our control but there are few things which are not in our hands. If others cannot accept me, I have no purpose in this life. I have served the purpose of this life. I think everybody has to accept crucifixion and pray for forgiveness for those who cannot feel light of the God within, so that they can see the light.

7. This was to dissolve my ego which was alive while I considered myself healing and changing people's future. I thought I want to teach people by writing my experiences. Till this time I was doing this with the intension of thinking myself controlling things in life. Biggest blow to my ego was that in past many years of healing there was not a single person to stand up and speak up his experiences of healing by me. This realization dropped any expectation from others and brought considerable liberation in my outlook and my work. I started working because I was guided to do so not because I expected appreciation from others.

8 So far I was also measuring my success in terms of people's acceptance, appreciation and material gains. I wasn't thinking of mentioning cases which had not succeeded changing their attitude in this very life or those who could not continue living in this very body. But that is not the true meaning of healing.

9. Healing is like reinstalling new program in your old out dated computer. Not only reinstalling new program in the computer is important but one also should show willingness to learn to work on it . If one is not able to bring changes in his attitude because of lack of flexibility yet if he has been healed, his past memory of some unresolved issues have been healed. Faulty out dated data has been replaced. Only thing he hasn't decided to work with his new program. He may be taking time to accept so much change in his overall thinking.

10. Same is with those who haven't been able to continue living in the same body. If the old system was too worn out to withstand the new program, we might exchange it for a new set.

The old thorny seeds have been replaced with new flowery fragrant seeds. Now all depends on the fertility of soil (their mind) how fast it can grow these flowers to give fruits. It could be in few months to few years or in next life. It depends on person's willingness and capability to accept this new programming in the mind.

11. There is no loss, nothing goes waste, it is only transformed and changed in form but some total of energy remains constant. Had that not been the case there wouldn't be unexplained cases of some fortunate born heir to millionaire or someone as beggars , someone with inherited defects and someone as genius progeny.

12. Death is not important for dissolution of physical body but is more important for dissolution of ego. Death is painful whether it's of body or of ego. Pain is ego's struggle to stay alive for its existence is threatened.

13. Alchemist is not only the one who can convert metal in to gold but the one who can change rusted, diseased system in to healthy body.

Real Alchemy is to heal, transform and bring new system in to being by generating healthy tissues ,new ideas and progressive attitude in the same body . Otherwise the same orthodox idea, same disease passes over to new body born in a distant new place, creating similar circumstances to deal with same old issues in the tissues in the name ***of hereditary and genetic defects, faulty planetary positioning and numerological calculations or psychic attack ,spirit possessions and black magic***.

Myths about healing / Spiritual Energy

It is important to discuss here the facts and myths about healing.

It is a myth that healer loses his energy while healing others, discouraging most people from adopting healing as a great service to self, God and humanity. Most disciplines / spiritual paths impress to conserve this energy for spiritual growth required for Kundilini awakening (dormant energy seed sleeping at the base of the spine)

The fact is that healer has to give his energy in terms of time and to still his restless mind to do healing, also his body becomes the channel to transfuse the energy. Though initially he may not be transmitting much energy yet every healing helps in cleansing up and opening up of his own channels resulting in increase in his energy transmitting capability. It is a both way process helping client get rid of his problem and healer's own growth.

Myth- Only rigid rituals, difficult postures of yoga, living austere life like renunciation and brahmacharya are prerequisites for Kundilini awakening or spiritual evolution. It is one of the means to prepare the basic foundation of the disciple to clear his energy bodies. These are not an end in itself , there are other ,softer ,more harmonious ways.

Myth -Magical power or psychic capability in a person is a result of awakened Kundilini and he is evolved spiritually.

Fact –Psychic capability is just a single reward (sidhi) for his dedicated effort (Sadhna) to one of many extrasensory perceptions. It does not mean he is spiritually much evolved or enlightened. There has to be balanced growth in overall spheres of life . Otherwise this capability may not prove to be beneficial in the long run and some time may spell even doom in his life.

Myth -Any Guru can awaken one's Kundilini making one spiritually awakened and powerful to control things and people.

Fact –Without proper knowledge on the part of Guru and preparation of the disciple, it is always considered full of danger and warned to be careful of such novice and greedy people. Who want self-gain at the cost of others or trying to control others.

Fact - Kundilini awakening is an automatic response to cleansing and free flow of energy channels, when sufficient energy is generated in an individual.

Fact -Without cleansing energy channels and proper spiritual growth trying to awaken Kundilini would be disastrous like causing short circuit and blowing away the fuse. Our body is a vessel, a channel. It has to be prepared gradually to encompass and contain the high voltage Godly energy required to cause rise Kundilini in full stream. There may be other ways but ***what better way than healing***, where one can kill two birds with one stone. Making healing a faster way to grow spiritually, doing great service to humanity and God Himself.

Myth – There is a risk of for healer to contract client's disease.

Fact -Healer may face some similar problem because while becoming channel for healing the client, healers, similar channel is getting touched. These may be some of his unresolved issues of which he isn't aware . Healers own memory of alike problem is also touched and resolving, problem, giving signal that it was there, but without really affecting him that deeply as it would have, had it not been healed along with his client.

Myth- There is a risk of more harm coming to client due to healing, his condition may deteriorate to worse.

Fact- The deterioration in such a condition may be due to already existing deep rooted grave problem coming to the surface as a result of healing as healing clears the problem from the root. The deeper the root of the problem the more time and more symptoms may appear while continuing healing. Making ignorant people sceptic and fearful of healing doing some harm to them and force them to discontinue healing.

Myth -Disease or suffering is karma, destiny, lords verdict thus cannot be cured and need to be endure. Meddling with karma will endure wrath on healer as well as the client.

Fact. Suffering is a consequence of karma; it is a self verdict to experience the emotion or the pain of the other person whom we may have harmed knowingly or unknowingly in the past.

It is not a punishment or abandonment from God. It is platform for learning some virtue which may be lacking in the victim.. It is a self guilt for doing wrong to other person as eventually there are no others, we all are one .

Healing is like extra coaching given to someone failed in the subject to understand the weak subject and save him from succumbing to the failure again by blaming others or developing guilt or feelings of worthlessness.

Why one truth is not accepted universally.

There is always contradiction and non-acceptance of any fact unanimously at a time. Even we our self go through a stage when what we rejected some time back, we may accept it now. We may not have been ready to accept it for lack of understanding or its importance in our growth . But now we might have come at an understanding and may be willing to accept it.

Why a statement is not accepted to be true has only two reasons . First one is that we have experienced it and it is over for us ,we don't need to hold on to its significance now because there are other things needing our attention at the moment. Such people will not reject it strongly but will just consider not important for them at the moment.

Others are those who will strongly oppose as they have not yet reached near this truth, not prepared the soil to accept the truth ,they are not ready as yet. It requires time ,intension and effort to cleanse our system ,make our heart accept the truth. Everything exists here and now ,whatever we may have heard is true at any point of time but only difference is that we are not able to accept it until we have arrived at that truth.

Pushpa's case is a clear example that her body wasn't able to withstand the high energy required for regaining back her health. Time was at an advantage for her. That is why I was getting guidance and continued her healing over such a long time, whenever I met her. Though there was no outward progress in her health because inwardly her injury was very profound and in acute stage. But my efforts did not go waste. Along with her, my own unknown cause was also being healed. Deepa also had the same problem, her same body was not ready for regaining health back because outwardly her circumstances were very unfavourable. It was a big blow to her ego, she wasn't able to accept herself as a failure. Time was not at advantage for her. But the old cycle has been terminated which she had seen in her first session itself that her new beginning is going to be pleasant and different from her present unpleasant state . Same thing can be said about other cases who might not have been transformed dramatically but their past memories have been deleted from the system and they might be taking time to get used to working with new program.

Chapter 5

Conspicuous Divine Plan

✤ ❋ ✤

You had promised to pay back my debts

1 Anjana 29th March 2006

Depression, Feeling neglected, no reward for her talent.

(Nadi Astrology at Vasant Kunj Delhi had predicted good future for me in Healing and spiritual field in the beginning of this month (March 2006). I had only wished, how wonderful it would be if all that is said, could come true! Predictions looked very interesting, and fascinating but seemed next to impossible at that moment ,as my healing centre was almost closing down due to unavoidable reasons. Anjana came to me at this time to reconfirm the earlier predictions made by Nadi Astrology, making me intrigued and wonderstruck.)

Anjana's Aunt Kanta, was Deepa's colleague (Deepa is my earlier case, in Chapter Three). Kanta called me on 29th March to fix up an appointment for Anjana. I was reluctant, as on Tuesdays I had almost stopped going to my Healing center, instead I had been going to do healing for Cancer Patients in Army Hospital nearby my house. But Kanta requested me to come along the same day as Anjana had come from very far and she cannot come again very soon. I asked them to come in the afternoon time. I was late by half an hour because for the first time in my life, I got stuck in the lift, in my building. In the meantime Kanta had hard time to keep Anjana waiting for me in my healing center, because Anjana was very disturbed due to her problems as well as she was very sceptic of healing doing any good to her. Since she had been to many doctors, pundits and Tantrics but she did not feel any better. As I reached there, I explained to them little bit about my healing through Reiki and regression, which they hardly understood anything. They were just interested in some remedy and relief in her condition somehow. Seeing her condition, I clarified to her that one session is hardly going to help her. She should also learn Reiki and must have few subsequent sessions.

Her session was self-guiding in the sense that I was guiding her to follow the conventional way to reach back to the origin of her present problems for the purpose of healing. But her mind was leading its own direction; she was viewing some different things unknowingly and unintentionally. I am writing her sessions as it happened without deleting or adding anyething. I will describe my observations in brackets or after the sessions.

Session 1 - She immensely missed her papa, who had died when she was twelve years old. She immediately reached back to her childhood time and was seeing herself at about eight years of age. Descending down the stairs of her house, her present Guru Tajender ji Maharaj came, he blessed her and pampered her very much. I guided her to reach the healing temple in inner century. She said, 'My Guru is taking me and I have reached the healing temple. It is open from top and all the light is falling through its open roof'. Now I asked her to focus on the energy exchange between her and Rajat, with whom she had affair for some time but now they broke up , making her depressed and filled with low self esteem.. Pure healthy energy was flowing from Anjana towards him but black energy was coming from his side. I cut both these cords connecting them. She said, 'he is crying and very sad on being separated from me'. I asked her to see both of them receiving energy from the /sky/source, to heal their raw wounds due to cord cutting. She said, 'after healing is complete now he looks calm and normal.'

(She was much infatuated by him and wanted commitment but he was a pragmatic ambitious man, not interested in settling down at this stage, as they both were pursuing higher education. After cord cutting there was a shower of healing energy from the sky on her. She was exclaiming in excitement by seeing the snowing of some white flowers like thing on her. "O, what is this"? Now she herself reached up in the heaven to her father. She said, "Papa has lifted me in his arms and is pampering me so much. I am about eight years old and am wearing a frock. Papa is loving me and making up for all those years absence. Papa is in a temple in the Inder Lok. (Inder Lok is one of the Higher /spiritual dimension / level of the heaven, according to Hindus). She Continued , "Papa keeps reading Gita there. I can hear the ringing of the bells, chanting of mantras". She described the scene of the place where she was seeing herself.

"In the temple there are many Idols. One red shining face is becoming alive and is coming forward. He is taking me to my hostel room and giving me one big crystal to keep it on my study table.(I thought her guide is giving me guidance to give her a crystal to keep in her room). I asked her, " do you recognize this figure '? She replied, 'he is Narender. He is blessing me".

Her future – She herself progressed to see herself in the future. She said, 'I am getting an award. My book is published. Mummy, Kanta aunty and you are also there. You hugged me and are blessing me. Everyone is so happy'. I asked her, 'when is this happening? She replied, 'its 2007-08 (or 2017/18) I am also taking classes in Journalism in some college'.

My present - Now she war murmuring something like this, 'people are taking undue advantage of you but the dedication and hard work is going to pay you soon. Your good deeds are getting accumulated. There is so much crowd outside your centre. People are eager to come in. I am having severe headache. Please, somebody let me go in first'. She sounded restless for a moment. She continued, 'you are going very far in your work. *This place is very small for you*. Soon you are going to open a Healing centre in a very posh area'.

My Future - Now she was startled and exclaimed, 'arey! You have a big show room type place. A big Budha statue is kept there. Had you thought of naming it Budha Center'? I had to respond to her question as she was waiting for my feedback on her vision. I softly said, 'no'.(Though I wanted to succeed in my venture that is why I had opened this center but this name has not come on the conscious level in my mind. I was surprised as she is sort of reconfirming predictions by Nadi Astrology) She insisted, 'but its name is something like this only'. Thus I was forced to ask her, 'where is this center'? 'Somewhere in the east, she showed with her hands directing towards east. Connaught Place in Delhi or some such place in Kolkata. Yes, this is Kolkata only. Outside wind chimes, crystals and some such other things are kept. I don't know all these names'.

Now she was sounding like a playful child and inquisitively asking, 'Is this called laughing Budha? It's so beautiful; will you please give this to me? ***This is your shop only'.*** Amused, I was listening to her without much interruption from my side.

My family -Her tone became slightly serious now as she addressed me directly, 'but why are you sad, there is something troubling you'? I always tried to keep a brave front but there are few things which we know that these are troubling us. So what first came to my mind, I blurted it out. I said, 'my mother in law can't see'. Now she was conversing with me as if she is directly seeing my mother in law. She said, "Oh, she is very old. She is wearing blue bordered white sari and is in her room lying in the bed". She said, "She has troubled you a lot". I quickly responded to negate her feelings by saying ' no'. But she insisted, "In your past life she had troubled you a lot but now she is repenting." I did not wish to waste time in arguing and make her feel offended. Instead I asked her, "Will she be able to see again"? She acted by opening and closing her own eyes as if she is trying to ascertain whether she can see or not and then pointed to her right eye, "Yes, she can recognize you with her soul's eye now, she is managing her affairs well and is happy with this" (as I always tried to heal her and wished deeply that she could see in this life time)

She announced, "One man is also there, he is looking towards you. I wanted clarification from her like who is he, what is his name? But she did not give any information on this, instead she said, "he is wearing golden framed spectacles, he is tall and healthy with round and full face". I asked her to recognize this face properly, "you may come across this man some time later". To this she asked, "but why does he get so angry"? Then she was answering herself, "he is saying, my ego used to clash with her (with me) that is why we had differences".

At this dramatic revelation, I got bit curious and posed her a question, "Who else is there '? On asking this she again was seeing herself in Kolkata like place in the healing centre. She said, "There are three people, Aditya, Anjana and Nirmala. Arey! Nirmala is your name only. This is your centre. All three of us are working together. There is one more person who has gone out from inside right now. Did you want to adopt a girl? Then why didn't you do so"? Without waiting for any answer from me she had moved ahead.

Inspiration for me --She reached to 2010 and declared, "You are also getting award for your book. It has blue colour cover with your photo in white sari. Many copies are sold". Sensing my disbelief at this revelation, she questioned me, "did you decide the blue colour for this book"? I just clarified my stand on blue colour saying, "blue is the colour of wisdom". She gave me further feedback saying, "I can see many copies are sold. Yes, you have got a prestigious award for your book. In fact you have brought out two books together". I could not believe my ears and she could sense it, thus she again clarified, "but you are already writing". I asked her, "what is the name of my book"? She tried as if to read in to the future and said, "something about life "life is like this also" (*aisa bhi jivan*)." I can see the first chapter is very beautifully titled, " Who is God"? Your son is also there. But he is not happy. Don't force him to follow this. He wants to do computer and go abroad. Again that spectacled man is there, he is telling me, "I should have got this award but you helped your didi (me) to get it. You could have helped me also."

Our Past -Now this was becoming too much for me to digest (healing center and all that was still my desires, writing a book was also at the back of my mind but not so soon and getting award was something beyond my imagination at that time) So I guided her to come back to the healing temple for her further healing but she was on her own and she asked me, "So you had decided to open your center in Manali? O.K, you wanted to fulfil your promise by paying back your debt". Not understanding the real meaning behind her words, I plainly refused because I had no connection and interest in Manali ,thus the thought of opening a healing centre there had never occurred to me. I told her my desire that I wish to open one in Shimla instead. She did not give much importance to my words and started murmuring in hushed and different tone. These are the proceeds of her intriguing session with me.

Anjana-***'we have met earlier too'***. I could not recollect where and when we would have met, so I asked her, 'where'?

Anjana- "Many many years back, at Manali". Before I could correct her that I have never been to Manali so far in my life, she continued, "but ***why are you (***tum***) touching my feet"***? (The session was in Hindi and so far she was addressing me aap(respectful address in Hindi) and now her tone and address has changed to tum.) Surprised at what she was seeing , she kept on elaborating further, "you offered me white flowers, people are worshiping me, ***no one talks to me but you are talking to me. I am an idol***, I had given you this crystal Necklace (mala), you had lost it somewhere, now you have got it back". (I could not make out anything from her irrelevant talk. I had no idea whether she is infatuated or have some connection with Manali, if she is talking about the same Manali, a famous hill station in Himachal Pradesh. If at all by any means she knows about my origin from Shimla, then why she is saying we met in Manali, where I had never been so far nor had any inclination to go there in future. It took me some time to realize that she is talking about some past life about which I am not aware. In spite of my intense desire and best efforts many times to experience my past life, so far I have never been able to do so.)

I told her the fact , rather I asked her, "why I could not see any of my past life"? She replied, "You will come to know everything by December." Amazed at her explanation, I curiously asked her, "who am I, what is my name, how do I look"? I became curious to at least know about my past life through some body, if I am not able to see myself.

Anjana- "you are very beautiful, full face and long hair, you are Vimmi, Nimmi is your name (I could not hear her clearly as she was talking in different and hushed tone.) You are troubled by your people and society. They don't allow you to walk the path you want to tread. You are asking me for help and saying, "***I will pay back my debt.*** Help me get rid of the bondages of this world". "Your Kundalini is not awakened as yet. You cannot meditate for long time. There is some obstacle in your path. And I have promised to help you. You are filled with gratitude and have promised to pay back the debt". And I am filled with ego ***and I snapped at you proudly, "Oh, what debt can you pay"?*** (*tum kya karz chukaogi*)" " Do you remember, you told me that story of "a rat and the lion"? She was waiting for some response from me. I told her the truth that I don't remember any such thing. Then she herself went on to elaborate that famous story of rat requesting lion to forgive and spare him once and promised when the lion will be in need, the rate will also help. The lion was also filled with ego at that time and said the same thing to rat but let him free. And then the rat really saved lion's life by cutting and freeing him from the mesh trap placed by the hunter". "***Nimmi, will you help me cut my ropes now ?*** I have also got trapped. Will you help me? You had promised me"? Then as if she was coming around from the trance into the present and said, "but I don't have money, I cannot come here next time". And she was in tears. I tried to re assure her," you will be able to come here; I will repay back my debt. I have to be free from your debt." She asked, "Can I turn aside"? She was having backache and her body had got tired after such a long session. Giving her positive affirmations, I brought her out of the session.

After the session, she was feeling surprised and even embarrassed at whatever she saw and said. She explained to me after the session, "I saw there is something troubling you. I saw you entering through a big hall and peeping in to one room. There was your mother in law with blue bordered white sari and I could sense her regretting now for her action in the past". She saw many things which she could not understand or elaborate for lack of time. She was moving forward and backward in time very quickly.

She wanted to know my response. When I told her that you were not listening to my instructions and thus we could not go to the origin of your problems and heal these. But at least you must have felt relaxed by releasing out whatever was trapped in your mind. She was now judging herself and said, "it means today's session has gone to waste. I don't think I will be able to come for another session". Seeing her condition and reluctance to come for another session, I asked her for her photo so that at least I can give her distance healing. I gave her one crystal rock as she had described, Narender had given one to her. I also gave her one locket to wear. I felt responsible for her as her session had made me marvel at the mysterious working of the invisible world. I wanted to help her in healing and teaching Reiki but here in the centre I could not do so because the centre was in partnership. And I could not do so without my partner's permission. I wrote the details of her session in my diary.

But we were willed to meet very soon as my partner became very interested after reading details of her session. He agreed to teach her Reiki and heal her from her problems saying that she has something special in her and we must help her in hour of need.

Next day she called me to inform that she is feeling very low and had been crying whole day. She said, "I cannot wear that crystal locket, it makes me very restless, I cannot tolerate it'. I did not know the reason for her this problem with crystal at that time. I told her that crystal helps to protect from negative energy coming to you and increases your energy level. I also informed her about my partner's willingness in healing her. Her first experience had given her the hunch to become ***conspicuous of the Divine plan for both of us***. Whatever she saw and felt in the session was not mere imagination and she could not dismiss it as useless. There definitely is some relevance in it. As for me, I was thinking that my higher self is showing me the way by confirming earlier predictions and experiences that there definitely is something in store for me. With gratefulness I was reminded of the truth behind this saying, which says, 'when one door closes, it opens the way for ten other doors'. Thus she started coming to healing center and I started healing and teaching her.

I was wondering who is Narender? She had said, a golden glowing face which became alive and took her to her room and gave her crystal. In her next meeting when I asked her about him. She described he was wearing a saffron turban and angrakha (Shirt). I intuitively asked her something like Vivekananda used to wear? She replied, "He was Vivekananda himself". I further wanted to know, "did you have some relation with him in the past"? She said, "no, you had been his disciple and he had come for you".

Session 2 – Next session 30th March.

She reached in one temple where far away one old man was doing prayers with rosary. There were few idols in the temple and it did not have roof top, it was open from top. Same Guruji came and took her to one cave. 'We have reached now in Vaishno Devi Temple' (Goddess temple in hills of J&k state) she started narrating what she was feeling and seeing. 'I am standing in the water. It's very cold. I am searching something there in that temple.'

For her present life relationship with Rajat, I asked her to see the cause in any of her past life.

Past life –She immediately started, "I am five years old, on the sea beach, may be in Goa. My name is Anu. Mummy is wearing a Sari. I am in frock. Rajat is younger to me and we both are playing. His name is Sonu. Now we have come home. It's a huge house, there are servants around. But we are only two of us and one very old man probably uncle (kaka). Mummy has given me something to eat. I kept share from it in a Tiffin box for Sonu". And she sounded as if she is weeping. I was surprised at this sudden change in her mood, I asked her, "why are you crying? In a childish tone, she complained, "mummy is scolding me. She is reprimanding me, asking me not to play with Sonu" I asked, why? "He is not of our status. But I like to play with him and share things with him".

"I am fifteen years old and studying in the school. Sonu doesn't go to school. He works with his father. We both are still friends. When I turn twenty one years, I am getting married. My bridegroom's name is Ajay. He is very tall and handsome. It's our departure and we are sitting in one decorated car. Sonu is standing quietly. Both of us are very sad. I am not able to control my tears. After travelling some distance, our car collides and tumbles down the deep gorge. We both are dead. From my body one spark appeared and reached that Temple and merged in that Idol. ***There after I was in that place only***. At this I asked her, "who helped you to reach that Idol and merge in that idol"? A- "That old baba, who was doing rosary in that temple where I had gone in the beginning". Whenever I asked her about the time and year, she always said, 'I don't know' (*pata nahi*).

In between life- "This is in Kulu, (A place in H P) my temple Vaagh Devi Veena Badini (Goddess Sarasvati). It is on a very steep hill. Now I am there. Small children are playing near this temple. Rajat is also there as a small child. His name is Bitu. I am watching him. He is also watching me. He doesn't know that I am there. He has come to stay in the shade of that temple (*chhaya lene aya hai*). He is eating my Prasad (Sweet distributed in the temple). He does not recognize my presence there but I care for him, he is my friend from the past life (*ye pichale janam ka dost hai*)."

Now I sensed that she is seeing that Life when ***she remembers as being worshipped as Goddess***. ***Or was she there in-between life*** stage ?(after death a spiritual existence ,a small halt after one earthly life ,the freedom from earthly laws, to enjoy the reward for the time earned by our deeds on earth ,time to contemplate and prepare till the time we are born again as physical beings) Had her consciousness merged in that Idol, till the time she was born again ?

I asked her, "Who all are coming there and how are you helping them "? She replied, "One woman has come, her name is Ahilya. She doesn't have any child. I gave her one flower. And she is blessed with a child". She was saying as if everything is happening now and here.

My past -Then suddenly she chirped and radiated, "Arrey, Nimmi also has come. She is very small. She is playing harmonium. Her father doesn't allow her to come here. She is crying. I am telling her, you don't cry. I gave her this crystal mala to wear. She comes here stealthily. She desires name and fame in music (*kala mei naam pana chahti hai*). She is remembering somebody". I knew now that she is talking about ***me*** so I asked her,"whom is she remembering"?

Anjana –"she wants to meet Lord Krishna (*Krishna ko pana chahti hai*) she is singing one Bhajan" (Devotional song). I inquired, "Can you listen, what are the wordings of the Bhajan she is singing"? Anjana- (*meri nayia paar lagalo*) " ***row my boat across***". (I had never heard this Bhajan before this, but there after it kept ringing in my ears and making me feel very connected to its deeper meaning. I was thinking, did I sing this song in my past life? But I am facing this situation now, feeling alone and seeking path for further evolution in this life. Was my situation same in my past life"?)

From there I guided her to go to the origin of her problem, probably her relationship with Rajat or some other reason for her miseries in this life.

Muslim life – Tantric work - To see her problems in this life, she went back to a life when she is a Muslim lady. She said, "I am a Muslim lady, I am married and have two children. I am still young but my husband is no more alive. There is one Butcher, his name is Akram. My name is Fatima. Akram keeps watching me while coming and going through the road in that small street. Once he has caught me from my hand. I slapped him and ran away from there. It is sin for me to even touch some other man. Now he is in the Mosque. I am also standing there. He is telling something to that Moulvi (Muslim cleric) I want this lady.(*mujhe ye Mohtrima chahiye*). Moulvi sent me away from there. He wants to protect me. This Moulvi is Rajat's father in this life. And he is same old baba who was in that temple.

Now Akram is going to one (Dargah) Muslim saint's grave. He tied one thread over there. He has wished for me through that thread. But I am married, I have kids, this cannot happen. But heart in heart I seem to have liking for him, after all he desires me so dearly. He has become old now; he has even left that work of a butcher. He is dead and has been buried. Now I am also dead. I am also buried at his side by same Moulvi. Because he had wished to get me. My mind was tied to him, though physically I could not be his while alive. And she recognized him; he is Rajat in this life.

I healed her from her that past by freeing from that thread where her mind had got attached to him. For healing purpose, I also rescripted the past in to a positive and full filling way. Giving her suggestion to feel and imagine that you both have got married in that life , you both have lived a very happy life, fulfilled all your wishes and desires and finally die as a satisfied couple. All the desires from that life had been fulfilled mentally, where there was memory for those unfulfilled desires has been erased now and replaced with fulfilment..

Now I asked her to go up ***in the sky to meet any guide***. She said, 'same guide Tajender ji Maharaj is there. And she started talking on her own giving subconscious feedback of our relationships from past life.

Our relationship in the past.

Past life- She continued, "We both have been together in many past lives. I am born in a poor colony (jhugi).You have come there searching for me. You are a British lady. You have chosen me and brought me with you. You want to educate and bring me up. Rajat is also there in that colony. He is much older to me. He is a doctor. You brought me to your home. Your family members are annoyed with you for bringing me to your house. You are not married yet. You have left your home and we have come to Manali. You have opened a school for the poor. Now you have opened a home for the destitute. Arrey, you have named it after my name! I asked her, 'what, Anjana'? She corrected me, 'No, no, ***Vaagh Devi Anathalya (orphanage)*** (Vaagh Devi is the name of Goddess).We have started many such schools. Now you have got married to one British man, he is your present husband. He is taking you away from there. You did not want to go. You have handed over to me all the responsibilities of schools and homes and gone from there. I am also growing old now, giving my entire attention to look after these schools. I die in my ripe old age. I have been buried in one grave. Many people are praying for me.

She had done Sadhna in many past lives

I was both confused as well as filled with wonder at this story. At one time she is a goddess and in another life she is a destitute. In one life she is helping me and in another I am bringing her up. So I asked her, "Why and how you got stabilized as that Goddess in that temple"? She explained, 'I have meditated in many lives(tapasya ki hai). I can see that I am in a white sari,sitting on some hill meditating in solitude. I asked her, "What did you achieve by such meditation"?

Anjana-"(Vaak Shakti, door drishti, divya drishti, sangeet) wish fulfilling speech, foresight, divine vision, and music".

Q –Who stabilized you in that temple?

Anjana- "That baba who was meditating in that Vaishno Devi temple , he was also that Moulvi and he is Rajat's father in this life".

Q- "Then why so many downfalls came in your life? Born as destitute and falling victim to black magic etc"?

Past life -Anjana-"This is the time of Sikh Gurus in Punjab. I am twenty years old. I have meditated in previous lives and I am doing Sadhna in this life also. I am knowledgeable in this life too. One sadhu is feeling hurt by seeing my knowledge. He doesn't want that I should progress further. I have a debate with him. His ego is hurt. He has cursed me. So now I am in to very miserable lives. I became Fatima. This Baba only saved me in that life time also. In today's life also he has blessed me so much because I had served him few months back when he wasn't well. He likes me so much and has blessed me that if not with Rajat, May you be happy, wherever you are"!.

I asked her to find out from her guide that why you both are together in many lives but could never marry and have a fulfilling relationship? She replied, "Guruji is saying, '***this cycle has been going on like this only and will continue to go on***'. I asked her, "Do you want to come out of this cycle"? She said, "I do not want to leave him. After all, he had wished for me. That is why he tied that thread around that tree in the *Dargah*. I also wanted him heart in heart but I was tied down by social customs. I was buried beside him." Now I had to convince her, "you never had a happy married life in your past lives. You both were never married in any of the earlier times. Now also he doesn't wish to marry you, we cannot force anybody to love us and commit to us. He has changed his mind now. There may be some good in this for both of you. May be you both would not be happy together in this life. Then why not be sensible and face harsh reality and take some firm decision". Somehow she became willing to cut away from him. I healed her and also gave positive affirmation to her subconscious mind. After that she was crying so much and I also let her cry, so that she could feel lighter.

Next meeting she told me that she kept crying for two ,three days that she felt weak and drained out. She did not eat anything because it wasn't easy to cut her relationship with Rajat. She was so devoted to him that if he would be willing, she would go out of the way to please him. She could not think of leaving him or somebody taking his place. But the problem was he wasn't willing for commitment now. She was awake most of the time and whenever she fell asleep, she would dream of some time getting drowned, somebody is tying her with ropes, somebody is pulling her back, she is falling in the gorge. She could not wear the crystal locket in her neck; the one I had given to her in our first meeting. The moment she wore it, she would feel much heat and restless in her mind, she would be forced to remove it.

Next Session - I asked her to see one by one all those visions and healed these by releasing into the universal fire for transmutation and purification. She went on to describe what all was being released from her.

She said, 1. 'Somebody is throwing broom on me. 2. Black thread is tied on to the tree. 3. One havan kund is burning . 4. One black lady is asking one tantric to do something on my head. 5. A black dog is licking my head. 6. A horse is standing, some body is throwing ashes on me. I am completely drowned in the heap of ashes."

I asked her, "How is it affecting you"? She Said, "My hands and feet are trembling, my body is listless, my heart is tied down. I have no strength to move. I can't think anything".

Source of negative attacks – I asked her to view the origin of all these things simultaneously, so that these can be released from her . She said, "it is my aunt,(taayi) asking this tantric to tie my mind so that I may not progress in life. Some nails are planted in somebody's house; the man of the house is requesting me to clear his house. And those nails have got stuck in to me'.

She was clairvoyant -Actually she had this gift from her childhood that she could see aura of people and pull out any such negative attacks on them. Some people had recognized her capability and were asking her to help them out. But same negative things were getting attracted and retained in to her. She had no protection and no means to clear herself from all these and were affecting her adversely. Though she was inclined towards worship/ rituals from her childhood and had done lots of mantra chanting, rituals and fasting. But all this didn't seem to protect her and she was falling into the clutches of negativity to the extent that she was even contemplating suicide. Known and unknown people were taking her help without giving her any due and worth reward, whereas her family members were oblivious to her talent. They always looked down upon her and taunted her.

Session 4th March – Today she was calm and composed. Again in her session she saw few other such things which were imbedded in her. I wanted to clarify, "are these same things which were released earlier"? She answered that the origin of these things are somewhere else, which were not cleared that day. After healing these, her Guruji Tajender ji Maharaj came. She said, 'He is giving me few limes, some mustard seeds, turmeric (haldi). He is giving me water'. I advised her to wash her face with it and also drink it. It is purifying, cleansing and energizing you. She did same thing and replied, "I am feeling much better and relaxed. There after she was being given higher wisdom described below.

Good or bad, you make it on your own.

Higher Wisdom – She said, "Now Guruji is giving me mud. He is taking me to a potter, there he is showing me ,how he is making different vessels from that same wet mud, "you can also shape up your life. With this mud, the surahi (long necked pitcher) and Gh-ada (short necked pot) are made. Water can also be kept in it and Alcohol can be stored in it. Same way you can shape up your body and life as you wish. *Good or bad, you make it on your own.* Now the past cycle is broken. So you are free to exercise your discretion". "He is giving me one small bag (batua) full of coins to keep it safely".

Hearing the higher wisdom of her guide come through her and her readiness to accept the past cycle break for better things.

Future healing -I asked her, "would you like to marry somebody else now'? Then you can visualize it is happening now. She affirmed, "It cannot happen, I cannot see it because there is some wall which is preventing me to view it". I sensed, it is her mental wall. I dissolved that with healing light. Then I asked her to see it again. She said, "Yes, he is Aditya. (**The one she had announced was at the healing center with her and me.**) He is the same Ajay with whom I had married when we both had met an accident and died in one life (she herself recognized this person and her past connection with him)". I asked her,"Where are you meeting Aditya for the first time"? She said, "There is a Talk show on radio and afterwards he is saying, he wants to meet me". I asked her to see how they are getting married. She said, "It is a simple court marriage". (**That is why future is probable,fifty percent is destiny and fifty percent are self efforts.** Whatever she saw her relationship and infatuation with ***Rajat***, it was created by her unfulfilled desires. She could not break free from him even though they both were poles apart. He was very dominating, pragmatic ambitious youth. She too had strong desire to prove to the world to be someone on her own.. They both would always be tussling to prove one worthy and not lesser than the other. She would not have a happy life ahead with him .Yet she wanted to continue this relationship because she was not free from mechanically following same cycle all over again.. Next probability was meeting Ajay and may be marrying him.

Our past connection – She moved on to see our past connection again. "I am a sadhvi (female saint). You are Meera (Krishna Devotee). You have come to me". I asked her, '"then why are we not able to fulfill our Sadhna in many lives"? She continued, "People, circumstances and distractions. We have been losing the insight and getting swayed away. A man---Rajat, in that life also I got infatuated with this man and left my Sadhna as I did in this life". Now she was addressing me, "Your mother in law is your mother in law from many life times. She was your mother in law during Meera's time too. She did not approve of your path of renunciation and devotion. She has got her own definition of woman's dharma. So in each birth you both meet to teach each other, you want her to mend her ways and she wants to teach you her ways of doing things".

Next verdict by Anjana was that your present husband is from the time when you were a British lady and you had brought me up. Your husband from Meera time will come to you for healing of abdominal problem later and you will be able to recognize him due to dream beforehand. I wasn't asking her much because **whatever she was revealing to me was far too much to accept and digest at this moment.** But in between she was going on telling something and I was taking note of it irrespective of my readiness to accept it at that time. Our conscious mind can never be unbiased and non-judgmental. This was the one important thing I had learnt and was trying to apply it in my life as much as by accepting things, I could easily digest.

In-between she was falling asleep for a long time that I had to get up and attend to some other work. Normally she wasn't able to sleep because of the problems she was having in life, forth coming exam, her disturbed mental state, worry about future and present financial crunch. During healing she would see her ***chakra being cleansed.*** She would see weird things coming out from her chakras, smoke, sand, mud, black cloth, thick black greasy substance, blood, wood ,wire, stones. After clearing all these things she would be in a relaxed state, free from all her worries and would go into deep sleep.

At times in sleep she would scream , 'somebody is crushing my head , somebody is scraping things from my mind , my head is bleeding , there is a hole in the centre of my head. It is paining there'. ***Her healing sessions were so exhausting that at times I too felt intense headache and felt drained out.***

Her guide always came sometimes giving her lime pieces, mustard seeds, honey etc. Sometime showing symbolic pictures of some events giving us higher wisdom and understanding of the mystic world. When I asked her whether her guide wants to give me some guidance about your healing, she always nodded in, 'no'. He is not saying anything about healing, leaving everything on you as you desire.

Her Visions giving proofs of healing -In between she described some of her visions. She said, "I a had vision that you are busy in writing a book and asking me to stay at your house as the work has increased too much. I am helping you in writing the book. I know that you are also writing my case in it. I am requesting you, 'please didi, don't write about me people will come to know and I will feel embarrassed'. You are telling me , 'you have given me future vision, through you I have received guidance that how I have to work and progress further, so your case is very important. I can hide your identity and change the name, that's what most writers do to hide the identity of the characters '. Convinced at this I go to the kitchen to make coffee and you start working on computer".

Vision –"Now I am in my hostel room and one of my colleague is asking me , 'how are you ? I tell him, 'no, I am not all right, I am thinking of committing suicide as nothing is pleasing me in my life". (This was a cleansing process, it was releasing negativity which was created by contemplating suicide as an alternative, not able to withstand the problems of life).

Distance healing -She also told me that she saw me doing her distance healing. I was surprised, I asked her, "how did you know that I was sending distance healing to you"? She replied, "I saw you were sitting in a white dress in your room and healing me in the morning. Some light vibrations were coming towards me, which were releasing some dark shades from my body, in turn I was feeling lighter and relaxed".

Sensing Mystic Energy Around us -Session –She was seeing negative energy in any of the above mentioned form and I was releasing it one by one by directing Reiki energy . She could see how cleansing is happening, which colour is entering and filling up while healing. She was opening me up for the truth about our energy body, our mystic influences without my realizing at that time. I had decided to accept everything as truth; it is that person's own truth. It is being revealed to me through her, it may have some purpose for me though not everything.

She was clairvoyant -Then one strange thing happened in one of her session which proved that she was clairvoyant and could see person's aura clearly at least when in regression session. I do not want to give more importance to this experience of her for the purpose of highlighting other person's negative traits but for the purpose of its importance in opening me up to yet another reality and ***verifying Ayan's revelations,*** which I had otherwise rejected thinking his conscious interpretation of my situation.

I was healing her and she was giving me feedback of the effect happening on her. Suddenly she started revealing something which I took some time to understand. She said, "Somebody has tied my nerves in my mind". I tried to open it with Reiki energy. She said, "yes , but somebody else is also cutting them open now". I thought maybe she is seeing the Guide who may be healing her (we all know that Guide takes over from healer when we are in deep healing meditation and healing happens in Higher dimension) I asked her to see, "who is doing it "? She said, "He is telling me, "follow me, and work for me". I thought such close encounter with Guides! I encouraged her to listen to him, maybe he is some Guide. Ask him what sort of work he wants you to do for him? She said, "He is telling me that you work for me, I want to hypnotize you. He is some earthly being and I seem to know him. His intensions are not good. He is staring at me with some strange feelings. His eyes are sending some very uncomfortable vibes. He is snatching the bag (*batua*) full of coins which my Guruji had given me. I am scared, shall I open my eyes? But why have I given my bag of coin to him"? She almost screamed. Now I got suspicious of this person,and I was trying to control the situation to get rid of his influence on her. In the mean time she questioned, "sir,you? He is Mr Kumar". I was startled and so was Mr Kumar, my colleague in healing center who was sitting there and pretending to heal her along with me. Hearing his name, he felt so caught up that he asked me to bring her back from regression and in desperation he got up. Her eyes were still closed yet she shouted loudly , " but why has he stood up? Tell him to sit down". I hurriedly brought her back. She sat up and very firmly and consistently asked Mr Kumar, "What were your intensions? I could see very uncomfortable vibes from your eyes". He was feeling very awkward and did not say much to her other than this that may be there was something in subconscious, 'what can we say of the subconscious mind'. (Now I realized that I was healing her and he was pretending to heal her sitting there but knowing about her capabilities as revealed by her through her sessions, he was trying to possess her by asking her subconscious to follow him, work for him and also almost snatched the bag of coin. (May be it was symbolic of collection of her powers, which she had gathered by doing Sadhna in many life times.)

As after this session my healing centre was closed forever. Logically there were many reasons, I had failed in my first project to open a healing center. But illogically it had served its purpose. I had learnt few important things and learning is a continuous process, failures teach more than success. I had to be opened to certain mystic truths in life, in which I did not want to believe because I had never had any experiences in any way negativity affecting me. Having positive outlook, I had concluded that everything is good. Good and bad always exists, as these are two poles of creation. If I wanted to tread further in this inward journey, I had to learn to accept everything and slowly I was being given the lessons in each topic, and I had decided to accept lame and tiger in me, so in everybody. Not to be judgmental, self-righteous moral guardian and become picky to condemn others.

Lesson* -1-*Honesty -To be successful in this obscure field, in the real sense, honesty is the key word. While healing session, it is not only the client who is opening up to his truth but he can also see things and access energy of others through and through. She was not only seeing her past and future but was sensing my aura also. So could have done Ayan and given me the feedback which I had not given much importance at that time. But now I was contemplating on his revelations more openly. Divinity was again giving me a chance to accept the reality of mysterious working of the invisible world.

2 Destiny – Her sessions confirmed working of conspicuous divine plan. Everything has some purpose. Nothing is useless. Nothing comes from nowhere. We are creator of our own destiny. My vision has some purpose, so were predictions given in Nadi Astrology to help me move in the right direction. We are so closely being guided and guarded by our Higher Self.

3. ***Confidence*** – We can heal anybody anywhere; this is proved and even can be shown to others also. This can bring confidence in our capabilities and be instrumental in realizing our responsibility. I had the courage and intension that is why without much knowledge, experience and finances I had opened a healing centre. If my intensions are pure, and I strive consistently without becoming the doer of the action, then I will be guided and protected. I don't need to fear anything from outside world but I have to be watchful of my inside (ego and desires).

4 ***Optimist*** -Practically proved that failure teaches more than success and all experiences are for learning. Nobody is to harm us, no failure is to break us. Failures are to teach us that there is still more to learn from. Negative people are the contrast background to teach us that duality will exist. ***They are for us to bring us face to face with this truth about life.*** The outcome entirely depends on our attitude to accept things sportingly and responsibly in our strides. In higher plan of hings there is nothing good or bad. Surrender and selfless action will manifest the best for our higher good. Self-pity, blaming others or God is not the syllabus of my class. Because everybody's higher self has created his syllabus, framed question paper and now we have to find answer and explanation to justify it.

5 ***Discretion*** – Life is a bit of everything but one bit is not everything. Every path, every subject has some truth to offer but not everything. One can take help from different agencies in times of confusion and delusions but not depend totally on any one thing. One has to use own discretion, our Viveka and also exert our human endeavour. She started giving feedback to me about my work in the direction of writing and healing at times through her Visions. Which didn't correlates all the time in terms of proclaimed time, Yet it was giving me direction to some extent. Devoting time to write a book so soon was influenced by her revelations in her first session. I was also seeking guidance through my inner self. Nadi Astrology had also predicted

that I will be doing research in energy, crystals, chemicals or medicine. But I will have to upgrade, modernize and work hard to make my knowledge acceptable to people. I understood it that my research is help people open to experience mystic energy world influences.

6 *Watching my steps* -One important cause of her suffering in this life was also this clairvoyance. People were getting benefited from her talent but she could not be benefited much and was very negative towards her life situation. Was she fulfilling the past prayers of people by revealing to them their future or remedy for the present problems? Why wasn't she able to benefit herself from this faculty? I was just learning and thanking universe for not desiring in me some miraculous powers which would make me miserable in longer run and thwart my growth. There are no short cuts for evolution but to learn from the situation.. Balanced growth in life is the sure short way to progress.

7 ***Endeavour*** -She revealed many things which were beyond our comprehension at that time. As she saw that there is one mountain and there is no path to reach there. She was seeing very distant probable future and I have to work towards that direction to reach there. I have been shown the destination but I have to chalk out my path . Thus I cannot totally rely on anything but seek inner direction and work hard in the direction of my destination. I understood the importance of human endeavour and not become fatalist. Time does not change; we have to make efforts to change time.

8 ***How conscious acceptance*** of facts seeps to become subconscious? When I asked her to see my guide,she surprisingly announced, 'it is pixy(my pet bitch) and you are saying that I will prove it'. I was consciously accepting my pets' presence as a teaching for me. She confirmed that how I had vowed to prove it to others subconsciously. She narrated the incident of one year back when I was healing and teaching Reiki to my husband's cousin, who was suffering from ptosis of eye lid. She said, "you are healing someone, who resembles sir, (my husband) but is heftier and has got moustache. But he doesn't believe what you are saying. You kept quiet and saying with-

in yourself that 'I will prove it'". She could narrate this much only and rest I knew what had happened? When I had opinioned that dogs (animals) are more closer to God because they don't have judgmental minds, he just wouldn't listen to any of my explanations and dismissed it my insanity saying that whatever you may say this Reiki and all, to some extend I can agree but I cannot believe that animals are more closer to God. Sensing no use in arguing with people who have closed themselves for certain facts I just kept quiet but internally I was sure of what I was trying to explain is true. Later, pets as my guides have been confirmed by few other people whom I had regressed.

8 ***Reinforced faith in crystals*** –Initially she could not wear crystal, that surprised me. Later once she herself gave me feedback of the crystal pencil used for healing, which had broken without my knowledge. She said, "it has turned black and breaking in to two pieces". I asked, 'why? She replied, "You are healing a man. for some other problem, probably head but he has got some other problem. His heart is blocked, his kidneys are weak. With his negativity, the crystal broke down." I had to agree that I had healed through distance healing my another brother in law who had head injury two years back. To doctors' surprised ,he had regained conscious within two months and improved eighty percent in six month. But he lacks self-effort and does not take any interest in his health by doing some exercise or yoga as advised by the doctors. In the month of August 2006, I had personally tried to heal him by regression and past life but wasn't successful as he could not concentrate on my voice and would become detached and thoughtless.'

9.Internal Vision -Now she stopped going to any of her past lives but started seeing her ethereal body for her problems, her chakras, and nadis and even her organs. She could see the cause of the problem, see healing happening to that part and remedial measure in the form of some medicine or diet and how it is helping her eradicate that problem. For example ***her obesity*** was due to her faulty diet. She eats bread, potato, brinjal and some such food. It is dry inside as she doesn't drink much water ,so the food is not getting dissolved and broken down to become energy and absorbed in the body rather its getting stuck to her body as fat.

Her ***thyroid problem*** looked as if there were tea leaves stuck to the sieve and obstructing flow of the hormone. Which were getting dissolved by sending healing light there as if slowly opening up the blocked holes allowing fluid flush through her entire body. Some of her nadis looked obstructed and blocked which were being cleared and opened while healing.

10.Substitute healing – She worked as a conduit for substitute healing for her mother. Her mother had cerebral stroke due to high blood pressure. She requested me to send her mother distance healing. She had lost her speech and the right side was completely paralyzed. Within a week her condition had improved and was able to lift her hand, which even surprised doctors there. After she was discharged from the hospital she came to me for her mother's healing by becoming a channel or substitute to heal her mother. She saw how and why her mother is getting attack? When she is visiting some hospital few days back , in the hospital some ***spirit had attacked*** her. Now she is becoming more negative and her body is becoming tense. On that fateful day she had gone to one of the neighbour's house where she is being offered water. That lady had very negative attitude towards her mother. As her mother comes home, she is feeling very uneasy and faints. When I asked her to see the origin of all these problems, she saw some box type coming out from her mind and ***declared it is her past deeds***. She saw how my healing was reaching her mother. She could see spirits getting dissolved by the healing light which we were directing at her distantly by us. Within a month she was back to her daily routine and could talk. While doing her mother's healing this way she saw that there was also a spirit attack on my mother in law. Which is making her negative towards my work in healing. When I wanted to heal the spirit possessing my mother in law she could not continue further session as she felt tired and unable to concentrate. So I understood that this is not meant to be healed by her.

If I start writing all her sessions then it would make one full book because for five years she kept coming to me for some or the other reasons . She herself kept informing me about her visions about me. Which are sometimes warning to me about a forth coming danger I do not deny significance of her vision simply because what she saw about my life, it did not manifest same way. I know it was probable occurrence and since I had taken her information as a warning and healed the forth coming probable event it had changed for better.

***Learning from* failures** –

Negative experiences are to teach us to accept the other side of the coin and practically experience the relevant truth. These are to open our blocked mind which is rejecting the multifaceted nature of life. I could have avoided writing incident where she could sense the energy around her during regression. (***Clairvoyant)*** because it describes some body's not so noble intensions. What I had learnt through her, I have to be honest to share it with others, because at times she had revealed things regarding my mental state making me feel uncomfortable but I had to accept it.

I don't want to hide anything as I learnt from Dolores Cannon (author Conversation With A Spirit and Prophecies Of Nostradamus) lecture that what we hide or mislead people, we have to come back to undo that again. So to clear my conscious and may be heal this person (my colleague) of the guilt by bringing it out in to the light.

-When I first started sharing some of my inner experiences with my colleague in my healing center. I felt he sounded suspicious or jealous. He discouraged me, why do you look outside, you must learn to go within. I felt upset as on my part I didn't know what is inside and outside. I was having such experiences because I was healing certain people and myself. I had requested my mind to accept any information which may be helpful in my progress but may be unpalatable to me because of ego. Thus his words were always ringing in my mind. Did this intension paved the way for accepting messages from various sources for myself progress rather than shine forth in my healing capabilities and guarantee remedy for any ailment and feed my ego.

-One of his sarcastic prophecies was that within few years you will have powers to heal anything by just touching or wishing to do so. I jokingly replied that I don't want to have any such powers within me so that somebody may kidnap me and force me to misuse this Divine power . Besides I don't believe in becoming a life saviour or a crusader rather my intension is to awaken everybody to their true nature and make him strive to work towards becoming their own master. I want to be like an honest teacher who doesn't want to teach his student to just pass the exam by any means. My idea is to teach child to understand the topic so that it will help in longer run not just somehow pass one single exam.

-He would try to influence me not to follow the importance of healing. Rather he was keen in meditation for gaining powers and experience spiritual growth. But reflecting and using my own discretion weighed the importance of healing and helped me go deeper in healing. Which was confirmed to me later in Gnostic teaching that we have to pay back our debt to humanity by doing service or healing humanity. We may erase our memory by meditating and healing self but we have to heal society by erasing memory of sufferings from the society. They have not forgiven us for the sufferings we had caused them in the past. That is why many highly evolved spiritual people suddenly are faced with some unbelievable allegations or have to undergo sufferings. They have definitely attained some spiritual heights in this life that is why they have so many followers. But because they don't want to accept their negative side at all or are not aware of their negative Karma in the past. Prarabdh karma, which we have accumulated in the long journey of life through millennium , which is their debt to the society. So the same person was showing me direction, same was creating confusion and misleading to go astray from the path. Also forced me to listen to my inner voice and use my discretion not to depend on outside sources to show me the path. Which weighed more on the side of healing people unconditionally at that time.

-Knowing about my intension of writing a book on my experiences, he had introduced me to one of his relative to seek some guidance, who had written/ translated a book on Astrology (Laal Kitab). This person's advice to me was that you must learn to write to sell yourself, otherwise nobody will buy your book. To which my conscious reply was , " I don't want to write to sell myself , I want to write because I really want to write something'. There after I had postponed about writing book in the later part of my life when I would be able to really write what I want to write. Was Universe listening at that time and testing my intensions? Whether I am tempted and allured by the outside world (name and fame) and ready to sell myself or my intensions are still deeper? Thus sending me guidance this way!(Anjana)

-My husband had warned me by seeing some of the topics of my first book that nobody is going to understand what you are writing. I had told him that it's not for everybody as everybody cannot yearn and afford pearls of wisdom but there may be some takers for this too.

-My dream that Guruma is asking me to close down the center saying ,' if you think that you will earn money from it, then you better close it. That time I could not follow the deeper meaning behind this dream but I was pondering upon its significance. If I wish to earn name , fame and money then I must close this center and Guru ma (My higher Self) tells everybody same thing. Because this is not the real purpose of life. If we listen to our Higher self, it will guide and take us through the roads leading to real purpose of life. I had totally surrendered to manifest the best for my higher evolution, which is more important for me than temporary name and fame. There were these revelations by Nadi Astrology and Anjana, where I had come to know about distant destination for me. It made me accept closing down of healing center not affect me as a conventional failure. I had learnt so much and I have to move on. Wasn't Divinity testing, guiding and making me reflect and assisting by verifying from outwards sources in drawing my own conclusion.

Truth has many levels –It is very important to understand here why truth has many levels making life confusing full of contradictions and paradoxes. As Shakespeare said, 'there are many things existing between heaven and earth unknown to man,' because there are so many things beyond our comprehension. Why Rajat was not interested in marrying her now, where as she says that in their past life he had so strongly wished for her. Or any other such case for that matter. She was seeing her reality, which may not be the truth for Rajat or anybody else. It is her truth that she remembers being worshipped as Goddess. Apart from her own Sadhna she also gives credit for it to Rajat's father for establishing her in that temple. Whether it was her in-between life existence or anything else, that is beside the point. Same way may be Rajat has been healed of his infatuation for her by any or other such means done by some other evolved soul. (That is why praying for others is emphasized in all the religions)

Criticizing and judging unknown things is a sin- just be non-judgmental

Here I want to draw attention to one important point of utmost concern. We worldly wise (Karma pradhan) pragmatic people always criticize and negate the importance of Sages or saints, who are only meditating and not doing anything productive in the worldly sense. If we believe in God or some superpower, we have to understand that everything is perfect at the moment, but trying to evolve further by breaking free from the cycle. Thief or saint all are part of that overall Divine plan. In any department/organisation some are doing active role, others are doing passive role. There are board of directors, who are not in direct contact with the general public. They are making rules and setting policies. Some are advertising, some are giving feedback. Some are collecting material, making data. There are only few implementing these policies by directly working in the public. Wordly action can be compared to this direct action and contact. But we cannot deny the importance of any of the above mentioned in the chain of events followed in the procedure. Same way some may be stealing or misusing the plan. These are instrumental in bringing out the loopholes in the plan, so that pilferage can be stopped and further improvements can be done. Now if the thief is causing loss and pain to others and also creating negative karma for himself then, he should be helped to reform /change for better. Punishing him to stop from repeating such misdeed is a step to maintain balance in the nature and break the cycle to evolve further. Same way how do we ***know which Saint is internally trying to heal, transform or is working to bring awareness in whom?*** I may have been helped to reach this understanding by many such selfless souls whom I do not recognize now. In the past ignorantly I may have also criticized them. But after becoming aware of the importance of the role each one is playing in this Divine plan, I ask forgiveness from them and show my gratefulness to every actor (saint or fraud) for teaching me valuable lessons of life. We all are only playing our part trying to perfect by becoming that character for the moment. We are becoming so involved with the character we are playing in this drama of life that we even forget that we are all actors trying to perfect our part. We are not only repaying back for our actual deeds (good or bad) we are also receiving repercussions for judging or blaming others without really trying to understand their role in the sequence of events shaping up our life in particular and society in general. We are only criticizing because the other person is just the reflection of us, may be a cheat or liar or the epitome of quality we admire but haven't yet achieved it. Either one should be inspired to do the good deeds of the saintly person so that one can become the recipient of reward for good deeds or one should learn from the thief not to hurt others so that he does not have to repay back later with regret and remorse. There should be only these two outcomes of our observations of things and people around us. This is the first step to practice non judgment. *)*

Important note –. Things which higher world wanted me to know were being revealed through Anjana ,so that I can take clue from it. It is not that anything I wanted to know consciously or Anjana would like to tell me, she would see. Though she was a clairvoyant, yet she was utterly miserable and felt very negative about her life situation on the whole. When it comes to taking any guidance for herself she could not see much. She was always shown very distant and probable future and she would feel frustrated as she was not anywhere near working towards that direction. She had to first solve her present problems. She confided in me later that whenever I have a problem and need some help in regard to finding some solution for myself, I start praying to show me some way out but instead of getting answer I start seeing you. Sometime you are facing some problem, sometime it's about your progress or unexplainable things and at times you are feeling very restless or physically unwell, some psychic attack being directed on you.

Today have you discontinued my healing ? She inquired me. 'You were saying that now you do your own healing' At time she really surprised me by giving such feedback. 'I acknowledged her revelation and said, ' yes, for past two months , I was taking your case as a first priority and today I decided to replace it because I have done enough for you and also taught you Reiki. So from now on wards you can do it yourself and not keep depending on me'.

Described my mental state - In one session she told me , 'now you are not that sincere in my healing. You have also become very irritable and don't allow anybody's interference in your work. In every life you had been forgetting the right path ahead and were always dragged in to the mundane world. But now you have started making forward movement. You start your progress from your family. All your people will accept you. Their time hasn't come yet , your time has come. Your interviews are coming up, articles are being printed. Your book is complete till page forty five but most of the material will be edited, new material will come up. You will leave this house very soon.

Seeing my inner world - she said, 'there is one beautiful lotus flowering on your head but then it closes. You are in the sky and all Devi, Devtas are standing in the circle and blessing you. But nobody is looking at me. She was sounding bit unhappy at being ignored and all attention being paid to me. I tried to cheer her up by saying, 'but I can't even see this beautiful sight, it is you, who is seeing it, ***so you are my eyes'.*** There is some black ribbon tied around your neck. And you are feeling stifled because of this. When I asked her to see why it is there and see it being healed. She stopped seeing anything at all and said I am feeling very heavy and tired. I realized I have to heal it myself and to my surprise I now know each step I had been given hunches about healing of my throat center.

Later also she had been informing me of her vision about me and herself and wanting clarification on that.

Similar circumstances in my present life.

1.My **husband** had taken me away from the work I was pursuing in that life. Which was my soul's calling. In this life also his strong logical mind was totally closed to appreciate any importance of healing and meditation and would oppose me in my learning initially. I was stronger this time ,I could argue ,stand up for my right and gradually show him proofs of my inner connection..After having Nadi Astrology prediction, I could accept his opposition more openly and convince him as it was revealed in it that initially he will oppose my work but as he will get more proofs and be convinced, he will come forward directly help me in my work.

2 *My Devotion* - I was realizing my awakening after coming to Mathura in 1999 to live there for three years, as if I am reliving the Bhakti yuga. I learnt Reiki and healed my past, modified my present and transformed my future, that is why I started getting such direct feedback on mysteriously working of our life. It may be my modesty if I feel hesitant to describe one of my fanciful verdict after watching Hindi film Meera in Mathura. I told my husband that I feel I am at least a fraction of Meera(Krishna Devotee princess of medieval times). And it is there after that I started searching for collection of Meera's Bhajan and hearing these. I started wearing tulsi (sacred herb) beads necklace. This was objected by my friends saying that only widows wear tulsi necklace signifying that they are wedded to Krishna. I resisted and continued wearing clarifying my stand that first I am wedded to Krishna ,who is even Lord of my husband (*mere pati ka bhi pat hai Krishna*) then only I am wedded to my husband. Because there are few things which even my husband cannot give me and that only our Lord can give. Though I must confess that

I came out of any extreme follower ship because of Reiki. I had to be practical and moderate in accepting religion and spiritual connection yet be devoted to the higher evolution. Changed circumstances of my this life were, as she said, your father doesn't allows you to come here, follow this path of bhakti. Contrary to that in this life it was my father's great influence on me to imbibe values as truthfulness, service ,charity, gratefulness, seeking and devotion to God. He could not give me much material things but always blessed me and advised to take all his books collection. I had taken his Geeta and *Rudraksh* mala from his collection and started reading a page or two as a routine and chant names of different Gods on the *Rudraksha* mala without much deeper understanding and devotion just to do my bit from my side to feel a higher connection. My father in this life has been my first Guru.

3. ***Relationship with my mother in* law** -I was reminded of my childhood as one of my cousin had innocently drilled his imagination in my mind that Radha,Krishna and all the Gods are hiding in the mountains and if we keep watching at this mountain in front of our home in the hills of Shimla , slowly we will be able to hear Krishna's flute and gradually they willappear and give us Darshan by coming out from their hiding I had announced my decision at very young age when nobody expect us to talk about such things that I don't want to marry ,I want to become Meera and find Krishna. I was sure to find Him one day. Later when I grew up and started thinking of getting married, I was scared of doing so much of adjustment. I wanted to marry a person whose mother will not be alive or lived around us. This was an unconscious feeling, without any apparent experience of seeing any discord between daughter in law and mother in law in the vicinity. It is well said that what we resist, it persists and our fear will come true. My mother in law would have not liked to stay with us but circumstances were such that from the time I am married she is staying with us. Though I fully accept the fact my mother in law is an excellent person and a perfectionist. She has appreciated my good qualities and always meant my good. But this is a bitter truth that she never liked my way of dealing with

any thing in life. She has criticized my restless nature,fickle mindedness, impatience, imperfection, loud voice and fast speech, very talkative, wanting to do many things at a time and later my excessive involvement in healing and meditation etc. She has shown me my true self. When one becomes aware and accepts his short comings, one is capable to start making changes for better after exercising his discretion. I do not deny in me all the above mentioned not so good qualities but again it was because of accepting and recognizing these that I have reached where I am today. Had I been opposite of all said bad qualities, I would be peacefully relaxing and enjoying good life and crying at the unpleasant situations ,blaming other people and unavoidable circumstances and my fate. It is my imperfection ,which never made me perfect in anything so that I could boast off it and get stuck to keep it going in me. I had the courage to practice and consider every activity as a play, not fearing failure in healing and taking up any challenging cases coming my way , without much knowledge and experiences. Sometimes I may have neglected my household duties, sometime not followed the method accurately. At times I may not have devoted proper time, yet intended to achieve positive outcome yet I did not lose hope when failure knocked my door. My restlessness never allowed me to feel at peace till I had achieved some inner strength to manipulate laws of nature for our higher good. I had this problem of wanting to learn many things at a time and give my heart and soul to it but would soon get exhausted and loose interest. I had excess energy which wasn't channelized in particular direction'. My fickle mindedness was a means to experiment various things and seek right direction through trial and error method. This is my experience that no activity, no knowledge, no short coming is useless. If accepted in right perspective every shortcoming, every strength is here to give us hunches to keep proceeding in the direction towards real purpose of our life.)

Note. I am not here to clarify or to validate what was the source of her information. Was she the Goddess and I her devotee or the sceptics may feel it was her imagination? Since she was saying something about my life and I am writing memoir of my inner journey ,I want to clarify my stand in this regard.

She remembered being the Goddess in her session that clearly showed that she was part of that greater energy (goddess in the temple) merged at that time. *(Collectively we are all God , part of that big whole. We are spark of divinity manifested in physical body ,trying to realize our connection to that collective conscious)* Now she is feeling separated and living an independent existence full of sufferings. Consciously she doesn't remember this yet from her childhood she had been doing many rituals, worshiping and chanting, without any body guiding her to do so. Few people had recognized some capabilities in her and were asking her for help or remedy for some of their problems with accurate outcome. But they were not rewarding her amply making her feel miserable and used. She could not seek much direction for herself from her this gift of clairvoyance. ***Then were these people reaping the reward for their previous births' Sadhna and dedication***?

I on my part cannot deny her presence in my life as God giving me feedback and direction on unforeseen eventualities. Now and then she was conveying her visions about me , many things which might have not come true but I cannot negate their occurrence altogether. Since what she was seeing were probable occurrences and I have the faculty to apply my discretion and heal the event to more appropriate outcome.

Looking back I now realize the pattern of cases being healed by me at times coincided with my own healing of such problems arising in life. Her guidance such way was sometimes hidden in to the obscurity and at times it would give clear indication of the probable event and its outcome after healing.

Imagination, fears, desires have some seeds, some source of origin somewhere in the mind. That is why everybody is unique because his desires, fears and imagination have its unique reason and origin. She was directly verifying my state of mind by telling me some unpalatable hidden truths about my life, which I will describe in detail in my autobiographical book.

Why she kept coming to me for so long?

In past five years she had unaccountable sessions with me. Apart from her own causes, she had been seeing many symbolic visions which some I understood, some were beyond my comprehension. Though higher purpose of her coming to me may not be logical , yet I can cite two reasons for her need to come to me for so long.

1. She is there to verify my experiences. She has this talent (clairvoyance) many things which were in my mind, she could see it. Being strong logical mind, I would relegate it to the realm of my imagination. Is she the Goddess, whom I had worshipped in the past or my higher self, giving me guidance this way regarding my inner quest, efforts and direction I am treading in this life? Any way is right in which way one may feel comfortable to believe it.

2. It requires conscious effort to bring changes in the attitude

After her past life memories were healed yet she was seeing her attitude, her tendencies forcing her to view only the negative side of life and felt miserable at times. It requires conscious effort to bring changes to curve our natural tendencies. Not going in to the depth of her problems on which I had no control. Only her free will, her will power, her wisdom and above all her intension to mould her life, would only do it for her. It was her tendency that any time she would sit in meditation to heal, being clairvoyant; she would start seeing everything as it was. She would also see things about me. I told her to keep record of it. Being busy in other pursuit in the present, she could not do so. She would waste her time and energy unconsciously on viewing such things which were not directly related to her or on which she had no control.

3. She wasn't conserving her energy,it was unconsciously getting exhausted in criticizing,judging and evaluating people. Sometime she would see people cursing and criticizing her, if she wouldn't listen to them and solve their problem because of lack of time and her own problem. Which would fill her with the negativity. She was positive in a moment and one such incident or blow to her ego would make her entirely negative and bitter towards life, making her drained and stand at the same place. It was also draining me a lot. I think she was taking time to accept the higher truth and replace it with the earlier truth. Enlightenment is a slow and arduous process, it requires dedication and discipline. It is perfectly fine to rest now and then. In asking for miracle, we are not asking something outside to change but something inside to change.

Session in March 2008 I am running away from the light

I asked her in the session, why do you feel still stuck in the same situation? Even though she had achieved so much after her first meeting with . She replied, 'I am again seeing myself in the same place where I remember being worshipped as a goddess. But now I am in my present body, roaming here and there'. I wanted to heal her and told her to feel the healing light fall on her. She said,' no, ***I am running away from the light***, I do not want to merge in it, it is very bright ,***I fear opening up of my eyes ,as it might harm me***'. She did not want to take that higher energy for she wasn't ready for it yet, that is why she was avoiding it. Even though it was made available to her.

She said, 'now I am at a sea level. There is water everywhere around me, I feel very uncertain and fearful '. Again I understood her apprehension of not venturing further in the water. I advised her, 'move ahead, water cannot harm you. You are not there in your physical body, that is your astral body and no harm can come to it from water'. She said, 'ok, I am trying; I am walking on the water. I reach at the other end, there is a mountain there. I climb that mountain; I find it hard to climb as if I don't have energy in me. I have reached the top but I don't know from there where to go? So I ***jump down from there as if unconsciously and land on the water bed again.*** I am continuously following this cycle. (She had earlier described to me her meditative experiences or dreams where she was doing exactly the same thing.)

Now I sternly told her to stop doing this. Be there on the mountain and pray for some higher guidance, I also started healing her silently.

She said, it's not even me, now it has turned in to a man who is doing this all over again. I understood that this is a symbolic vision, ***signifying how a man is caught up in this mechanical cycle, running with the full force***, without our really being aware of it, thus we find difficult to beak free. It is termed kaal or wheel of karma. What we are not aware of is controlling us. I asked her to stop turning round and round mechanically get out from this cycle. Get out from that place. There is some road and start walking on it. She expressed her inability to do so.

Present condition of her life was exactly reflected in this symbolic vision. She would feel an achievement in one sphere and another sphere of her life would appear lacking and making her again very negative and forget all her achievements. I counselled her to keep account of all her achievements as a gesture of self reward and feel encouraged in time of certain failure in another sphere.

Her session after three years 20th Feb 2009

I am struggling since beginning without knowing for what.

She has recognized me which is why she is doing all this for me.- Anjana

She was doing her PHD, naturally there was lots of pressure on her, on top of it there were minor family problems and being sensitive she would take such things very seriously. Though she declared that she had brought so many changes in her attitude. She would say,' I give full credits to self-Reiki and healing sessions, yet I cannot deny the fact that problems are still chasing me with the same intensity,I feel exhausted and at times I feel devoid of any will and strength to live life. After all how much can one take on.

Session -Her main worry was that why she wasn't able to concentrate on her studies and why she gets swayed by other things, which aren't important right now? I asked her to see it for herself. She said, 'I am seeing ***my head has inflated like a very big balloon***. Inside it there is one big library with heaps and heaps of books and books are also scattered here and there on the floor , on the table everywhere in that library. This is making me very confused and burdened that I don't know from where to start my work. Which book to select? I gave her suggestion, to feel intuitively guided to pick up the right book, open the selected page and start working peacefully. She herself said, 'yes, now the balloon is deflating and I am sitting in my university library and peacefully working.

Taking her deeper in the session, I asked her why are you still so confused and get disturbed easily. She got connected to herself as a girl in this life. Who is confused and depressed. She said, I am a small girl wearing frock in my home town in this life. I just keep struggling and struggling as if I don't know for what. I am not at peace and I feel insecure.

I am grown up now,still struggling and confused, walking on the street (it's a symbolic place) a busy cross road. I am meeting one lady on the road. This lady is very tall, she has got very tall legs but very slim. She is making me sit on the rickshaw and bringing me home. At her home she is giving me bed to lie down, I rest there for some time. She gives me food to eat, gives me one bag with some money in it. When I asked her about the identity of this lady, she expressed her inability saying , 'no I do not know her personally . Because she is very tall and her legs are very slim and slender just like a doll.. But ***she says that she has recognized me. That is why she is doing all this for me'***.

I asked, ' what else is happening now'? She said, '***she is holding my hand and taking me towards a big mountain*** through a very rough road. Its taking so long, I am feeling tired and I cannot walk with her. I feel like giving up'. I advised her to feel already arrived at the place where she wants to take you. She replied, 'now we have arrived at the top of this mountain. But there is a very big ground there. There are many people there, some are weak, crippled, some miserably sick..

Slowly all of them are separating in to three categories. One side are children and handicapped people, one side are sick and miserable ones and one side normal people. We are doing something there. Some people from there are also coming forward and helping us in our work. Q What work are you doing there? A- As if we are creating a big butterfly design embroidering with thread. As the work is progressing this butterfly is becoming more prominent and bigger. At last all the people standing there are holding it and releasing it higher up as we fly kite. Flying higher and higher in the sky till what we had created had disappeared.

She is the same girl

I asked her to find out what is the exact significance of this vision, who is this lady ,who had recognized you but you are not aware of her identity?

She said, 'now again I see myself in a stone statue of Sarasvati Goddess in a small temple. This place looks to be very ancient and statue is also worn out, dull faded. One old man is trying to brush and clean the moss and grass grown on this statue. I am seeing statue now many years back when it was very bright and lots of people are coming to worship it. This lady is a small girl then and she comes here to pray. Oh, ***she is the same girl , I had seen earlier a***nd now I have recognized her . This is the same statue situated in the same old temple where ***I was being worshipped at that time.***

Q Why she comes to you, what is she asking? A- I can feel though I cannot see , there is some unrest ,some problem in her house. People do not listen to her. Though she means good to them, she wants to reform them. She is feeling very helpless and miserable. She prays for help and I help her. Q- How you helped her? A- I do not know but now people are listening to her. They are peaceful and happy now.. I keep waiting for her. She seems to have got busy with some other work now. She doesn't come to pray there anymore. She prays from her home only.

Now people come and throw stones at that statue. I am feeling hurt. Now it's broken and I have also left that place.

Q Did you recognize this lady now? She said , ' yes, now I recognized her, she is the same girl who use to come to pray to me when I was worshipped in Vaagh Devi temple in Manali. She is getting reward for helping me. She is getting fruits; I can see unimaginably very big size Keenu fruits.

She repeated her story in this session, which she had seen three years back but a little different this time. Realizing her problems and getting convinced of our deep connection in the past, I ask her, 'why do you see things more negatively and then get threatened by it? She replied, 'actually it's a very big hollow tree or tunnel type thing. I am stuck inside it and its dark there. That is why I see every negative aspect of life threat'. I asked, ' if it is dark and negative is part of it, then why I am not able to see any such thing?'. She said, 'because ***you are outside this hollow tunnel, you can see light***. But you also know there is negative and ***you avoid looking down to the darker aspects of life'.*** Q-'What is our role in the grater divine plan? There are guides, god, goddesses, angels and many such fictious characters and phenomena really existent. I wanted to know who is your or our guide at present ,who is relaying all this vision to you? A-'There is a very giant figure Guide, I don't know His identity, He is so big that I look to be smaller than His finger nail, if He places his finger on me I will be totally covered in it. Q-What is our connection with Krishna? A–It looks to be a very great form of Krishna as if He is covering the whole of cosmos, I am the crown giving it a shape and you are the jewels giving the shine, the glory to that crown'.

(I think that is the reason why some people see the glass as half full and others will notice only it half empty. It is not really their fault as we call such people pessimistic and all that. It depends on the location in the journey of life, where they have arrived at. If they have not crossed the hollow tunnel, where it is dark, naturally they are filled with uncertainty and fear ,criticism, rejection etc. Is also for this reason that there are many dimensions, many levels. Which are difficult to comprehend

by our logical faculty at a time? We are working to unfold one particular dimension at a time. But our intuitive faculty always knows there is some truth in another person's experiences also. Strong adherence to one's knowledge explains that person is not yet ready to progress further from there, as he is stuck in that situation. As he will be ready, he will start searching for new path, new knowledge and tread on it.)

She is a very imaginative and ambitious person and has struggled her life to claim an identity of her own. After these earlier sessions I asked her to see any future event as she used to see earlier. This time she expressed her inability to see anything in the future. Actually by now her many phases had come to an end and a new phase was beginning. Now a days she was again filled with depression , no will to live, weakness and old memories resurfacing. She had seen the reverse of what she had seen in her earlier session. Where she unconsciously claimed me indebted to her and gave me an opportunity to clear my dues. With the result she is seeing that now I am growing spiritually and also guiding her to a new direction ,which is leading her to her evolution. It is a both way process for both of us. I cannot deny her presence in my life nor can she claim to be more knowledgeable and powerful than me.

Healing of my kidney cyst

In Dec 2008, after one of routine meditation session she informed me that she had seen a small cyst or a sac type in my kidney area. I could not make out anything from it. I may have presumed that by healing myself in past many years along with my clients, I am totally reformed by now. But this was the fact that in past five years I had occasional high BP which had increased in frequency and intensity in past two years. Which I had mentioned in Pushpa's case. I requested her to heal it. I am just presuming it to be the cause of high BP. She did do her job well as I did not feel that discomfort and helplessness thereafter as I had been feeling in past few years when my BP would rise occasionally.

As I was also clearing my phase where I owed my debt to my family, many people and my goddess. Gradually I was feeling free from any guilt and yet living my life in the present and enjoying whatever life has to offer me. I am only doing my role without expectation or burden on my part just considering myself the actor of the Great director, trying to perfect my part.

Am I living the next phase of my life? New and last life, which Nadi Astrology had predicted for me in another time and place. Where I will not have the challenges of first preparing my family and people around me to approve my desired action. They would support me whole heartedly from the beginning. Since I am neither preaching nor I am proving anything, I am simply writing memoir of my inner journey, so I have the liberty to express my own views. I do not expect anyone to believe in my experiences whole heartedly. Just consider this as my fanciful idea, and how many times I am surprised, how many of my fantasies have proved realities? Yet I am not in a hurry to live that life now nor I want to delay my life by one more birth. I am ready for whichever is suiting to my higher self.*(Death is not only in terms of energy body separating from physical body and dissolution of its five basic elements back to its origin. But the ultimate Death is of Ego, where an issue separating us from grater reality by creating wall of illusion continues to haunt us many life times. Until this wall of separation is broken and we experience our connection back to our origin. In Reincarnation process of reintegrating of our being we actually find more life. Why do we celebrate prophets and saints' anniversaries, like Krishna, Jesus, Nanak ,Mohammad and all. Isn't it to reincarnate their goodness through our physical being? To become integrated with our greater self and feel the lightness, vastness and unity of that bigger, greater , higher reality)*

I had taken up healing as a medium to progress spiritually yet when I ventured in to it completely, I started thinking healing as my main aim and healing humanity is my destination. Slowly this realization is dawning that I am not to heal anybody, I cannot be any body's life guard. I don't have to desire such things. Let life flow uninterrupted. In the journey of life, healing is a mile stone, a small halt. I had recognized it and energized my being and also had taken valuable guidance in changing my direction towards the final destination (completion of life cycle). My family is aware of my evolution, truth behind my dreams, and intuition interpretations. I did not get dejected, disappointed by failures, criticism, lack of feedback or rewards. Now onwards I am my own Guru, I will do what naturally comes to me, I will not get tamed by any organization and promotion.. I am pure conscious; I was only trying to find out who I am? When I am what I am, I need not prove anything to anybody including me. I am a tap, pure conscious flows through me. Who wants to be benefited, will open this tap and be benefited. For others, who do not wish to try and open the tap doesn't have any purpose.

Is her meeting with me my reward or paying back my dues?

Was divinity rewarding me for my devotion and prayers? Anjana being spark of divinity from that collective consciousness (our source) of which we both were part of. Has she come to remind me of my past deeds and association with my higher self (my past life Goddess) coming as my guardian angel to guide me in time of uncertainty and confusion? Lest I might slip and miss my way this time too. As Anjana had confirmed, "your circumstances were always same, your family's objection to your path, social bindings on you. I had promised to help you, you had also promised to pay back your debt". I was not aware of my that past but my present circumstances were replica of the same.

Was she crediting her debt from me, for saving me from my miseries in the past life by coming to me for her healing? I, on my part did all my best to bring her out from the mess in her life. As she had demanded, "you had promised to pay back your debt". Yet this question is as mysterious, debatable and disputable as asking whether hen came first or egg, whether God created man or man creates God by his faith? Life loses its meaning if we don't believe in immortality and continuity of life. I was amazed at the beginning but was becoming aware of the conspicuous divine plan, I am trying to grasp heuristic insight from the evidence of fiction fusion in life. God is as far from us as much we think He Is and He is as near to us as we are connected to everybody and everything around us (subconsciously) within energy world, which is store house of raw material of manifested world. We are only substitutes, subdivision and extension of our Soul, our higher self on this earth; we are unaware of our higher connection because of distance from our source and gap which is claimed by unconsciousness.

So there is no enemy, no friend. Our soul /God / Universe speaks to us internally as our intuition and foresight and outwardly He confirms it through the words of saint, fraud , friend or enemy, whose words may echo in our mind or touches the chord in the heart. And depending on our wisdom (Viveka) we will reflect on those messages and apply in our life as per the powers or control we have on our life. Leave aside things we don't know, we are not able to exercise all good things we know in life, because of not having control on ourselves. The fact is that the one committing crime also knows that he is doing wrong but because he doesn't have the power to control himself , thus he is forced to do so. Empowering self to control oneself is very important. Nothing is served on the platter; we have to earn everything, wisdom, intellect, power, health, wealth, happiness to become a (serv gun sampan) perfect multifaceted human being.

2nd Case -This is your Lesson from Higher World

You already know everything

Shahnaz 4rth April 2006 -Thyroid, Obesity, Weakness.

Shehnaz was a forty years old lady, moher of five children . She worked as a cook for me just for two months. In those two months she use to go to hospital to take medicine for thyroid problem. Once I told her that I can avail the medicine prescribed for her free of cost as my husband is a doctor. Deepa was staying with me at that time , she jokingly told Shahnaz that in this house everybody is a doctor. Why do you have to outside for medicine? There after she insisted that she wants to experience my healing, I warned her that it would take one to two hours weekly sitting followed by another three to four weeks. I was a bit hesitant as she wouldn't give me that much time but finally I gave in. We proceeded with the healing.

Session – She prayed for her guide, and she started seeing him. She said a very long name of her guide which I could not remember. He is walking with me on the marble stairs and is blessing me. I am in a beautiful garden, sweet smell of flowers and very soft touch is making it a very pleasant experience.

Happy moments -When I asked her to go back to the origin of her problem ,she reached back to her childhood as girl of five years living in her house in Bijnaur. We are playing hide and seek,my brother Tayyab is few years elder to me. Now I am seeing my wedding, I am dressed in very beautiful sari and flowers are on my hair. There are many people who are enjoying the feast. We are a well to do family of that place. After feeling pleasure of her happy days, she shifted to watching painful memories of this life.

Painful memory -Now I am admitted in the hospital for my fourth delivery. I am in labour pain, nurses and ayahs are around in the ward but nobody is attending to me. I am screaming in pain,they are shouting back at me and very vulgarly telling me, 'did we ask you to take this trouble? With our permission you are producing more children? I am requesting them to help me. They are threatening me that they will send me to another hospital where they will perform a big operation by opening up my whole abdomen. I am helpless, I am pleading to them, and one nurse has injected some injection in me. Slowly my whole body is getting swollen. Now I have been taken to another hospital. (Ram Manohar Lohia). I am naked, they are really performing an operation on me. Doctors and nurses are standing and attending to me. The baby has come out but they have not shown me. They have exchanged my baby. At this I asked her, 'you don't love your child? She replied, 'no, I love her so much, whatever eatables I get, first I give it to her. She continued further, 'now my husband has come searching for me. He is aghast at seeing my swollen body, I am telling him everything, he is complaining about nurses and ayahs to big doctor. Doctor is scolding all of them.

I have come home now. I have cooked rice and dal as I ate it ,I started vomiting, I am feeling giddy, I am feeling very weak. I am again back to the hospital. She herself started giving her history, 'I had tonsils in my childhood for which I had taken some medicines. After having this child, I had weakness and giddiness. There are few tests done in the hospital. The doctor is saying, 'it is hyroid ,you have to take medicine life long. Otherwise hormonal imbalance will create weakness and giddiness. I am nodding in agreement, 'ok doctor sahib, I will do as you say.' 'Because I am fearful of going back to the same condition, I am very regular in taking medicine'.

At this I asked her to go back to the origin of her this sickness and her living in fear of becoming weak and giddy , may be in some past life. She replied, 'no, ***it is coming from this life*** only. And she started describing what she was seeing and I was dissolving simultaneously with Reiki energy and she was giving me the feedback of the healing happening -

-There is one tantric, he is rotating one road and sprinkling something.

-My sister in law (devrani) is stitching something in my children's mattress. She is also giving me something to wear. But I don't trust her. Now she is putting something in the food, which we are going to eat. She is wearing something from head to toe to harm me (invisible but at this moment she can see it) (may be negative black aura to harm her). One black lady, I have seen her somewhere around this area, she is standing outside my husband's cycle shop and digging in the corners and saying in words that ***this shop should not run***. She wants that instead her shop should get more customers. I healed all whatever was coming up. She saw one by one everything was burning. She told me that my sister in law is inside one round ring type and something is burning inside it. I put protection ring around Shahnaz also and she saw that something outside this ring is burning but it is not able to penetrate in and harm her. The food also was cleansed by Reiki energy now ,the dark look of it had transferred to healthy clean look. By sending healing light outside her shop where the lady had dug it, it started burning inside the soil. And the words which this black lady was uttering were burning and disappearing as soon as she was uttering those harmful words. Thus I ended the session.

Note - I thought that she is full of suspicion for her sister in law so I asked her, 'do you remember what all you saw and said? She surprised me by saying, 'no, I feel as if I was in deep sleep and now I am waking up. All I remember is as if in a dream there was something burning in some different looking fire. But I am feeling light and relaxed.

He belongs to everybody & he is praying for your family also.

-Second session was very important and went something like this.

I told her to pray for her guide to be with her to help you in this healing. She said, 'yes, he is here and he looks like a Maulavi with very calm, serene and loving look'. She named him but I could not understand as it was very difficult and long name. 'He has brought me to you'. I asked her, 'where is he?' ***'He is standing behind you'*** as she said so, I was bit nervous and felt shiver down my spine. She herself continued, 'ask what you want to ask about her? I was surprised why she is talking to me like this ? I questioned her, 'about whom should I ask you '? She replied, 'ye, Shahnaz, she has something coming from her home to harm her. Her sister in law doesn't have children na, You are healing her correctly; you have told her that you will give her those stones (Crystals) that will be better, her house also needs protection, and there is something in her husband's shop. That lady wants to take over from his shop. She (Shahnaz)is becoming healthier and active. Now she is working in two houses, earlier she could hardly work in one. She needs three to four healings and will be fine. She has already stopped taking medicines'.

As she was revealing all this, I felt guided to ask her more about guide, 'where is He now?' she replied, 'He has gone to Medina to pray Namaz.' I asked, 'what and for whom is he praying'? She said,

'He belongs to everybody, He is even praying for your children and family.' At these words, I felt a surge of emotion choking my throat and my eyes moistening with gratitude and I conveyed it to him through her.(Even now also whenever I remember or read that incident , I am filled with gratitude and same emotions.)

Healing - I asked her to see where all the negativity is affecting her. She saw that her nerves in he brain are tied , with healing it is getting released and she felt lighter and relaxed. I cleaned and healed each chakra one by one and she was giving me the feedback of what was happening in her each chakra.

Crown –nerves are tied, Third eye - black thick smoke. Throat – thread, Heart –smoke, Solar – fire, Sacral –fire, in Root chakra she felt something moving out with pain like she had in the hospital while having delivery, but did not see any shape or colour.

She saw her children one by one, they were screaming and restless. I healed them and when the turn to heal her husband came, she saw there is already a protection ring around him. Because I had healed him previous day for burning in the eyes and feeling depressed because his shop was not running well. This was sort of a feed back to me that protection shield given by me is effective)

After completing healing and putting protection ring around her she felt relieved.

After ending the session, I again wanted feedback from her about the Guide, the chakra healing and her children but her reply was same. I only remember as if I am waking up from a very deep sleep but as I was about to wake up, I could see my children coming one by one and fire around them was burning something in them.

This is your Lesson from Higher World

Third session was more intriguing. By now I had become familiar with her Guide's presence, His direct communication and His love for humanity. This made me feel secured, confident and comfortable.

In this session we continued healing from wherever it was left in previous session. I felt guided to ask her,'why I am doing your healing? And she went on, 'this is a lesson for you '. (Lesson, I thought punishment or paying back for some misdeed)I could not understand what she meant by it. So I asked her, 'what is the meaning of lesson? 'As if she was waiting for this response from my side and she started, (*ye upper se sabak hai ,tumhain sikhane ke liye*) '***This is your lesson from higher world, to teach you***, because you are so pure hearted, I can see some very nice thing on your head, a flower and a beautiful hand. Your soul looks so white. Your Guru is there behind you.' I was dumb founded, I asked her in surprise, 'who is my Guru? How does he look'? 'He is wearing pant, shirt, and is in Delhi. You are working with him. But they are not telling his name'. I further asked, 'where am I working? In his place or some hospital'? 'No, this looks to be your own place. There are other people also with you. You are working so sincerely'. I asked her to find out about the place so that I can take guidance as to where should I work? She said, 'the talks are going on about a ***place for you up there***'. I asked her, 'will I be healing anybody else here in this place? She replied, 'no, but you will be helping lots of people in another places'. I felt more curious and posed one more question, 'will I be working only in Delhi? She said, 'you will be going to different places. You will be helping lots of people. ***But you already know everything,***' was her final answer. And the truth was that by this time I had known quite a bit about my self . I became conscious and not to distrust any of the sources revealing things to me in this way , they had common purpose in letting me know. So I should not waste my and their time in repeating it make them feel as if I don't trust them.

After the session she remembered few things and was explaining to me in more details what all she saw internally. I asked her what you were talking about my soul. She replied, 'I felt compelled to speak few things which I even don't understand. Flower was flowering on your head, there were some beautiful hands placed on your head but I don't know what it meant.

Her guide directly talked to me   Shahnaz April 2006

This guide appeared through Shahnaz, whom I was healing for ***thyroid***. Her case sort of confirmed my belief in negative energies in the form of tantric work, psychic attack etc. Really exists. Though by now I had already encountered such phenomenon but I had no proof to prove it to others. Though I had sent this experience to Reiki Healing Foundation and it was published in the monthly magazine. Another person by this time being healed with such problems was Anjana. She was revealing so much of such things that it was beyond my comprehension to understand one suffering with so much negativity to such extent. I still presumed it her mental imagination and creation of such things because of her belief system. Though off course in the beginning Ayan had revealed it all but I did not understand what to make out of all this.

I had so many reasons to believe Shahnaz's revelations.

-After the session, she would not remember what she had said or seen, and felt as if she is waking up from sleep and felt very light and relaxed.

-Her symptoms were subsiding and she was losing weight and becoming active.

-Her guide would directly talk to me about her as if she is a third person. The tone and language was hers but wordings were something like this, 'she has problem coming from her home, her sister in law is jealous of her, as she doesn't have children. Her sister in law has also given something to her children to eat etc.' During healing I was patiently accepting whatever she was saying and releasing it. After the session I wanted to take feedback and every time she said, I don't remember anything, I feel as if I was in a deep sleep and waking up now. All I remember is as if in a dream, there was something burning. Next session I decided to record her session to make a proof to myself and show it to her also. In third session she remembered few things. I could not do any further sessions with her because I had to shift my house from that area to another location. She had already given me positive feedback within these three sessions itself. Had she thought it more useful she could have come to my new location.

3rd Case ***Wandering Souls doesn't let me come in.***

Sujata May 2006 - Depressed and abusive husband, negativity in the house

I had healed Sujata's husband through distance healing for his depression, alcohol addiction, and abusive behaviour. They both never had good relationship but off late she was finding it difficult to bear as it were affecting her teenage children. Her sister in law was learning Reiki at that time and suggested her to try distance healing for him She agreed and would give us positive feedback every week about his progress, which was not only a pleasant surprise for her but was a positive reinforcement for me too. She was so impressed that she had agreed to come to learn Reiki. Without knowing anything about Reiki and distance healing she had agreed to get her husband healed and felt it is effecting him and their life positively . After a month she had a severe backache, she shocked me by asking us not to send her distance healing because she feels giddiness and totally numb in the mind. She did lots of treatment for her backache but wasn't cured even after seven month. Her sister in law on her visit to her house in Chandigarh tried healing her through Reiki and to both of their surprise she was completely healed of her ailment. Coincidently at that time her husband also became suddenly so abusive that he hit her and she fell unconscious for some time. Her sister in law threatened him and brought her to Delhi and also suggested her to come to me for personal session and also learn Reiki. Later she confided to me that whole night I was so fearful and thinking that am I doing something wrong? Then why I have to learn it stealthily? Had it not been for my sister in law, I would have changed my mind. After talking to me she felt relieved that it will not harm her in any way.

Session – She soon slipped deeper in her mind and reached her childhood at her maternal uncle's house. She was sensing invisible negative energy and was describing, 'there is one dark lady downstairs in the open, making chapattis and frightening me. I am a small girl, very scared and running upstairs to hide in some room. But in every room there is something dark and frightening. There is no safe place here ', she was feeling unsure of herself, how to feel protected . I released the spirit of that lady by directing healing light at her. She gave me feedback, 'the lady is screaming and trying to escape from light but light is more focused and powerful, slowly she is engulfed in this light. Then she saw in all the rooms something is burning and now she is feeling its bright and secure there.

Guide - I asked her to make a request for her guide to be present with her so that she will feel secure. She went on to narrate whatever she was viewing,'my papa (late) has come. I am clinging to him and crying ,he is consoling me, don't lose hope, now I have come, everything will be all right now.' I enquired from her,' why didn't he do something till now? She replied, 'he is saying, ***wandering souls in front of your house are not allowing me to enter inside'.*** Now we both are standing in front of my house in Chandigarh. There are many souls lined up and stopping us to enter in. One of them is my father in law, who had died of heart attack ,few years back at a place where accidents had claimed many lives. I healed them to be released from there. She said, 'all are getting easily dissolved in this light but my father in law is angry at me. He is saying, '***I will not go anywhere , this is my son's house***. I tried to explain to him through her but she said, he is crying and doesn't want to listen anything, he says, my son is in danger,he has many enemies'. I tried to instil sense in him that how can he help him, what power does he have to help him? She reported, 'now frustratingly he has left that place'. As I had to heal her for her own problems so I proceeded from there to heal her further.

(Next day when I asked her to see him again, as he had not been released yesterday. She said, 'he is roaming in our village. I tried to convince him to accept release and move ahead. Today he was more willing and was immediately engulfed in the healing light and disappeared from her sight. At that time she saw that her husband in her home in Chandigarh is feeling very light and relaxed. He is feeling very guilty for his anger and earlier behaviour. He is telling her , 'you know I am like that only, you should understand me'.

Cause for his behaviour – Lower level spirit -I asked her to see the cause for his irritability and anger outburst. She started seeing herself in her in-laws village, when few years back there was one function in their family to celebrate one dead person being worshiped as a devta. She started narrating that day's scene which came alive now in her mental screen exactly how it had been then. She said, 'people are running here and there in preparation, offerings are being made, our pundit is performing ritual of calling our devta and now telling us that Devta is coming. I can see clearly that the person being worshipped is coming there, people are bowing with devotion, but I don't feel any such feelings in me. Because I can see crookedness in his eyes. ***I know he is not any pious soul.*** Later when I am sleeping in my room, this so called devta spirit is entering my room and throwing my *duppatta* down from my body. I am very angry at this and he is laughing wickedly. I told my husband this and he too did not like this behaviour from a spirit who is held in high esteem by the villagers. He is also filled with suspicion towards this spirit and has stopped worshipping him. Now this spirit is trying to take revenge on both of us by troubling us. He incites my husband to trouble family members; ***he instigates him to commit suicide.*** My husband has become so coward that he can't even go to the market alone. He is totally dependent on me but still ***harasses me by putting blames***, 'have you given my *supari*, do you want me murdered?' To hide his fear and frustration he remains lost in drinks and ***chases children far from him*** so that they may not know his real self.

Cause for alcohol-(Past life) -Where is the cause for his alcohol? I enquired, she responded, 'this is from past. But now in the village his friend is telling him, 'drink little more, all your problems will vanish away.' And he is drinking it thinking as a remedy for his problems.

Relationship with her brothers- (tantric)Now I asked her to see the cause for many of her problems in this or in past life. She said, ' I can see my younger brother's wife and her mother sitting with one tantric. She is telling this tantric, 'do something so that her husband (Sujata's brother) should not keep any relation with his brother and sister'. Tantric is giving one black thread and assuring them, '***keep this thread with you and it will keep affecting from here itself.***

Backache – Psychic attack –'After burning that thread, I asked her to see the reason for prolonged backache, which was healed only few days back through Reiki healing by her sister in law. She said, 'it is Navratra celebration in October month. One of our colleagues Mrs Sethi has celebrated the festival for nine days in the school by erecting a *pandal* and decorating and worshipping properly. It is last day of the festival. Prasad is being distributed. I am taking Prasad and coming out from the room. Mrs Sethi is running after me and asking me to halt for a while. She applied vermillion on my forehead. I have come to my class room. As I bent down to pick up something from the floor, suddenly I get a severe pain in my lower back. I am unable to move even. I asked her, 'what was there in that *tilak* which caused you so much pain?' Mrs Sethi had prayed to Goddess to grant her the wish that she should become a number one teacher in the school. That can happen only if I leave this school. Because I am a number one teacher of my school. Finally I had to leave that school because of backache and her wish got fulfilled.

Healing – I asked her to see what was there in her back which caused her so much pain? There is some black patch type at my lower back area where I had pain. When my sister in law is touching it, it is slowly dissolving and I am feeling relieved.

Proof of distance healing - I also was curious to know, In spite of positive feedback about her husband's healing initially, why did she reject her own distance healing?

She said, ' I can see some white hands as if giving support to my back, I can hear my sister in laws voice, Sujata, you are getting better. I also feel some comfort by this. Q-Then why did you object to healing? A-When that healing energy reaches me, because there is so much negative in my mind ,its running here and there making me disturbed . A voice is telling me in my head, ' healing is not going to help you ,it's no use , go to the doctor, get your x-ray done, take some injection. I am so confused, my head starts spinning and I feel numbness in my brain and become helpless and loose hope that Reiki cannot heal my problem. Thus I became negative and refused to accept healing.

Guide – I asked her to find out from her guide, how long will he stay with her? He is saying, my work is almost over now. You are free from very strong negative phase and free to progress further. Thus ended her session enriching me further in accepting the mystic mysteries affecting our life.

Note – she was also clairvoyant to some extent as she told me that she had already seen some spirits on her husband whenever he was angry. Even that day when he hit me hard, it was something this sort of force in him which hit me so hard. Whole night there was something trying to dissuade me from learning and getting healing sessions, creating some doubts and fear in my mind.' But her direct healing through my sister in law filled me with some confidence that I might not be harmed any way'.

We all believe in some psychic phenomenon, there is no two way about it. We know death is the destination of life but still we fear death and wish to hide it or push it behind our mind, same is case with psychic phenomenon. Another reason is that it empowers some and frightens few. In our culture there are different ways of showing our connection to mystic world. In Sujata's culture any dead person wishes to speak through some living being after death and he really speaks giving some details or future incidents. In different society all such phenomena are prevalent. Inwardly everybody is curious and believes in it but outwardly one rejects as intellectually wants to keep the pace with the modernity and doesn't want to be labelled orthodox and out dated. But soul and mystic world which is our original place is out dated rather undated, timeless phenomenon only. We as human body and physical world are just the zerox copy of that original piece which is not conceived by physical senses but can be perceived by sixth sense.

Summary- H*ow* can I avoid to be conspicuous of such cases. Gradually mystic mysteries were being opened to me which would not be acceptable immediately? Every case was as if stepping on to next higher step and making me able to see more clearly than what was visible before.

Wandering Spirits is a term used for those souls who have relinquished physical body (death) but have not accepted transition due to various reasons and remains attached to earthly existence. We need not fear them. They have some purpose. They are of following types -

1 Ignorant – Just as there are ignorant people out on the road meeting us in physical form asking us the way as they don't know ,where is the way ahead. So do some ignorant spirits not knowing their abode as after relieving from physical body what lies ahead. By accidents or before being ready for departure, their life might have been cut short. Most souls even while alive are not aware or don't want to accept the reality that physical body is temporary, so they are not preparing them for journey ahead of their death. Thus remain lost and after a time they feel bored of this aimless existence and then try to touch somebody asking for help. Though death is a subconscious act, one reaches where his awareness, the energy of his intension takes him. Thus lost or confused souls remains scattered and don't catch up with higher energy as if out of fear or just pure ignorance.

2-***Purposefully unwilling to move on***- Who died accidentally, or before finishing something important from the higher purpose of things, may remain attached to earth plan either out of revenge or trying to finish that work by finding some way out. Independently they have no power. Thus they need some vehicle that they can influence and direct towards accomplishing that work.

3- ***Ghosts*** or some powerful spirit having negative attitude in their life while alive. After death one doesn't become extraordinarily wise, our desires and wishes all remains the same. These notorious spirits either out of habit are trying to exert their control on living people around them or karmically linked people are the victims of their wrath.

Tantric work – Black magic is another invisible negative energy around us by selfish and powerful Tantrics to just prove their control on others or out of some real revenge to harm other person.

Psychic attack is energy of strong negative intensions by negative attitude personality to show his upmanship or wish person some harm. But as it is well said that you get back what you put out. So with what force the negative intensions are sent out this way, same will attack back with many fold.

Lesson – She was very instrumental in showing me ***the variety of souls existing amongst*** us. One doesn't need to fear them ,as all are not harmful ,some are trying to find their release through us , some obstinate ones are ignorant of the fact that they are halting and harming self by remaining attached to the earth plan. She also proved to me that how can a person see his ***healing happening in person or though distant Reiki***. Because if one can see the cause and ***intension of negativity*** on him, one can also view ***positive intensions*** as in healing or praying to higher energy.

5th Case **GoddessDurga is sitting here in this room**

Alcoholic husband and step father to her daughters, have bad intension on them.

Minu 40 years October 2008

History -She has three daughters, three sons, of which two daughters and one son are from her deceased husband and rest from present one. Raja, her present husband is alcoholic and doesn't support her at all financially and morally he has bad intension for his step daughters. She is so god-fearing and has been fasting for requesting god to solve all her family problems. She spends so much on worshipping

Goddess Durga (jagrata) during Navratra and would go out of her way to help anybody in need.

Session- I asked her to pray and seek permission, guidance and protection from her deity. She felt a bit nervous and asked me will there be any harm to me if I want to know the cause of my problems in past life? I assured her that if you are ready to accept your part good or bad in your past life openly and to ask for forgiveness from people whom you think are the cause of your suffering in this life, willing to make amends because you want to come out of the sufferings you are facing and then there is nothing which can harm you. If you are not ready to accept all these things then there is no use your undergoing session in this way. She agreed and we proceeded.

I asked her to go through a path and reach in one garden but she said, no, I am standing on the river bank. I then asked her to go and have bath in this sacred river so that all your blockages are opened, all your tensions are released and you feel energetic after being thoroughly cleansed. She declared, ‘ I am climbing stairs but no, it's not me, it's one fairy who looks like me. She is not wearing anything,but white dress and feather how the fairy generally have. She is plucking flower and now going to the temple in that garden itself. There are two people, greeting her on the door. One of them is pundit and she has gone inside the temple with these people. Now she is sitting and weaving garland for the Goddess. There are many idols in the temple, Hanuman, goddess Durga on lion, all the other gods whose names I don't know properly'. I asked her to make a request for her guide to be present there. She said yes, ‘ my guide has come. She is a girl of ten twelve years old. She is Goddess herself incarnated in a girl form. She is saying it's all my karma which is causing me suffer this way'. I agreed with her and asked her to find out the cause so that it can be erased from the origin.

She said,‘ I cannot see anything but debris /mud getting collected in front of me and turning in to a hill. I can see one eye of some animal staring at me. Slowly this animal got released from this hill, it is an eagle (cheel). It is flying now. There is one man working in the field and this eagle is flying here and there. Suddenly it snatches the food from this farmer. The farmer is running after and chasing eagle to get back his food. But it is very high and far from him. The man is very disappointed and angry as he is hungry. At this she herself recognized this farmer and said, 'he is my husband. I think I am that eagle. Now some people have thrown stone on the eagle and hurt her leg. It cannot fly as it is growing old and gradually getting buried inside that hill from where I could see its one eye'.

Many lives vision-. I healed that vision from her mind. She said , 'now that eagle is freed from that debris and again flying in the sky. After death people are burying it near the temple'. I asked her where did the consciousness of that eagle remain after its death. She replied, ' in that temple, as a fairy. Now I am again in that temple as same fairy. There are many ladies, some of them I know now also. My friend Rita, Sunita etc. They are all dancing and weaving flowers to make garlands for Goddess. Arti is going on, plate full of Diya is being circulated in front of idols. Now I am that pundit who was bringing that fairy in. Yes, I was a pundit doing worship of Goddess Durga in that temple. But I died in an accident, I had many children, they are crying for me. I am also feeling bad for them, who will look after them'.

Healing her husband

Now I asked her to see her husband, so that she can ask forgiveness from him. She said, 'he is not in his senses because of drinking heavily'. So we proceeded to bring out the debris from his mind which is making him senseless and addicted to alcohol. She said, 'so much white snow type thing is coming out; now something greasy blackish substance is coming out. So much dirty substance is flowing down his feet. After enough has come out, now Hanuman is hitting his head with his weapon (gadda) at one side. There are many fairies dancing on his head spreading so many colorful thin muslin clothes (chuneries).Flowers are flowering on his body. Now he is sitting peacefully. I am asking him forgiveness and we are forgiving each other, he is also asking forgiveness from me. He is also feeling so lighter now'.

I asked her to see again Goddess Durga in that temple not as an idol but in original form. She said, ***Goddess is here sitting in this room*** pointing to one direction. Such a big statue and you are sitting and meditating in front of Her. She opened her eyes to see whether she can see with physical eyes and pointed to me that here in the center, I saw Goddess Durga. She was awe stuck.

Giving positive affirmation, I brought her back and she was folding her hands and filled with gratitude again and again at having such a wonderful sight. Next day she told me that her husband for once didn't scold any of her children today. I convinced her of gradually getting healed but she has to forgive and accept few of his traits not meant to hurt her but part of his cultural conditioning and not expect him to change because it doesn't suite her cultural background. She agreed.

Lesson-

1. Nobody is excused from pay back of past deeds. Eagle snatching farmer's food and now the same person is having bad intension on her children, living in the same house as her closest person. She is threatened by his intension towards her daughters same way as eagle must have threatened and pained hungry farmer by stealing his food

2. She was an eagle, a fairy, a pundit and now she is a poor lady. Yet she is very religious. It signifies her previous life's tendencies making her worship Goddess now in this life with great enthusiasm. She could never have imagined that she would have been any of these but after seeing now she was trying to convince me of her inner experience.

5th case Its All That Baba's doing

Blood tears are rolling down papa's eyes

Anirban 6th July 2006 -

Accidents, Fear, Obstacles

Anirban is twenty years old boy who have met unaccounted accidents and faced unusual obstacles. He also lacks concentration in studies, yet try to work hard. Last year he was preparing for his final exam when suddenly he had severe pain and was diagnosed as renal stone and had to be operated in emergency. Thus he could not appear for exam which made him loose confidence and he became depressed.

Session- He slipped deeper in his mind and reached one temple near his ancestral house. His deceased grand parents came as his guides who are standing outside that temple. They always use to warn him not to go to that temple and he invariably went there to play with his friends and siblings. The temple is very small hence nobody can enter inside it. There is nothing inside this temple.

To find out the causes for fear and accidents etc, I asked him to go to the origin of his these problems. He reached back to his ancestral house where he had lived as a young child for about eight years of age. He saw ***many glimpses of his childhood*** which somehow have been ***contributing to his present problems***.

- I am six year old. One of the neighbour lady is giving me tea, Inside the glass it looks blackish in colour; she seemed to have put something in this. She is also sounding words from her mouth wishing me harm which are coming towards me. Now I feel it was jealousy for me.

- My late cousin brother's picture wearing white kurta payajama is appearing in my mind.

-Now I am having a dream which I use to have in my childhood about one baba (sadhu). I am again seeing it, the baba is in our house, I feel, his looks are not saintly how he appeared then, I feel suspicious about him as I see he is hiding something in the corner of that room where I am sleeping. Seeing that dream I am so scared that I woke up from the sleep. I could not sleep alone in my room thereafter and went to sleep with my parents that night.

-I am seeing the accident which our whole family had met few years ago. I was ten years and very fatally injured.

-In my childhood one tantric had come near our house. Out of curiosity we had gone to see him. Now I can see that tantric is calling us to the jungle near our house. He is digging something in the soil there. That is causing ***blood tears come down from my father's eyes*** and his hands are pierced with nails and are bleeding. (*I think going to jungle was symbolic ,that tantric must have cast his spell on them and done some such ritual that he feels, they have been asked to come to the jungle and his father will suffer so much later that he will weep blood tears and his hand will bleed and pain. Because when i askd him later ,he said, we never went to that jungle in reality)*

Now he announced, ' ***it is all that baba's doing*** **.** I asked, 'how'? He elaborated, 'because baba resembles that tantric now. (In my opinion Tantric and black magic is the outcome of past deeds. That is why karmically linked person faces their wrath)

Tantric work causing accident

Q- How did that tantric whom you called baba caused that fatal accident? (First he started seeing what led to this accident.) A- 'Papa is driving the car, we all are sitting. Papa's hands are becoming weak and losing control, so is his mind not able to react and slow down the speeding car. It is banging a tree. We all are injured very badly. My left hand and leg is entangled in the door very badly'.

Q- 'How is baba responsible for this'?(Now he shifted his focus to invisible subtle negative influence coming to create that accident)

A- 'There is Puja ritual going on in that baba's Ashram. He is chanting some mantras and making offerings in the fire. Dark vibrations from there are travelling towards us. Papa's hands and mind are totally covered by this darkness and losing control resulting in accident. I healed all these memory from his mind.

Tantric causing murder -Moving ahead in the session I asked him, 'How did he harm your cousin , as you said it's all this baba's doings? Answer –'my cousin Brother is eight, nine years old, this baba is at our home. Brother does not like this baba's attitude, thus ignorantly he replies back to baba. Baba is feeling insulted. Papa is intervening by asking forgiveness from baba and is defending my brother by saying, 'he is bit kiddish and spoiled child ,otherwise he is going to grow up to be very well.' Baba is saying, ' it's all right, ***that you will know only when he will be twenty two***.' ' Nobody understood the deeper meaning behind his words that time'. Q- What was the deeper meaning? A- 'I can see brother is tied down with ropes, and placed in front of an altar. Baba is crookedly laughing and telling, 'you were talking too much that day, now see the fun' Q- How is it affecting your brother ? 'Brother is drinking alcohol excessively. He is not in his senses. He is very restless, he gets angry very soon, he is arguing with everyone and picking up fight with us at home'. Q- But how did he die? A- 'His hands are tied, he is crying, ***his head is beheaded and offered at the altar***.

Now he is fighting to let free from three four people at his work place. But he is not in his senses and they hit him and he is dead. His body is lying there but he is standing and roaming here and there. He is very disturbed'. Q-It means he is not released? A-'No, he is saying, I want to take revenge, I wanted to live more, I will not spare them'.

Releasing his brother -I tried to explain to his brother through him that you cannot do anything now. You don't have physical body; people cannot see or hear you. You have no power to take revenge. It is no use wasting time like this. Life never ends, move ahead in life. Things on which we have no control, we leave it to God to do justice for us.. Anirban said, 'now he is accepting and getting touched by the light and dissolving slowly. He has completely merged in the light, which is moving up in the heaven. He is in the sky, looking happy and waving us from there.'

After the session I asked him about this baba. He did not know much about him except that few years back his father was very devoted to this baba. Even he had been taken to baba's ashram as a child. Q- Then why your father is not going there now? A- 'Baba is very short tempered and demanding. Our family doesn't likes baba much. So slowly papa stopped going to him. Baba still keeps sending messages and calling him there'.

(I told Anirban what I could understand from the whole situation. Baba was trying to exert his power to control them by creating accidents and adverse circumstances, so that they will turn to him for help and reconciliation. I told him to convey it to his father. He conveyed it or not, whether his father took it his imagination or some trick on my part to create some inexistent facts and present it as truth, I have no idea. But he continued coming to me for subsequent sessions

A face is coming Alive in the mirror

Session 2 – He reached to one Gurudwara near his house to see his Guide. He is standing inside and feeling peace full and secured. I guided him to the origin of his problems.

He said, 'Now I am in my field and watching one coconut which was lying there and I had touched it accidentally. I also feel now, some body is watching me. It looks as it was placed to wish harm to me'. Q –What harm has it done to you? A-' A black rope type is coming from my mind. My legs are also tied with some rope as if that is why I cannot step forward and progress'. It was healed by dissolving it in thc hcaling light.

Spirit possession – I asked to him to see any other cause. He said, 'I am back to my ancestral house when I am two -three years old. I am standing in front of a mirror and there is so much light coming from it. As we see when mirror reflects back the light ,when it is placed facing the light from the sun'. I asked him to see why this mirror is giving so much light ,is it placed in front of sun. ? A – 'No, the room is dark. I am feeling bit scared. ***Now I see a face coming alive in the***

mirror, it's my aunt. Q –'What is her age at that time'? A –'I haven't seen her, she had died much before I was born.' Q – 'Then what is she doing in the mirror at the time when you are a child'? A- 'She is in the room and now she is in the *verandah*'.

I asked him to see the circumstances of her death. He said, 'she is lying on the bed in that house. Now she is placed on the floor, my grandmother is crying, other people are also there. But I can see her; she is standing in the corner of the room. Now she is sitting on the bed. ***She has been in that house ever since.*** I use to feel some shadow behind me in my childhood and get frightened when I could not find any one behind after looking back. I know that she used to be standing behind me.

(I was surprised at his revelation. If she had died long time back then why is she there when he is a young child? Slowly I realized that she had been wandering there and not released.

Releasing his Aunt– So, I asked him to see her getting dissolved in the light, which we are directing at her. He replied, 'she is getting very angry, she is saying, I will not go any where. She has got very heavy and frightening voice'. I tried to release her by directing healing light on her but he said, 'she is running from it'. 'I tried to convince her that you are harming not only yourself but your loved ones also. Everybody has moved ahead, and you are left behind'. He said, 'she is crying and running out in the *verandah*. She has jumped down from the window and standing on the lawn looking very disillusioned. Her hair are scattered around her face giving a very frightening look. I again tried to touch her and speak directly to her, 'even your parents and many others who left body after you, have gone much ahead of you. You are alone wandering in the darkness and uncertainty'. Slowly she was coming around to accept our advice and getting ready for release. Light started dissolving her in to it. After she was totally merged in the light, light was rising up. He said, '***in the sky my grandparents are there to receive her.*** She is happily going to them and they are blessing and thanking us from there'.

This was quite an experience for both of us, so after healing him for some time and giving positive affirmation, we ended the session.

After the session, I enquired about his aunt. He said,' I had not seen her and I don't know how she died. Yet he was surprised to see her in his session and this definitely added to telling him to his father about all that transpired in the session. His father came to meet me and was startled by what Anirban had told him. ***How could he see her***? Because she had died at a very young age and we had done all the Sanskara (last rites) even taking her ashes to holy rivers and feasting many pundits and all that. He did not like my opinion that she had been wandering spirit. He said, ' she was very spiritual girl, even at such a young age she was reading good scriptures and had become disciple to one famous baba of that time. She used to write to him and ask queries about higher wisdom. People were surprised at her this keen desire to seek higher things.

Then on his own ***he narrated one incident*** when all of a sudden this bright young girl with such keen desire to seek higher wisdom or salvation ,had one unpleasant experience. One day she was looking very beautiful wearing saffron dress which her mother had stitched for her as her birth day gift. She was giving a trial and showing it to everybody how she looked in that dress? All of a sudden ***she had a tremor and fell on to the floor rolling here and there*** with so much force that four five people also could not control her. After doing much *totkas*(trying things), she regained her normal state. There after she became very depressed and at times got such convulsions. She had written in a letter to that baba that she feels life is not worth living and may be by the time he receives this letter, she may not be alive. This really proved true as she was consumed by this trouble and died within few months.

Now he also talked about his baba and confirmed the revelations by stating that even I had started suspecting his intensions, besides he is so arrogant and demanding that it's difficult to please him. Any way now I have got proof that he is doing more harm than good. What has happened cannot be undone but I will be careful in the future as

I was deciding to pay him visit once in a while because he so desired.

Attraction of magical powers

He also told me how he had ***got impressed by this baba's magical power*** few years back. His friend told him that baba has miraculous powers, so to see it for himself he visited Ashram far from any market. It was night and Baba asked them what would they all like to have for dinner? They said *parathas*! Baba further asked them to decide clearly, how many and what stuffing *parathas* they like? It's difficult to get things from such far of place again and again. They told some number and within few minutes the potato *parathas* were there before them and they were eating with great curiosity. There was also one small bowl of *Kheer* (rice milk sweet dish) to his surprise everybody ate to his full and that small bowl was still full as it was in the beginning. This incident had made him ardent admirer of baba and he started going there finding another such miracles happening every now and then.

I cannot call it a mere coincidence, his father coming and giving this feedback to me. Because I was confused as to why should a highly spiritual girl become a wandering spirit? But very soon I was to get an answer for it. Next day Anirban informed me that he was sitting and dozing off on the sofa in the afternoon when suddenly he felt very scared. Even though he has been worrying and feeling depressed , but it was something more than that. I was also thinking why should he feel so scared now , when the soul possessing him has been released, he wasn't that scared earlier even , he wasn't aware of any such thing happening to him other than excessive worry depression and accidents. I asked him to come for another healing session as soon as possible.

Spirits Possession -- two in one –

Session –In the session, he again reached to his ancestral house. I asked him to see his aunt there. He said,'no she is not here anymore, she is higher up in the sky, very grateful to us and blessing us from there'. Q- Then why have you come here? What is there to cause you this excessive fear in you? He surprised me by saying, 'I can see somebody wandering in this house, probably a lady. Her hair are scattered over her face, her face is so dark that it is beyond recognition.' (Whatever it may be I decided to release this so I asked him to see her being released). He said, 'she is threatening me, I am so scared, she is shouting, I will not go'. I consoled him to be patient and let her listen to me. I told her that we don't mean to harm you; we want to help you because you are trapped. By hearing, consoling and loving words, he said, 'she is crying, she says, ***no, I don't want to go, I have small children***. They need me'. I told her, 'your children are so grown up, they don't need you now. Look at you, they cannot recognize you and may be frightened of you. See how much time has passed. Now she came around and realized, so the light started falling on her and she was slowly dissolving in it and finally disappearing up in the sky.

(Now I understood that his aunt was possessed that fateful day by this very old and probably not revengeful but not ready to move on spirit because of infatuation for her children. That is why the aunt could also not find release after her death as she was already under her influence and depressed. This spirit had possessed him in his childhood itself. First day his aunt was under her influence and resisted a bit but when convinced, she got released. But the other more powerfully attached to earthly existence was still not ready to move because we had not expected her to be here and thus not addressed her. After his aunt was released ,she must have felt lost and lonely and frightened him. When we traced her in another session she wasn't ready to be released because she was stuck in the time, when she must have died leaving her small children. Whom she thought still needs her. By hearing convincing and assuring words ,she too must have come around and realized her situation It is like somebody is not seeing the other side of the things and doesn't realize what lies there but if somebody shows him the face of another side he will be ready to see and move ahead)

Ghost Spirit caused the accident

Past life - We still had time left so I asked him to see any other cause for his present life's problems

.He reached back to his past life '.My guide resembles one of the business tycoon who appears in one advertisement of gutka and pan masala. I don't know him personally in this life. I don't know why he has come as my guide. I am five years old, wearing school uniform. I am sitting in a big car, its taking me to school. It is St Andrews School Bangalore. My father is a big business man. My name is Rahul. I have an elder sister and her name is Priya. She is my sister in this life too. After finishing studies, I have joined my father's business, we are in cloth business in Bangalore. He sounded very sure of recognizing the place. I am constructing a very big house at one secluded place outside the city. That place was graveyard earlier. There are still some graves. One soul is disturbed and roaming here and there. It is telling me not to disturb them. Q- How is it telling you? A-' By creating many accidents and causing unpleasant experiences while construction work is going on. But I don't believe in all these things. We have shifted to this house. Now this spirit has started troubling us in our house. Q- How? A –'By doing unusual things. We are not peaceful at all. I have gone to my sister's room , I am aghast to see she is hanging from the ceiling fan. ***She has committed suicide.*** I bring her down. I can see that spirit is sitting on the window and watching all this happen. It has turned its feet towards the back (I was reminded of stories of ghosts having their feet turned towards back, does it mean they are turned or fixed at their back (past). Q -Why did she try to commit suicide? A- She had become pregnant and she is not married yet.

My sister is saved but she is behaving very abnormal now. Some time she doesn't recognize us. Some time she leaves the main gate open. One day she left the gas cylinder open and she herself went out of the house. Cylinder got burst and all three of us died'. (After death he stayed back to see what Priya is doing?) 'She is entering the gate. She is laughing a wicked laugh. Now she is in her room but now she is crying and missing us. I can see that spirit is standing at the corner of that room. (I askd him why Priya is doing this double trick?) He said, after the suicide attempt, she has changed so much. She only caused this accident. (Now I understood that she is possessed by the spirit. At times she takes revenge through Priya and sometimes Priya comes to her senses and misses her family).

After the session- I asked him about his sister. He said, she is happily married and blessed with a child, but she had a difficult time to preserve her pregnancy. She is very religious, keeping many fasts and wearing *rudraksh* mala etc.(I was relieved that at least she is not facing same circumstances in this life. She must have been healed, may be in between life stage when we are in higher dimension after death. May be somebody healed that place and she got healed automatically or may be some of her good deeds brought some higher awareness and released from there. Her truth only she can reveal but she had no problem so she wouldn't even like to believe what he has seen and we cannot force her to believe it).

I am showing my gratitude by accepting it as reward from Divinity -

I have heard people enjoying material gains in this life express their gratitude declaring that that they must have donated pearls in their past life (*moti daan kiye honge*)that is why they are blessed with such good life . I cannot feign ignorance on the truth behind this utterance in my life. It is true, there is nothing free in this world, otherwise why would one be born as a beggar and other one with silver spoon in his mouth. ***I have to make a confession*** here to break my ego of pretending modest, humble and ignorant and show my gratitude to Divinity. I acknowledge that I have earned this obsure knowledge that is why I am retrieving it back in such simple and practical way and also becoming instrumental in eradicating the negativity from earth's surface. It was like eating my cake and having it too. I also marvel at those artists, for grasping insight in to this obscurity in such realistic way depicting for us in books and pictures. But we prefer not to listen, relegating it to the realm of figment of imagination of the artist or just avoiding its existence altogether. But I could not do so now and I must mention my reason for it.

First -My transcendental experience where I had been taken from outside of constellation below one invisible bridge type place. There I saw few people as if their bodies including eyes are smeard with mud. Seeing them I am compelled to speak that you are healed and the person opens up his eyes and starts looking at me ,I know that he is healed and that I have to heal all these people.there .

Second – My research in to such work by various other people in my first book. It has been proved to me that everything exists here and now but will only be revealed to us as much we are ready to take and how much we are in a position to accept.

Third – There after such people coming to me for healing and revealing what lies beyond physical eyes. I also want to mention my reason for writing my research book first and then describe cases in my second book. Was it only to convince people? No, who wants to be convinced, will be convinced who doesn't want to, he will not be, until he comes face to face with this reality by becoming victim himself. I wrote that book to convince myself, to break my own mental barrier and keep it as a proof in case I again fall back to the strong logical mind's fancy of forgetting my experiences which are hunches given by my soul.

Lesson

Reconfirmed capabilities of subconscious mind, and connectedness at subconscious level. Records of every incidents is in Akashic memory and can be accessed by connecting to it subconsciously. Mind which is akin to a computer in its working, if we can connect to any desired site through internet connection, why can't we do so through our minds internet connection?

Proofs of Healing this is not simply to diagnose, do research and add more information to the piling list of our problems but also to eradicate the cause . Obstinate spirit, hidden psychic attack or powerful tantric trying to empower him where ever and how ever powerful it may be. He revealed everything is getting healed and released in to universal fire for purification and recycling.

Karmic Debts – The family is recipient of the wrath of tantric. Subconsciously we are connected to everything and everybody but consciously we are connected to near and dear ones and people who are affecting us in any way. Proving beyond genes, it is person's karma (memory of past unresolved issues) influencing to be born in a particular family to undergo certain experiences of failures , genetic illness, suffering, destiny in term of fortunes or misfortune .

We all are psycho

Moral of the story is that imagination has got some seeds somewhere that is why different people imagine different things. What we imagine is truth for that moment. Otherwise in esoteric terms this world is nothing but imagination. (Brahm Satya jagat mithya) The physical body and senses are mortal and illusionary but soul and consciousness is truth and eternal.

Life is a paradox that is why everything is realty for those who are experiencing this facet of life at the moment. It is as real as somebody suffering from malaria or cancer. As these ailments are diagnosed by sophisticated instruments, invented by highly intellectual research oriented approach of mind. Same way this inner disease is also diagnosed by mind of the victim by experiencing unusual things. Also by people whose mind is attuned to this frequency can diagnose and predict presence of such things on a person, place or a thing like psychic, spiritualist and clairvoyant. Those who cannot see or feel it, they call it as mere imagination or prefer to give it derogatory names ,calling them mad , mentally sick or psycho . '.

We all are psycho. Because we contain this element called psyche / consciousness/ soul / spirit.

For experiencing life in fullness we have to come face to face with every facet of life. Those who are not acknowledging it today may face it tomorrow by becoming victims. In my opinion such experiences are also to bring awareness in the victims that such mysterious truth does exist, we can not shrug these back to the non-existence. Irrespective of ones faith , anybody whose time has come to face this reality will be having such experiences and seeing it with his soul's eye. There is nothing real at the end of the journey. Just as it is not true that every mosquito bite will cause malaria. We only have to be aware of such possibility and try means to prevent and eradicate it.

Aim is to awaken not to frighten

I am not explaining it to frighten you or asking to succumb to such things but asking you to be aware and accept it positively ,in case you come across somebody suffering with negative influences I have found that everything could be diagnosed through regression and Reiki healing by focusing the mind on the frequency in which this heavy energy vibrates. I am not denying that there may not be some other softer ways to be healed and freed from it. .

1 I am also not putting all the blame on ***Tantrics and vampires.*** Because I had asked from the subconscious of many people facing this wrath, why is he doing this to you? The answer I have got is , ' that he has to do it, he is forced to do so'.This Force is nature, tendency of attracting like energy. Law of karma, action and reaction. Give and take.

2 Many people sending ***psychic attack*** have said internally that I will not leave you. This means they have something to give and take with the victim from the past.,the karmic give and take coming to individual as dues of his karma.

3 Same is with spirit possession, nobody can enter your house unceremoniously, you have to know him and then only somebody enters your door. The spirit which has got something to give, teach you or take from you and frighten you will be able to manage to enter your aura.

In this book I have dealt with chapters on (1) *Inner calling makes us reflect at the* (2)*Intriguing Beginning, Leads life* (3)*stumbling through obscurity*,(4)taking *A step forward*, (5)*unfolding conscipicuous Di-*

vine plane.

Following chapters will continue in my next book *LIFE CONTINUES UNDER DIVINE PLAN* ***–(1) grasping heuristic insight (2)from evidence of fiction fusion in life. (3) History repeats*** as we quantify and reproach our own actions(,4) ***mythology is resurrected*** to intercept mysterious messages from oblivion, for we are ironical characters from scriptures. . We are journeying since ages, still ***(5) juggling with karmic lapses.*** Navigating obscurity to obliterate pain (separation)

Seeking Purpose

Truth That Sets Us Free is on what, why and how of our spiritual connection. This is an advertisement to interest you, desire you to seek that mysterious inner world, stir your soul to reveal the Kingdom of Heaven within ,, oneness with All That Is.

So this is for all those who are curious yet confused or sceptics for lack of any personal experiences in this obscure field. For those who are seeking remedial measures for any form of suffering. One may be inspired to install 'The art and science of inner connection' in life by learning different healing techniques and become "Interior decorator of the body, the abode of our soul ".

Am I doing this only for others? No, the greatest paradox of life is that nobody is doing any sacrifice by doing things for others, nor is anybody so selfish that he is doing things for himself alone. Because we are never alone, spiritually we are all one. It is like our hand removes the thorn from the path and the feet walks that extra mile towards our destination.

As for me, I have learnt that Ignorance is a curse, not wanting to gain knowledge is a sin, the greatest sin is not to share it with others. So I want to save myself from the greatest sin.

As today I live with this prayer -

I am happy, I spread happiness. I am healthy, I facilitate health.

I am Enlightened, I encourage Enlightenment.

I have glimpsed our Real Home, I aim to show the way back Home.

Healing Meditation Script

This meditation is designed to suit busy people with much of stress and less time to practice long hours in clearing and meditation. Voice record this script in your mobile or IPod and just play it twice.. While inhaling chant / affirm ,imagine and intend with full devotion, positive words entering and rejuvenating your whole being....

While exhaling release forcefully through your out breath clearing your system from all that is negatively affecting you

Importance of Breath -When breath wanders, the mind is also unsteady, when the breath is calmed, the mind becomes still. Therefore learn to control the breath.

Inhale and God approaches you, hold the inhalation and God remains with you. Exhale and you approach the God; hold the exhalation and you surrender to God.

So let's start -You may count each affirmation 5 to. 11 times as per your need.

1 - Breathe in LOVE and Light

Breathe out - Darkness and Delusion. .

2 - Breathe in unconditional Love and Light of God... Breathe out Darkness and delusion of conflicting thoughts

3 - Breathing in Purity, Power and Protection from the Source.

Breathing out all levels of Stress and Strain, Fear and Pain.

4 - Breathing in,clearing, cleansing, activating, healing, charging, with the light from the source.

Breathing out.. darkness, delusion, disconnection, depression and diseases

5 - Breathing in --Sensitizing, Awakening, Rewiring, Reconnecting, and Rejuvenating the central nervous system.

Breathing out disintegrating, dissolving, transmuting, transforming, transferring, turning tendencies upwards towards the source.

6 – Breathing in Joy, Ease, Grace, Abundance, Pleasure …

Breathing out cutting the chords of Repeated Mechanical Patterns.

7 – Breathing in Virtues of Love Hope Faith, Charity …

Breathing out as if uprooting all unconscious Elementals.

(AMEN. OUM. TATSAT. SOHAM. IAM THAT I AM

8 - Here Is a Mystic Healing session Script, you can read it and practice it.

What is Healing -

Healing is a God's Grace descending through Healing hands/ Healer / Facilitator/ channel ,in response to a plea sent to the Divine ,by the deserving soul to alleviate his suffering.

Disease means some blockage at the spiritual part due to illusion of separation from the Source of our Origin. Healing means reconnecting back to that Source. Anybody intending and desiring healing is, asking for help to find his way back our Real Home.

Why need for healing -- Healing is a by-product in achieving main goal i.e. Enlightenment. (The purpose of incarnation on earth is to learn and integrate from all the experiences of life, to help us evolve and achieve Oneness with All That is!)

Without being fully healed ,one cannot be enlightened on the purpose of life and Empowered on how to merge back ,seek union with our Father ,our Mighty I AM Presence, Holies of holy , The creator of All that is, The God Most High of the universe, The Supreme Being. So healing is this much important.

Why need for Healer / Facilitator--

Doctor stitches the wound and God heals it --is an old saying. There is only one healer and that is God/ The Creator of All That is. Any Earthly being claiming to be a healer is only a facilitator of that Universal Energy flow in to the recipient part, which has forgotten its original state of Perfection' Oneness with All That is'. (Mirror is to show our image, the healer is to take you to that blocked part.) Going for healing is like going to a -Soul Spa.

The facilitator has been trained (done Sadhna) to break this thin veil of illusion of separating physical from spiritual dimension . His/ her body is imbued with healing energy from the Source as s/he becomes a receiving channel for the healing energy to flow on behest of recipient's request for the healing of a person or a situation, thus he is called a medium /channel /healer.

I like to give analogy of a Healer with a Bank Manager or a Sales Representative of any Company. He knows the rules and regulations and has access to the Higher Officials of his department to present forward your case. I have also proclaimed myself representative of God's Company ,'CREATION 'in the department of LIFE.

Fundamental of healing -- Healing is not given but taken. One has to tap in to the universal store house or become a channel to receive this Grace, or seek for the channel /healer.

How to receive Mystic Healing – Write your request on a page, you may mention what you are wanting to heal. It could be a physical pain, mental ailment, relationship issue or any difficult situation you or your loved one is experiencing in life. Write detail on a piece of paper to keep it with you, till some amicable solution has been achieved

-Sit comfortably at a fixed free time. Intend, affirm and be the recipient of the energy from the Source / Divine intelligence/ Supreme Being /God or whatever your connotation of your spiritual connection is.

- Ask your ego not to criticize, doubt, judge or interfere in the process. You have every right to get what you want, yet be open to accept alternative outcome. Healing does not happen from our logical perspective but commences from Higher Self, which knows all the causes, conditions, cures and solutions for our Higher Good.

- Take a glass of water, charge it with positive affirmations (success in your venture) and drink it .Intend and affirm that this charged water is filling your aura with strong positive vibes and also absorbing like vibes during the session, which are being transmitted to you from the Universe.

Use of crystals also empower our aura to be more open and receptive.

Preparation – Making yourself comfortable, disconnecting from external stimuli, noise. Tell your mind that I will not be disturbed for half an hour and will fully receive healing.

START — by clearing your mind from clutter and any and all form of stress, strain – by taking deep long forceful five breaths. You may also inhale in through nose and exhale through mouth by making a heavy, sighing noise.

Once you feel lighter, focus on your breath and start by taking deep comfortable breaths, which are long, deep connected. See that your belly rises when you breathe in and when you breathe out it flattens.

Break away from physical conditionings— allow yourself to be in a beautiful, seren place ,full of pure light, your inner century. The amazing thing about this place is that it has no limitations of place, time, shape and size. It totally works with your intension and imagination. So it's a most beautiful place, with sun shine, comfortable temperature, birds chirping sounds, water rushing down through spring lake, gentler breeze whistling across your body.

(We have many layers of Aura (energy bodies) around and inside of our physical body, which are invisible to naked eyes. Just like we cannot see our blood vessels, our bones, or organs with our naked eyes. We need some instrument to see them, x-RAY, MRI- Sonography. Etc. Same way to see ,feel ,clear and heal we need some tool in our hand/ mind)

So breath is first the powerful tool .Our intension and Imagination is our tool too. So by these tools we are asking God's help. Which is readily available when asked with pure intent and focus.

1- First layer we are clearing, cleansing, mending, rearranging beautifying, just like one of the many layers of clothing put on our body, so this is first layer. As we Breathe in, intend and feel ,visualize, imagine, that our breath is dusting something down from our first covering of our energy body. Below our feet is a sack, a container which is attracting this dust into itself as vacuum absorbs dust with force in to it.

2- Now we are cutting and separating our aura from outside energy continuity from its surroundings. Just as we make a wall or fence, or draw curtain while bathing. To have our privacy and to avoid intrusion from outside energy in to us. One oval shaped /egg shaped form is formed around our being.

With a powerful Crystal wand we are slicing this oval shaped form of our aura into 10 equal parts. Longitudinally slicing, absorbing, and flushing – from front to back covering full range and disposing excess and waste in to the container below our feet. 10 times longitudinally 1-2-3-4-5-6-7-8-9-10; cut and separate, absorb and release, dump.

3- Now we are combing up our aura, with a fine crystal comb or even our fingers are so powerful crystals that we are combing our aura up and down. Taking care of each part. Starting at the right side, combing down wards, releasing in to the knapsack, coming upwards as we comb our hair. 1-2-3-4-5-6. You may do it more time if your aura is not cleared in that much time.

4- Now all our powerful tools are coming in our hands – dragon Bugle , pink and violet crystal wands, shivashakti Yantra, Archangel Michael's/ Durga/ kali;'s swords. Let these tools slide up and down our aura clearing, cleansing, reconnecting, and mending our Nadi meridians. Our focus is on breath and intension is that I let go from my being which does not serve me anymore. Taking care that all released up energy is automatically collected in the container and it is connected to universal incinerating chamber, where everything waste and excess is transmuted and transformed in to pure light once again and recycled back in the universe.

5- Now a most magnetic mesh net is sent down from the universe right at the top of our head spread on whole aura. This net is sieving, sifting, burning, transmuting, flushing, and clearing any form of incompatible energy (misclassified).

6- Now Bring our attention to soul star chakra above our crown(-head)

A golden ball of energy is forming there as we focus our attention there and make intension of forming a strong connection with our soul and our Higher Self.. This ball of energy starts rotating, becoming active and coming into its full form

5- Bring this energy down to our crown chakra- this ball of light is clearing, cleansing, activating, healing, charging, protecting, expanding, spreading and radiating in to Gold colour.

6- 3rd eye—throat—thymus—heart—solar—naval—sacral—root-knee- ankle—sole of the feet—our connection in the earth -one feet below the feet.

7- Now we are chelating the energy through our main power current – in the spinal canal -Ida, Pingala, Sushumna.

Staring at the base of the feet with our breath, we are bringing the earthly energies up the front of body taking through chakras and meridians reaching up till the brain. Spreading in the mind and sensitizing, awakening, rewiring and reconnecting nervous system. Bringing it down through the spinal column this golden energy filling up, spreading each and every atom of your being.

8- Bringing our attention to our heart and seeing there violet light forming pink, light of divine love, blue of divine wisdom and yellow of divine power. Transmuting and transforming all form of disqualified energy. Affirming, the energy of divine love, wisdom, divine power is permeating every cell molecule, atoms and protons of my body, until my whole being is transformed in to a Light being. Be there till e feel sufficient light has spread there and on our entire being.

9- Moving down to below our feet and intending that we are connecting chakras to each other's, by making a double spiral –forming a continuous figure of eight criss crossing each chakra outwardly taking up till another chakra till soul star. We start -below the feet,-ankle—knees—root—sacral—naval—solar—heart—thymus—throat—third eye—crown - soul star..

10- After finishing this bringing down energy through our aura forming an oval shaped Golden white light cylinder around us . Knowing that this is semi permeable protective layers, a ring of violet, pink and yellow light.

11- Feeling some grid lines become active and extend to earth connecting to corresponding earth chakra on the earth.

12- Its automatic energy exchange now -healing that part, that issue from our body /life which was earlier bereft of this connection and this energy. Taking our time to heal our issue, being there, open and ready to come out of the situation, which feels strangling our soul, binding our steps, blocking our vision ready for the change of direction in life. With a great big hug come out of it and put our hands on our eyes for few seconds. Now we open our eyes.

Author BIOGRAPHY

Mrs Nirmal Mozumdar is a Seeker /Light Worker /Healer/Teacher. After a Mystic Experience in 1998, in her quest she became a Reiki Grand Master, Magnified Healing Master, Past Life Regression Therapist ,Shaman, Pranic Healer, Dowsing, Crystal Ball Gazing, Angel Therapy, Yoga, Elemental and Fairy Realm Healer. Since then she is a dedicated practitioner and teacher of alternative Energy healing Techniques named as Mystic Healing Yoga.

During her journey as a, Healer and Teacher,,she was guided to keep record of few memorable dreams, Inner Visions during healing and meditation and few important cases through Past life Regression session.

Then came the direct guidance from the Universe in the form of intuitive thoughts, Deep meditative experiences (Astral Travel) Guides speaking through Regression session (Channeling), Thumb Impression Astrology (an ancient future reading system prevalent in southern India).That time a clairvoyant colleague's constant company revealed her feelings, thoughts, prayers and healing directly getting communicated to universe and their feed back. She had clear direction and strong inclination to do research on her work. The cases she attended were like her assignments from the Universe. She lived every case though her, as healing, meditating, contemplating and compiling her cases in her books.